Fodor's 2001

Bermu[...]

D1415176

The complete guide, thoroughly up-to-date

Packed with details that will make your trip

The must-see sights, off and on the beaten path

What to see, what to skip

Mix-and-match vacation itineraries

City strolls, countryside adventures

Smart lodging and dining options

Essential local do's and taboos

Transportation tips, distances and directions

Key contacts, savvy travel tips

When to go, what to pack

Clear, accurate, easy-to-use maps

Background essays

...vel Publications
...ors.com

Fodor's Bermuda

Editor: Alice K. Thompson

Editorial Contributors: Ron Bernthal, Rachel Christmas Derrick, Honey Naylor, Vivienne Sheath, Dexter Smith, Judith Wadson

Editorial Production: Stacey Kulig

Maps: David Lindroth, Inc., *cartographer;* Rebecca Baer and Bob Blake, *map editors*

Design: Fabrizio La Rocca, *creative director;* Guido Caroti, *art director;* Jolie Novak, *photo editor*

Cover Design: Pentagram

Production/Manufacturing: Angela L. McLean

Cover Photograph: David G. Houser (Jobson Cove, Warwick Parish)

Copyright

ISBN 0-679-00623-0

ISSN 0192-3765

"America's Rebel Colonies and Bermuda: Getting a Bang for Their Buckwheat" is excerpted from *Bermuda Journey,* by William Zuill. Copyright 1946 by William Edward Sears Zuill. Reprinted by permission of the Estate of William Edward Sears Zuill.

"Bermuda's Hidden Landscapes," by William G. Scheller, first appeared in the May/June 1991 issue of *Islands.* Copyright 1991 by William G. Scheller. Reprinted by permission of the author.

"Off Bermuda's Beaten Track," by Ben Davidson, was originally published in the November 1987 issue of *Travel & Leisure* and is reprinted with permission. Copyright 1987 by American Express Publishing Corporation. All rights reserved.

Special Sales Fodor's Travel Publications are available at special discounts for bulk purchases for sales promotions or premiums. For more information, write to Special Markets, Fodor's Travel Publications, 280 Park Avenue, New York, NY 10017. Inquiries from Canada should be sent to Random House of Canada, Ltd., Marketing Dept., 2775 Matheson Blvd. East, Mississauga, Ontario L4W 4P7. Inquiries from the United Kingdom should be sent to Fodor's Travel Publications, 20 Vauxhall Bridge Rd., London SW1V 2SA, England.

PRINTED IN THE UNITED STATES OF AMERICA

10 9 8 7 6 5 4 3 2 1

Important Tip

Although all prices, opening times, and other details in this book are based on information supplied to us at press time, changes occur all the time in the travel world, and Fodor's cannot accept responsibility for facts that become outdated or for inadvertent errors or omissions. So **always confirm information when it matters,** especially if you're making a detour to visit a specific place.

CONTENTS

Contents

Maps and Charts

ON THE ROAD WITH FODOR'S

EVERY VACATION IS IMPORTANT. So here at Fodor's, we've pulled out all stops in preparing *Fodor's Bermuda 2001*. To guide you in putting together your Bermuda experience, we've created multiday itineraries and neighborhood walks. And to direct you to the places that are truly worth your time and money in this important year, we've rallied the team of endearingly picky know-it-alls we're pleased to call our writers. Having seen all corners of Bermuda, they're real experts. If you knew them, you'd poll them for tips yourself.

Ron Bernthal's feature articles have appeared in numerous U.S. and European publications, and he writes and produces a weekly travel segment for National Public Radio station WJFF, the only hydro-powered radio station in the country. Ron is a professor of history and environmental tourism at Sullivan County Community College in New York. Ron updated the "Exploring Bermuda" and "Nightlife and the Arts" chapters, and visits the island as often as possible so he can "ride the ferries all day just watching the beautiful sea and sky."

New York–based freelance writer **Rachel Christmas Derrick** has been revisiting Bermuda for more than 15 years. Her articles about this island and other locales around the world have appeared in numerous newspapers and magazines, including the *New York Times, Washington Post, Boston Globe, Los Angeles Times, Travel & Leisure, Islands, Newsweek, Essence,* and *Ms.*

Honey Naylor's feature articles have appeared in *Travel & Leisure, Travel Holiday, USA Today,* the *Times-Picayune,* and *New Orleans* magazine. She has traveled extensively throughout the Caribbean, but there's no place she prefers to Bermuda, which she calls the most civilized of the islands.

Award-winning British journalist and freelance writer **Vivienne Sheath** researched and fell in love with Bermuda while working as a business reporter on the island. Vivienne worked with husband and coresearcher Nicholas Mayer to update the "Destination: Bermuda," "Lodging," and "Shopping" chapters for us this year.

Beaches, sports, and cruising updater **Dexter Smith** was sports editor at Bermuda's daily *Royal Gazette* newspaper from 1991 to 1994 before moving on to the weekly *Mid-Ocean News*. He covered the 1992 Olympic Games in Barcelona, Spain. Dexter's professional work has coexisted with sporting interests that have taken him all over the world representing Bermuda in both table tennis and cricket.

Bermuda-born **Judith Wadson,** our restaurant updater, has written about Bermuda and other destinations for numerous publications, including *The New York Times, San Francisco Examiner, The Robb Report,* and *Yachting* magazine, where she worked as a staff photographer and writer. She is author of *Bermuda: Traditions and Tastes,* a book about the island's culinary ties. She is also a chef who has trained in New York City and at Alice Waters's Berkeley, California, restaurant.

Don't Forget to Write

Keeping a travel guide fresh and up-to-date is a big job. So we love your feedback—positive and negative—and follow up on all suggestions. Contact the Bermuda editor at editors@fodors.com or c/o Fodor's, 280 Park Avenue, New York, NY 10017. And have a wonderful trip!

Karen Cure

Karen Cure
Editorial Director

Bermuda

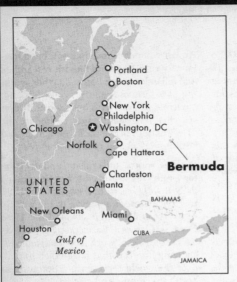

Portland
Boston

New York
Philadelphia
Washington, DC
Chicago
Norfolk
Cape Hatteras
Bermuda

UNITED
STATES
Charleston
Atlanta

BAHAMAS

New Orleans
Miami
Houston
CUBA
*Gulf of
Mexico*

JAMAICA

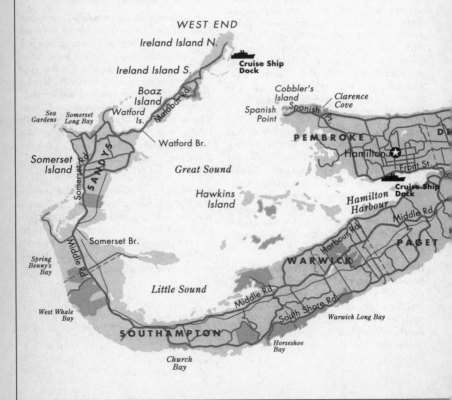

WEST END

Ireland Island N.

**Cruise Ship
Dock**

Ireland Island S.

*Cobbler's
Island*
*Clarence
Cove*

*Boaz
Island*
Maldbar Rd.
Watford
Is.
*Spanish
Point*
Spanish Pt.

*Sea
Gardens*
*Somerset
Long Bay*
Watford Br.
PEMBROKE
DE

Hamilton

Somerset Rd.
SANDYS
Great Sound
Front St.

*Somerset
Island*
*Hawkins
Island*
*Hamilton
Harbour*
**Cruise Ship
Dock**

Middle Rd.

Somerset Br.
Harbour Rd.
PAGET

Middle Rd.
WARWICK

*Spring
Benny's
Bay*
Little Sound
Middle Rd.
South Shore Rd.
Warwick Long Bay

*West Whale
Bay*

SOUTHAMPTON
*Horseshoe
Bay*

*Church
Bay*

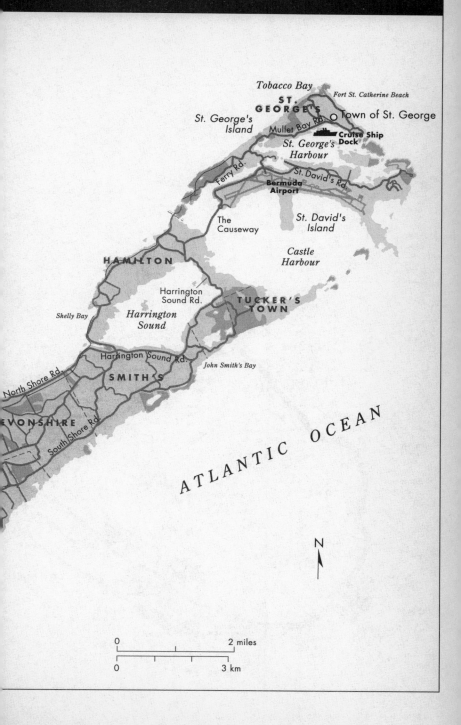

Tobacco Bay

Fort St. Catherine Beach

ST. GEORGE'S

St. George's Island

Town of St. George

Mullet Bay Rd.

Cruise Ship Dock

St. George's Harbour

Ferry Rd.

St. David's Rd.

Bermuda Airport

The Causeway

St. David's Island

HAMILTON

Castle Harbour

Harrington Sound Rd.

TUCKER'S TOWN

Shelly Bay

Harrington Sound

Harrington Sound Rd.

North Shore Rd.

SMITH'S

John Smith's Bay

EVONSHIRE

South Shore Rd.

ATLANTIC OCEAN

N

0   2 miles

0   3 km

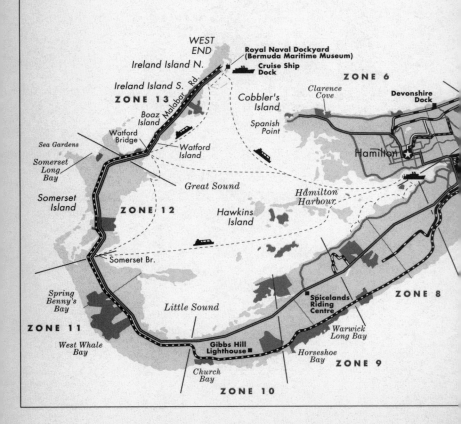

ATLANTIC OCEAN

WEST
END

Royal Naval Dockyard
(Bermuda Maritime Museum)

Ireland Island N.

Cruise Ship
Dock

Ireland Island S.

Clarence
Cove

ZONE 6

Devonshire
Dock

ZONE 13

Cobbler's
Island

Boaz
Island

Spanish
Point

Watford
Bridge

Hamilton

Watford
Island

Sea Gardens

Somerset
Long
Bay

Great Sound

Hamilton
Harbour

Somerset
Island

ZONE 12

Hawkins
Island

Somerset Br.

Spring
Benny's
Bay

Little Sound

Spicelands
Riding
Centre

ZONE 8

ZONE 11

Warwick
Long Bay

West Whale
Bay

Gibbs Hill
Lighthouse

Horseshoe
Bay

ZONE 9

Church
Bay

ZONE 10

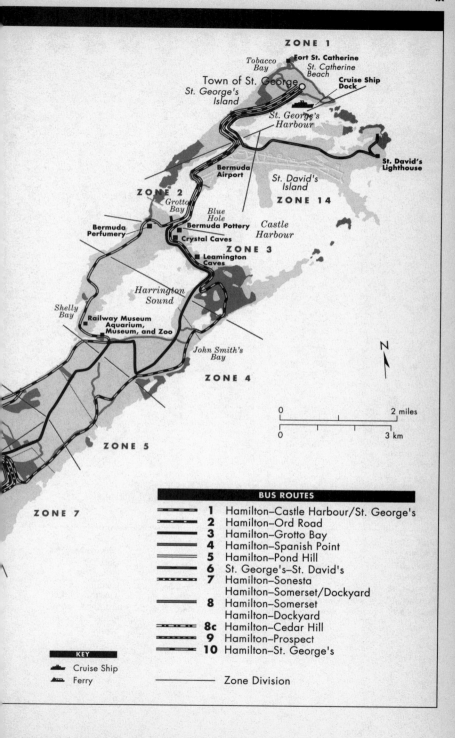

ZONE 1

Tobacco Bay

Fort St. Catherine

St. Catherine Beach

Town of St. George

Cruise Ship Dock

St. George's Island

St. George's Harbour

St. David's Lighthouse

Bermuda Airport

St. David's Island

ZONE 2

Grotto Bay

ZONE 14

Blue Hole

Bermuda Pottery

Castle Harbour

Bermuda Perfumery

Crystal Caves

ZONE 3

Leamington Caves

Harrington Sound

Shelly Bay

Railway Museum Aquarium, Museum, and Zoo

John Smith's Bay

ZONE 4

N

| 0 | | 2 miles |
| 0 | | 3 km |

ZONE 5

ZONE 7

BUS ROUTES	
1	Hamilton–Castle Harbour/St. George's
2	Hamilton–Ord Road
3	Hamilton–Grotto Bay
4	Hamilton–Spanish Point
5	Hamilton–Pond Hill
6	St. George's–St. David's
7	Hamilton–Sonesta
	Hamilton–Somerset/Dockyard
8	Hamilton–Somerset
	Hamilton–Dockyard
8c	Hamilton–Cedar Hill
9	Hamilton–Prospect
10	Hamilton–St. George's

KEY	
⛴	Cruise Ship
⛴	Ferry
———	Zone Division

World Time Zones

Numbers below vertical bands relate each zone to Greenwich Mean Time (0 hrs.).
Local times frequently differ from these general indications,
as indicated by light-face numbers on map.

Algiers, **29**	Berlin, **34**	Delhi, **48**	Jerusalem, **42**
Anchorage, **3**	Bogotá, **19**	Denver, **8**	Johannesburg, **44**
Athens, **41**	Budapest, **37**	Dublin, **26**	Lima, **20**
Auckland, **1**	Buenos Aires, **24**	Edmonton, **7**	Lisbon, **28**
Baghdad, **46**	Caracas, **22**	Hong Kong, **56**	London
Bangkok, **50**	Chicago, **9**	Honolulu, **2**	(Greenwich), **27**
Beijing, **54**	Copenhagen, **33**	Istanbul, **40**	Los Angeles, **6**
	Dallas, **10**	Jakarta, **53**	Madrid, **38**
			Manila, **57**

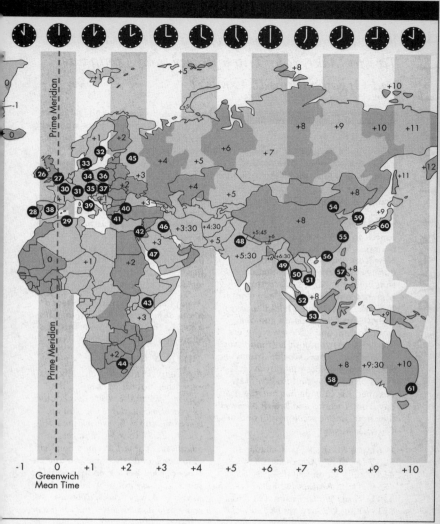

Mecca, **47**
Mexico City, **12**
Miami, **18**
Montréal, **15**
Moscow, **45**
Nairobi, **43**
New Orleans, **11**
New York City, **16**

Ottawa, **14**
Paris, **30**
Perth, **58**
Reykjavík, **25**
Rio de Janeiro, **23**
Rome, **39**
Saigon (Ho Chi Minh City), **51**

San Francisco, **5**
Santiago, **21**
Seoul, **59**
Shanghai, **55**
Singapore, **52**
Stockholm, **32**
Sydney, **61**
Tokyo, **60**

Toronto, **13**
Vancouver, **4**
Vienna, **35**
Warsaw, **36**
Washington, D.C., **17**
Yangon, **49**
Zürich, **31**

SMART TRAVEL TIPS A TO Z

Basic Information on Traveling in Bermuda, Savvy Tips to Make Your Trip a Breeze, and Companies and Organizations to Contact

AIR TRAVEL

BOOKING

When you book **look for nonstop flights** and **remember that "direct" flights stop at least once.** Try to avoid connecting flights, which require a change of plane.

CARRIERS

American offers several nonstops to Bermuda, with two daily flights from New York and one from Boston during the April–October high season. Frequency drops November–March. **Continental** flies daily from Newark, New Jersey. **Delta** has two daily flights from Atlanta and one from Boston, and **US Airways** offers daily service from both Baltimore and Philadelphia. **Trans World Airlines** flies nonstop to Bermuda from St. Louis on Monday and Friday, May–October. **Air Canada** has one flight a day from Toronto and **British Airways** flies four times a week from London's Gatwick Airport.

➤ Major Airlines: **Air Canada** (☎ 800/776–3000). **American** (☎ 800/433–7300). **Continental** (☎ 800/231–0856). **Delta Airlines** (☎ 800/241–4141). **Trans World Airlines**(☎ 800/221–2000). **US Airways** (☎ 800/428–4322).

➤ From the U.K.: **British Airways** (☎ 020/7897–4000; 0345/222–1111 outside London).

CHECK-IN & BOARDING

Assuming that not everyone with a ticket will show up, airlines routinely overbook planes. When that happens, airlines ask for volunteers to give up their seats. In return these volunteers usually get a certificate for a free flight and are rebooked on the next flight out. If there are not enough volunteers, the airline must choose who will be denied boarding. However, even during Bermuda's busiest season (summer), travelers are rarely bumped. This is because the airline usually simply switches to a larger aircraft. In the unlikely event that passengers are bumped, the first to go are those who checked in late and those flying on discounted tickets, so **check in and get to the gate as early as possible.** At many airports outside Bermuda, travelers with only carry-on luggage can bypass the airline's front desk and check in at the gate. But in Bermuda, everyone checks in at the airline's front desk.

Always **bring a government-issued photo ID to the airport.** You may be asked to show it before you are allowed to check in.

CUTTING COSTS

Airfare to Bermuda is generally least expensive November–March, the "off season," when the weather is coolest. However, no matter when you are traveling, you will save the most if you purchase round-trip tickets in advance. It's smart to **call a number of airlines, and when you are quoted a good price, book it on the spot.** The same fare may not be available the next day. Always **check different routings** and look into using different airports. Travel agents, especially low-fare specialists (☞ Discounts & Deals, *below*), are helpful.

Consolidators are another good source. They buy tickets for scheduled international flights at reduced rates from the airlines, then sell them at prices that beat the best fare available directly from the airlines, usually without restrictions. Sometimes you can even get your money back if you need to return the ticket. Carefully read the fine print detailing penalties for changes and cancellations, and **confirm your consolidator reservation with the airline.**

➤ CONSOLIDATORS: **Cheap Tickets** (☎ 800/377–1000). **Unitravel** (☎ 800/325–2222). **Up & Away Travel** (☎ 212/889–2345). **World Travel Network** (☎ 800/409–6753).

ENJOYING THE FLIGHT

For more legroom, **request an emergency-aisle seat.** Don't sit in the row in front of the emergency aisle or in front of a bulkhead, where seats may not recline. If you have dietary concerns, **ask for special meals when booking.** These can be vegetarian, low-cholesterol, or kosher, for example. On long flights, try to maintain a normal routine, to help fight jet lag. At night, **get some sleep.** By day, **eat light meals, drink water** (not alcohol), and **move around the cabin** to stretch your legs.

FLYING TIMES

Flying time to Bermuda from New York, Newark, Boston, Philadelphia, and Baltimore is about 2 hours; from Atlanta, 2¾ hours; and from Toronto, 3 hours.

HOW TO COMPLAIN

If your baggage goes astray or your flight goes awry, complain right away. Most carriers require that you **file a claim immediately.**

➤ AIRLINE COMPLAINTS: U.S. Department of Transportation **Aviation Consumer Protection Division** (✉ C-75, Room 4107, Washington, DC 20590, ☎ 202/366–2220, airconsumer@ost.dot.gov, www.dot.gov/airconsumer). **Federal Aviation Administration Consumer Hotline** (☎ 800/322–7873).

RECONFIRMING

The airlines flying to Bermuda do not generally require you to reconfirm your reservations either outbound or returning. It's not a bad idea, however, to call your airline a day or so ahead just to double-check that your reservations are in order. And although the route into and out of Bermuda is not known for delays, calling just before leaving for the airport to check the status of your flight is smart. If there is a major delay on your flight, it could save you hours of waiting time at the airport.

AIRPORTS

Bermuda's gateway is **Bermuda International Airport,** on the east end of the island, approximately 9 mi from Hamilton and 17 mi from Somerset.

➤ AIRPORT INFORMATION: **Bermuda International Airport** (✉ 2 Kindley Field Rd., St. George's, ☎ 441/293–2470 ext. 4814).

DUTY-FREE SHOPPING

While you can certainly find discounts in china, crystal, woolens, and other European imports, duty-free shopping in Bermuda is limited. To qualify for duty-free (or in-bond) liquor prices, you'll have to buy at least two liters or five 75-centiliter bottles. However, each U.S. citizen may only bring back 1 liter of alcohol duty-free. You can arrange for duty-free liquor you buy at stores to be delivered to the airport, or you can purchase it at the airport itself (☞ Customs & Duties, *below,* and Chapter 8).

TAXIS AND SHUTTLES FROM THE AIRPORT

Taxis are readily available at the airport. The approximate fare (not including tip) to Hamilton is $21; to St. George's, $12; to south-shore hotels, $28; and to Sandys (Somerset), $35. A surcharge of 25¢ is added for each piece of luggage stored in the trunk or on the roof. Fares are 25% higher between midnight and 6 AM and all day on Sunday and public holidays. Depending on traffic, the driving time to Hamilton is about 30 minutes; to Sandys, about one hour.

Bermuda Hosts Ltd. has round-trip transportation to hotels and guest houses aboard air-conditioned 6- to 25-seat vans and buses. Reservations are recommended. One-way fares, based on zones, are as follows: Zone 1 (to Grotto Bay Beach Hotel), $6; Zone 2 (to the Flatts Village area), $7; Zone 3 (to Cobb's Hill Road), $9; Zone 4 (to Church Road), $10; and Zone 5 (westward to Dockyard), $15.

➤ BUS TRANSFERS: **Bermuda Hosts Ltd.** (☎ 441/293–1334, FAX 441/293–1335).

BIKE TRAVEL

You'll be in the minority if you choose to ride around Bermuda since most two-wheelers on the island are mopeds. Some steep hills and winding roads (particularly those going north–south) mean that bikers need a lot of pedal power. However, with so many scenic waterside and countryside roads (including the tranquil old railway trail that is reserved for pedestrians, pedal bikes, and mopeds), bicycling in Bermuda is particularly rewarding. Bicycle rentals, mainly mountain bikes, are limited to a few moped shops around the island, so you should **reserve your bike in advance** (☞ Bicycling *in* Chapter 7).

➤ BIKE MAPS: For a map of the route along the old Bermuda Railway, get a hold of a copy of "The Bermuda Railway Trail Guide," available free at the Department of Tourism and all Visitors Service Bureaus (☞ Visitor Information, *below*).

➤ BIKE RENTALS: Day rates for rentals range from $10 to $20 per day on Bermuda. If possible, try to reserve bikes a few days in advance to avoid disappointment. For a list of rental shops, *see* Bicycling *in* Chapter 7.

BIKES IN FLIGHT

Most airlines accommodate bikes as luggage, provided they are dismantled and boxed. For bike boxes, often free at bike shops, you'll pay about $5 from airlines (at least $100 for bike bags). International travelers can sometimes substitute a bike for a piece of checked luggage at no charge; otherwise, the cost is about $100. Domestic and Canadian airlines charge $25–$50.

BOAT & FERRY TRAVEL

Ferry travel around the island is convenient and enjoyable. Ferries sail every day from Hamilton's ferry terminal, with routes to Paget, Warwick, and across the Great Sound to Somerset, in the West End. On weekdays, the Paget and Warwick ferries run until 11 PM; the last ferry from Hamilton to Somerset leaves at 5:20 PM. Sunday service is limited and ends around 7 PM. A one-way fare to Paget or Warwick is $2.25; to Somerset,

$3.75. You can bring a bicycle on board free of charge, but you'll pay $3.75 extra to take a motor scooter to Somerset, and scooters are not allowed on the smaller Paget and Warwick ferries. Discounted one-, three-, and seven-day passes are available for use on both ferries and buses. The helpful ferry operators will answer questions about routes and schedules, and will even help get your bike on board. Schedules are available at the ferry terminal, central bus terminal, and most hotels, and are posted at each landing.

FARES & SCHEDULES

➤ BOAT & FERRY INFORMATION: **Hamilton Ferry Terminal** (☎ 441/ 295–4506).

BUS TRAVEL

Bermuda's pink-and-blue buses travel the island from east to west. To find a bus stop outside Hamilton, look for either a stone shelter or a pink-and-blue striped pole. For buses heading to Hamilton, the top of the pole is pink; for those traveling away from Hamilton, the top is blue. Remember to **wait on the proper side of the road.** Driving in Bermuda is on the left. Bus drivers will not make change, so **purchase discounted tokens or carry plenty of coins.** The fare depends on your destination.

In addition to public buses, private minibuses serve St. George's. The minibus fare depends upon the destination, but you won't pay more than $5. Minibuses, which you can flag down on the road, drop passengers wherever they want to go in this parish. They operate daily from about 7:30–midnight, April–October, and 8–8 the rest of the year.

FARES & SCHEDULES

Bermuda is divided into 14 bus zones, each about 2 mi long. Within the first three zones, the rate is $2.50 (coins only). For longer distances, the fare is $4. If you plan to travel by public transportation often, **buy a booklet of tickets** (15 14-zone tickets for $24, or 15 three-zone tickets for $15). For long-term visitors, a monthly pass is available for $40. Ticket booklets and discounted tokens are available at the Hamilton bus terminal and at post offices. One-, three-, and seven-day adult passes ($10, $21, and $34, respectively) are available at the bus terminal and the Bermuda Department of Tourism in Hamilton and at the airport. Passes for children (ages 5–15) are $5, $10, or $15. Passes are accepted on both buses and ferries.

Hamilton buses arrive and depart from the Central Bus Terminal, a small kiosk open weekdays 7:15–5:30, Saturday 8–5:30, and Sunday 9:15–4:45. This is the only place to buy money-saving tokens.

Buses run about every 15 minutes, except on Sunday, when they usually come every hour. Bus schedules, which also contain ferry timetables, are available at the bus terminal in Hamilton and at many hotels. Upon request, the driver will be happy to tell you when you've reached your stop. Note that it is considered rude in Bermuda to ask a bus driver a question, such as the fare or details on your destination, without first greeting him or her.

➤ BUS INFORMATION: **Central Bus Terminal** (✉ Washington and Church Sts., Hamilton, ☎ 441/292–3854 or 441/295–4311). **St. George's Minibus Service** (☎ 441/297–8199).

BUSINESS HOURS

BANKS & OFFICES

Branches of the Bank of Bermuda and the Bank of Butterfield are open Monday–Thursday 9:30–3, Friday 9:30–4:30. Bermuda Commercial Bank (opposite the Anglican Cathedral on Church Street in Hamilton) operates Monday–Thursday 9–3, Friday 9–4:30.

MUSEUMS & SIGHTS

Hours vary greatly, but museums are generally open Monday–Saturday 9 or 9:30–4:30 or 5. Some close on Saturday. Check with individual museums for exact hours.

SHOPS

Most stores are open Monday–Saturday from around 9–5 or 5:30. Some Hamilton stores keep evening hours when cruise ships are in port. In high season (March–November), many Front Street retailers that participate in Harbour Nights are open late on Wednesday, and many street vendors sell their wares that evening only. Shops at the Royal Naval Dockyard are generally open Monday–Saturday 10–5, and Sunday 11–5.

CAMERAS & PHOTOGRAPHY

➤ PHOTO HELP: **Kodak Information Center** (☎ 800/242–2424). *Kodak Guide to Shooting Great Travel Pictures,* available in bookstores or from Fodor's Travel Publications (☎ 800/533–6478; $16.50 plus $5.50 shipping).

EQUIPMENT PRECAUTIONS

Always **keep your film and tape out of the sun.** Carry an extra supply of batteries, and **be prepared to turn on your camera or camcorder** to prove to security personnel that the device is real. Always **ask for hand inspection of film,** which becomes clouded after repeated exposure to airport X-ray machines, and **keep videotapes away from metal detectors.**

FILM & DEVELOPING

While a roll of color print film costs about the same as in the U.S. ($6–$8 for a 36-exposure roll), developing that film is another story. If you're in a hurry to see what you shot, plan to dish out a whopping $28 per roll for 36 exposures, whether or not you choose speedy three-hour processing.

VIDEOS

Blank videotapes run about $4 each for six hours of tape and $6 for eight hours.

CAR RENTAL

You cannot rent a car in Bermuda. A popular alternative is to rent mopeds or scooters (☞ Moped & Scooter Rental, *below*), which are better for negotiating the island's narrow roads.

CHILDREN IN BERMUDA

When children need a break from the beach or pool, there is plenty to see and do in Bermuda. From the carriage and maritime museums to the aquarium and botanical gardens, sights and attractions of particular interest to kids are identified in this book with a duckie (🦆). Bermuda has no fast-food chains, except for a lone Kentucky Fried Chicken, but children will have no trouble finding familiar menu items in welcoming settings, especially at the more casual restaurants.

BABY-SITTING

For baby-sitters, check with your hotel desk. The charge is usually about $17 for the first hour and $10 for each additional hour. These rates may go up after midnight and they may vary depending on the number of children. Sitters may expect paid transportation.

FLYING

If your children are two or older, **ask about children's airfares.** As a general rule, infants under two not occupying a seat fly at greatly reduced fares or even for free. When booking, **confirm carry-on allowances** if you're traveling with infants. In general, for babies charged 10% of the adult fare you are allowed one carry-on bag and a collapsible stroller. If the flight is full, the stroller may have to be checked or you may be limited to less.

Experts agree that it's a good idea to use safety seats aloft for children weighing less than 40 pounds. Airlines set their own policies. U.S. carriers usually require that the child be ticketed, even if he or she is young enough to ride free, since the seats must be strapped into regular seats. Do **check your airline's policy about using safety seats during takeoff and landing.** And since safety seats are not allowed just everywhere in the plane, get your seat assignments early.

When reserving, **request children's meals or a freestanding bassinet** if you need them. But note that bulkhead seats, where you must sit to use the bassinet, may lack an overhead bin or storage space on the floor.

LODGING

Families with children find Bermuda's larger hotels, housekeeping cottages, or holiday apartments the most comfortable and convenient. Along with pools, beaches, and family-friendly restaurants, most of the island's beach hotels offer summer children's programs. Parents can drop the kids off to participate in sand castle competitions, treasure hunts, face painting, and arts and crafts, or send them on trips to the aquarium or botanical gardens, or on a ferry ride. Activities on the premises are gener-ally complimentary, while there is an additional charge for off-property excursions. Most children's programs are divided into two groups, one for preteens and teenagers, the other for younger children. The age ranges vary from hotel to hotel.

Although **Pompano Beach Club** does not have a children's program, the facilities seem designed for families with younger editions. The very shallow beach and the "kiddies" pool beside the larger pool put parents at ease when their children hit the water. Paddleboats and rafts are available at the boat house. A clay tennis court is on the premises and there is a minia-ture golf course nearby. The spacious two-room suites are popular among families.

Two smaller properties (with smaller price tags) are also excellent choices for families with children. **Whale Bay Inn** offers one-bedroom apartments and is within strolling distance of the beach. **Salt Kettle House** has homelike cottages (with fully equipped kitchens) and a hearty breakfast is included in the rates.

Most hotels in Bermuda allow children under a certain age to stay in their parents' room at no extra charge, but others charge for them as extra adults. Be sure to **find out the cutoff age for children's discounts.**

➤ BEST CHOICES: **Elbow Beach Hotel** (✉ Box HM 455, Hamilton HM BX, ☎ 441/236–3535 or 800/223–7434, ℻ 441/236–5882, www.netlinkber-muda.com/ElbowBch). **Grotto Bay Beach Hotel & Tennis Club** (✉ 11 Blue Hole Hill, Hamilton Parish CR 04, ☎ 441/293–8333 or 800/582–3190, gro@bspl.bm). **Marriott's Castle Harbour Resort** (✉ Box HM 841, Hamilton HM CX, ☎ 441/293–2040 or 800/228–9290, www.marriott.com). **Pompano Beach Club** (✉ 36 Pompano Beach Rd., Southampton SB 03, ☎ 441/234–0222 or 800/343–4155, pompano@ibl.bm, www.pompano.bm). **Salt Kettle House** (✉ 10 Salt Kettle Rd., Paget PG 01, ☎ 441/236–0407). **Sonesta Beach Hotel & Spa** (✉ Box HM 1070, Hamilton HM EX, ☎ 441/238–8122 or 800/766–3782, resmgr-bermuda@ibl.bml, www.sonesta.com).

Southampton Princess (✉ Box HM 1379, Hamilton HM FX, ☎ 441/293–8333 or 800/582–3190). **Whale Bay Inn** (✉ Box SN 544, Southampton SN BX, ☎ 441/238–0469).

BABY SUPPLIES

Major American brands of baby formula, disposable diapers, and over-the-counter children's medications are widely available. However, prices are steep.

COMPUTERS ON THE ROAD

There is no problem bringing personal laptops through customs into Bermuda. It would be a good idea to bring proof of purchase with you so you will not run into any difficulty bringing the computer back to the States, especially if it is a new machine.

The following resort properties have in-room computer ports for Internet access: Elbow Beach, Grotto Bay Beach Hotel, The Fairmont Hamilton Princess, Fairmont Southampton Princess, and Sonesta Beach Resort. The Rosedon and Waterloo House are also equipped with in-room computer ports. Most properties will charge connection fees each time a laptop is hooked up to the Internet ($3 to $10), with additional charges (10¢ to 30¢ per minute) during the connection. The Southampton Princess has a fully equipped business center where guests can use hotel computers for Internet access (connection charges still apply). The 44-room Newstead Hotel in Hamilton has added a new Business Center to the property. In addition, the hotel has voice mail, a data port, and high-speed Internet access in all guest rooms.

GETTING E-MAIL

Visitors may receive, and send, e-mail at three locations in Hamilton: **M. R. Onions Restaurant and Bar** (✉ Par-La-Ville Rd., Hamilton, ☎ 441/292–5012, FAX 441/292–3122, www.bermuda.bm/onions); **Freeport Seafood Restaurant** (✉ 1 Freeport Rd., Dockyard, Sandys, ☎ 441/234–1692, freeport@ibl.bm); and **Twice Told Tales Bookstore** (✉ Parliament St., Hamilton, ☎ 441/296–1995, FAX 441/296–6339, pfowkes@ibl.bm).

TECHNICAL PROBLEMS

If you experience technical problems with your laptop in Bermuda, here's a list of computer sales and service agents on the island. **Bermuda Computer Services** (IBM), (✉ 20 Dundonald St., Hamilton, ☎ 441/298–1276); **Applied Computer Technologies** (Apple and Compaq), (✉ Williams House, 20 Reid St., Hamilton, ☎ 441/295–1616, FAX 441/292–7967); **Gateway Systems** (Gateway 2000/Dell), (✉ 10 Queen St., Hamilton, ☎ 441/292–0341, FAX 441/292–0455); **Bermuda Best Buys** (various brands), (✉ Washington Mall, Church St., Hamilton, ☎ 441/236–2648, FAX 441/292–2329, bbb@ibl.bm); **Independent Consulting Solutions** (various brands), (✉ Mill Creek Rd., Pembroke, ☎ 441/295–3806, FAX 441/295–6034, bobmcc@ibl.bm).

CONSULATES

Only the United States has consular representation in Bermuda.

➤ U.S. CONSULATE: **U.S. Consulate** (✉ 16 Middle Rd., Devonshire DV03, ☎ 441/295–1342).

CONSUMER PROTECTION

Whenever shopping or buying travel services in Bermuda, **pay with a major credit card** so you can cancel payment or get reimbursed if there's a problem. If you're doing business with a particular company for the first time, **contact your local Better Business Bureau and the attorney general's offices** in your own state and the company's home state, as well. Have any complaints been filed? Finally, if you're buying a package or tour, always **consider travel insurance** that includes default coverage (☞ Insurance, *below*).

➤ BBBs: **Council of Better Business Bureaus** (✉ 4200 Wilson Blvd., Suite 800, Arlington, VA 22203, ☎ 703/276–0100, FAX 703/525–8277, www.bbb.org).

CRUISE TRAVEL

Cruising to Bermuda gives you the benefits of an inclusive package. Your transportation, meals, and lodging are usually included in the cruise fare with a typical land package (the ship acts as your hotel while you explore the island). Not all cruises to Bermuda are the same, however. **Check where you will dock in Bermuda.** The traditional port is Hamilton, the capital and the island's most commercial area, the best choice for shoppers. Many ships tie up at St. George's, where you walk off the vessel into Bermuda's equivalent of Colonial Williamsburg, a charming town of 17th-century buildings, narrow lanes, and a smattering of small boutiques. The West End, Bermuda's third port of call, is fast becoming the preferred one. Its Royal Naval Dockyard, an erstwhile shipyard that was the British Royal Navy's headquarters until 1995, has been beautifully restored as a minivillage with shops, restaurants, a maritime museum, an art gallery, and a crafts market. There are also occasional special events and a marina, with rental boats, submarine cruises, parasailing excursions, and a snorkeling area.

To get the best deal on a cruise, **consult a cruise-only travel agency.** Weeklong cruises to Bermuda leave from New York, Boston, and other East Coast U.S. ports. For a complete rundown on the ships visiting Bermuda, *see* Chapter 2.

CUSTOMS & DUTIES

When shopping, **keep receipts** for all purchases. Upon reentering the country, **be ready to show customs officials what you've bought.** If you feel a duty is incorrect or object to the way your clearance was handled, note the inspector's badge number and ask to see a supervisor. If the problem isn't resolved, write to the appropriate authorities, beginning with the port director at your point of entry.

IN BERMUDA

On entering Bermuda, you can bring in duty-free up to 50 cigars, 200 cigarettes, and 1 pound of tobacco; 1 liter of wine and 1 liter of spirits; and other goods with a total maximum value of $30. To import plants, fruits, vegetables, or pets, you must **get an import permit in advance from the Department of Agriculture and Fisheries.** Remember, though, that merchandise and sales materials for use at conventions must be cleared with the hotel concerned before you arrive.

➤ INFORMATION: **Department of Agriculture and Fisheries** (✉ HM 834, Hamilton HM CX, ☎ 441/236–4201, FAX 441/236–7582, www.ag-fish@bdagovt.bm).

IN AUSTRALIA

Australian residents who are 18 or older may bring home $A400 worth of souvenirs and gifts (including jewelry), 250 cigarettes or 250 grams of tobacco, and 1,125 ml of alcohol (including wine, beer, and spirits). Residents under 18 may bring back $A200 worth of goods. Prohibited items include meat products. Seeds, plants, and fruits need to be declared upon arrival.

➤ INFORMATION: **Australian Customs Service** (Regional Director, ✉ Box 8, Sydney, NSW 2001, ☎ 02/9213–2000, FAX 02/9213–4000).

IN CANADA

Canadian residents who have been out of Canada for at least seven days may bring home C$500 worth of goods duty-free. If you've been away less than seven days but more than 48 hours, the duty-free allowance drops to C$200. If your trip lasts 24–48 hours, the allowance is C$50. You may not pool allowances with family members. Goods claimed under the C$500 exemption may follow you by mail. Those claimed under the lesser exemptions must accompany you. Alcohol and tobacco products may be included in the seven-day and 48-hour exemptions but not in the 24-hour exemption. If you meet the age requirements of the province or territory through which you reenter Canada, you may bring in, duty-free, 1.14 liters (40 imperial ounces) of wine or liquor *or* 24 12-ounce cans or bottles of beer or ale. If you are 16 or older you may bring in, duty-free, 200 cigarettes and 50 cigars. Check ahead of time with Revenue Canada or the Department of Agriculture for policies regarding meat products, seeds, plants, and fruits.

You may send an unlimited number of gifts worth up to C$60 each duty-free to Canada. Label the package

UNSOLICITED GIFT—VALUE UNDER $60. Alcohol and tobacco are excluded.

➤ INFORMATION: **Revenue Canada** (✉ 2265 St. Laurent Blvd. S, Ottawa, Ontario K1G 4K3, ☎ 613/993–0534; 800/461–9999 in Canada; FAX 613/ 957–8911, www.ccra-adrc.gc.ca).

IN NEW ZEALAND

Homeward-bound residents 17 or older may bring back $700 worth of souvenirs and gifts. Your duty-free allowance also includes 4.5 liters of wine or beer; one 1,125-ml bottle of spirits; and either 200 cigarettes, 250 grams of tobacco, 50 cigars, or a combination of the three up to 250 grams. Prohibited items include meat products, seeds, plants, and fruits.

➤ INFORMATION: **New Zealand Customs** (Custom House, ✉ 50 Anzac Ave., Box 29, Auckland, New Zealand, ☎ 09/359–6655, FAX 09/ 359–6732).

IN THE U.K.

From countries outside the EU, including Bermuda, you may bring home, duty-free, 200 cigarettes or 50 cigars; 1 liter of spirits or 2 liters of fortified or sparkling wine or liqueurs; 2 liters of still table wine; 60 ml of perfume; 250 ml of toilet water; plus £136 worth of other goods, including gifts and souvenirs. If returning from outside the EU, prohibited items include meat products, seeds, plants, and fruits.

➤ INFORMATION: **HM Customs and Excise** (✉ Dorset House, Stamford St., Bromley, Kent BR1 1XX, ☎ 020/ 7202–4227).

IN THE U.S.

U.S. residents who have been out of the country for at least 48 hours (and who have not used the $400 allowance or any part of it in the past 30 days) may bring home $400 worth of foreign goods duty-free.

U.S. residents 21 and older may bring back 1 liter of alcohol duty-free. In addition, regardless of your age, you are allowed 200 cigarettes and 100 non-Cuban cigars. Antiques, which the U.S. Customs Service defines as objects more than 100 years old, enter duty-free, as do original works of art done entirely by hand, including paintings, drawings, and sculptures.

You may also send packages home duty-free: up to $200 worth of goods for personal use, with a limit of one parcel per addressee per day (except alcohol or tobacco products or perfume worth more than $5); label the package PERSONAL USE and attach a list of its contents and their retail value. Do not label the package UNSOLICITED GIFT or your duty-free exemption will drop to $100. Mailed items do not affect your duty-free allowance on your return.

➤ INFORMATION: **U.S. Customs Service** (✉ 1300 Pennsylvania Ave. NW, Washington, DC 20229, www.customs.gov; inquiries ☎ 202/354–1000; complaints c/o ✉ Office of Regulations and Rulings; registration of equipment c/o ✉ Resource Management, ☎ 202/927–0540).

DISABILITIES & ACCESSIBILITY

The Bermuda Chapter of the Society for the Advancement of Travel for the Handicapped produces information sheets for travelers with disabilities. You can also get this information at any Bermuda Department of Tourism office.

➤ LOCAL RESOURCES: Bermuda Chapter of the **Society for the Advancement of Travel for the Handicapped** (SATH; ✉ 347 5th Ave., Suite 610, New York, NY 10016 USA, ☎ 212/ 447–7284). **Bermuda Physically Handicapped Association** (BPHA; ☎ 441/295–7376; 441/293–5035; 441/ 293–2099).

GUIDE DOGS

If you plan to bring a guide dog to Bermuda, you must **obtain a permit in advance.** Application forms are available from all Bermuda Department of Tourism offices. Once your application is approved, the Department of Agriculture and Fisheries will send an import permit to the traveler; the permit must accompany the dog at the time of arrival.

LODGING

The most accessible hotels are the large resorts, such as Elbow Beach, Marriott's Castle Harbour, the Sonesta Beach, the Hamilton Princess, and the Southampton Princess.

When discussing accessibility with an operator or reservations agent, **ask hard questions.** Are there any stairs, inside *or* out? Are there grab bars next to the toilet *and* in the shower/tub? How wide is the doorway to the room? To the bathroom? For the most extensive facilities meeting the latest legal specifications, **opt for newer accommodations.**

➤ INFORMATION: If you're looking for a vacation apartment suitable for a traveler with a disability, contact **Mrs. Ianthia Wade** (✉ "Summer Haven," Box HS 30, Harrington Sound HS BX, ☎ 441/293–2099, summerhaven@ibl.bm). Mrs. Wade can also assist with transportation and sightseeing arrangements.

TRANSPORTATION

Public buses in Bermuda are not equipped for wheelchairs. However, the Bermuda Physically Handicapped Association (BPHA) has volunteer-operated buses with hydraulic lifts. Make arrangements in advance. Note that you may have to be patient if more than a few travelers with disabilities are visiting Bermuda at once.

➤ COMPLAINTS: **Disability Rights Section** (✉ U.S. Department of Justice, Civil Rights Division, Box 66738, Washington, DC 20035-6738, ☎ 202/514–0301 or 800/514–0301; TTY 202/514–0301 or 800/514–0301; FAX 202/307–1198) for general complaints. **Aviation Consumer Protection Division** (☞ Air Travel, *above*) for airline-related problems. **Civil Rights Office** (✉ U.S. Department of Transportation, Departmental Office of Civil Rights, S-30, 400 7th St. SW, Room 10215, Washington, DC 20590, ☎ 202/366–4648, FAX 202/366–9371) for problems with surface transportation.

TRAVEL AGENCIES

In the United States, the Americans with Disabilities Act requires that travel firms serve the needs of all travelers. Some agencies specialize in working with people with disabilities.

➤ TRAVELERS WITH MOBILITY PROBLEMS: **Access Adventures** (✉ 206 Chestnut Ridge Rd., Rochester, NY 14624, ☎ 716/889–9096, dltravel@prodigy.net), run by a former physical-rehabilitation counselor. **CareVacations** (✉ 5-5110 50th Ave., Leduc, Alberta T9E 6V4, ☎ 780/986–6404 or 877/478–7827, FAX 780/986–8332, www.carevacations.com), for group tours and cruise vacations. **Flying Wheels Travel** (✉ 143 W. Bridge St., Box 382, Owatonna, MN 55060, ☎ 507/451–5005 or 800/535–6790, FAX 507/451–1685, thq@ll.net, www.flyingwheels.com).

➤ TRAVELERS WITH DEVELOPMENTAL DISABILITIES: **New Directions** (✉ 5276 Hollister Ave., Suite 207, Santa Barbara, CA 93111, ☎ 805/967–2841 or 888/967–2841, FAX 805/964–7344, newdirec@silcom.com, www.silcom.com/newdirec/). **Sprout** (✉ 893 Amsterdam Ave., New York, NY 10025, ☎ 212/222–9575 or 888/222–9575, FAX 212/222–9768, sprout@interport.net, www.gosprout.org).

DISCOUNTS & DEALS

Be a smart shopper and **compare all your options** before making decisions. A plane ticket bought with a promotional coupon from travel clubs, coupon books, and direct-mail offers may not be cheaper than the least expensive fare from a discount ticket agency. And always keep in mind that what you get is just as important as what you save.

DISCOUNT RESERVATIONS

To save money, **look into discount reservations services** with toll-free numbers, which use their buying power to get a better price on hotels, airline tickets, even car rentals. When booking a room, always **call the hotel's local toll-free number** (if one is available) rather than the central reservations number. You'll often get a better price. Always ask about special packages or corporate rates.

➤ AIRLINE TICKETS: ☎ 800/FLY-4-LESS. ☎ 800/FLY-ASAP.

PACKAGE DEALS

Don't confuse packages and guided tours. When you buy a package, you travel on your own, just as though you had planned the trip yourself.

ECOTOURISM

Bermudians are, on the whole, extremely proud of their island and fairly fanatical about protecting its natural beauty. Still, the concept of "ecotourism" has yet to find a firm footing. Although the government has been extremely successful in such endeavors as limiting cruise-ship traffic, banning rental cars, and protecting the offshore reef environment, the typical Bermuda vacation still consists of days by the pool or beach, a few rounds of golf or some watersports, shopping, and (for the adventurous) zipping around from sight to sight on a moped. That may be changing, as evidenced by the new **Daniel's Head Resort**, which opened in 2000 with 120 "eco-tents." Located on a secluded peninsula in Sandys Parish, the whole concept for Daniel's Head is rooted in a carefully considered environmental impact plan. The tent cottages, raised on stilts, are designed to have the lowest possible effect on the surroundings, both terrestrial and marine. Water recycling and solar-power generation are part of the village's day-to-day operation. Recreation is strictly nature-powered: swimming, small sailboating, and sea-kayaking in the calm, clear waters. Prices at Daniel's Head range from $135 to $250 per day. For reservations and information contact Resorts Management Inc. (☎ 800/225–4255 from the U.S. and Canada, ☎ 203/602–0300 elsewhere, rmiresorts@juno.com, www.islands-specialplaces.com).

ELECTRICITY

Local electrical current is the same as in the U.S. and Canada: 110 volt, 60 cycle AC. All appliances that can be used in North America can be used in Bermuda without adapters.

EMERGENCIES

➤ DOCTORS & DENTISTS: Contact the hospital or the **Government Health Clinic** (✉ 67 Victoria St., Hamilton, ☎ 441/236–0224, FAX 441/292–7627) for referrals.

➤ EMERGENCIES: **Police, fire, or ambulance** (☎ 911). **Air/Sea Rescue** (☎ 441/297–1010, FAX 441/297–1530, operations@rccbermuda.bm, www.rccbermuda.bm). The Government Emergency Broadcast Station is FM 100.1 MHz.

➤ HOSPITALS: **King Edward VII Memorial Hospital** (✉ 7 Point Finger Rd., outside Hamilton near the Botanical Gardens, ☎ 441/236–2345, FAX 441/236–3691) is open 24 hours.

➤ PHARMACIES: **Clarendon Pharmacy** (✉ Clarendon Bldg., Bermudiana Rd., Hamilton, ☎ 441/295–6144), open Monday–Saturday 8–6. **Collector's Hill Apothecary** (✉ South Shore Rd. and Collector's Hill, Smith's, ☎ 441/236–8664 or 441/236–9878), open Monday–Saturday 8–8, Sunday 11–7. **Hamilton Pharmacy** (✉ Parliament St., Hamilton, ☎ 441/295–7004), open Monday–Saturday 8–9. **Paget Pharmacy** (✉ Rural Hill Plaza, Middle Rd., Paget, ☎ 441/236–2681 or 441/236–7275), open Monday–Saturday 8–8, Sunday 10–6. **Phoenix Centre** (✉ 3 Reid St., Hamilton, ☎ 441/295–3838), open Monday–Saturday 8–6, Sunday noon–6. **Robertson's Drug Store** (✉ York St. and Customs House Sq., ☎ 441/297–1736 or 441/297–1828), open Monday–Saturday 8–7:30, Sunday 4–6. **Woodbourne Chemist** (✉ Gorham Rd., Pembroke, on outskirts of Hamilton, ☎ 441/295–1073 or 441/295–2663), open Monday–Saturday 8–6.

ETIQUETTE & BEHAVIOR

Bermudians tend to be quite formal in attire as well as in personal interactions. Casual dress, including bathing suits, are acceptable at hotels and resorts, but locals never venture into Hamilton in anything less than slacks and sports shirts for men, and dresses for women. Most restaurants and clubs request that men wear jackets, and more formal establishments

Food & Drink

require ties during dinner, although it's almost unheard of that someone would be turned away for not arriving in proper attire.

In downtown Hamilton, the classic Bermuda shorts are often worn by banking and insurance executives, but the outfit always includes high black socks, dress shoes, and jacket and tie. One should **remember that it is still an offense in Bermuda to ride cycles or appear in public without a shirt.** This rule may seem arcane, but most Bermudians appreciate this decorum, even as the rest of the world goes topless.

Courtesy is the rule when locals interact among themselves. **In business and social gatherings one should use the more formal Mr. and Ms. instead of first names,** at least until a friendship has been established, which sometimes takes just a few minutes. Always greet bus drivers with a friendly "Good morning" or "Good afternoon" when you board public buses. This is an island custom, and it's nice to see each passenger offer a smile and sincere greeting when boarding and exiting the bus.

Bermuda seems to be one of the few places in the world where respect is given to public servants in general. Although one underlying reason may be the fact that the residents of this small island seem to know one another, and personal greetings on the streets are commonplace, it also seems that a genuinely upbeat and friendly attitude is part of the national character.

FOOD & DRINK

The major culture influences that have shaped modern-day Bermuda—British, Caribbean, and American—have left their mark on its food as well. Truly local specialties are few and far between, but do search out mussel pie, shark hash, and the succulent Bermuda spiny lobster (available September–March).

Eating out, like most everything else on the island, is quite expensive, but the quality tends to be high and the range of options—from extremely casual pubs and local beach shacks to top-rated hotel dining rooms and elegant colonial-style restaurants—is typical of an area that caters to visitors. One thing you won't find on the island are fast-food chains, with the exception of a lone Kentucky Fried Chicken outlet.

Many hotels offer a choice of meal plans to visitors. Those willing to give up a little culinary independence in exchange for convenience, and often substantial savings, should investigate these options when booking. In addition, there are numerous "self-catering" lodgings available, and visitors up to doing some shopping and cooking on vacation can certainly eat—and drink—for considerably less.

For more information on eating out in Bermuda, and reviews of the island's best dining spots, see Chapter 4. The restaurants we list are the cream of the crop in their price categories. Unless otherwise noted, the restaurants listed in this guide are open daily for lunch and dinner.

PAYING

Most restaurants on Bermuda, even smaller ones, accept all major credit cards, but always check first if you are relying on this. **Be aware that a 15% service charge is automatically added to your restaurant bill.**

RESERVATIONS & DRESS

Reservations are always a good idea. We mention them only when they're essential or are not accepted. Book as far ahead as you can, and reconfirm as soon as you arrive, especially in high season. Also be aware that many restaurants close—or curtail hours or days of service—in the off season, so **call ahead before setting out for lunch or dinner.**

Bermudians on the whole are a dressy lot, and dinner attire is no exception. Even when not required, a jacket for men is never out of place in upscale restaurants. In our restaurant reviews, we mention dress only when men are required to wear a jacket or a jacket and tie.

WINE, BEER, & SPIRITS

Bermuda is known for its fine rum and spirits, and in addition many restaurants now have extraordinary wine cellars as well. There are numerous wine and spirit merchants along

Front Street that do a good business catering to cruise passengers, and many towns on the island have shops that provide excellent bottled rum varieties at reasonable prices.

Gosling's is one of Bermuda's oldest companies, and its Hamilton liquor shop was established in 1806. Their most famous product is Gosling's Black Seal Rum, which had been sold in barrels until just after World War I, and inherited its name from the black sealing wax that sealed the barrel corks. Black Seal, in its 151 proof variety, will test the strongest drinker, although it can also be purchased in the standard 80 proof. Black Seal is used in the popular Bermudian drink called a "dark n' stormy," which consists of a mixture of carbonated ginger beer and rum. The drink is available at bars and also in premixed cans at many of the island's liquor stores. Bermuda's "rum swizzle," another popular drink among visitors, also uses the ubiquitous Black Seal Rum. Gosling also produces three liqueurs which are big favorites—Bermuda Gold, Bermuda Banana Liqueur, and Bermuda Coconut Rum. These liqueurs can be ordered everywhere, from poolside bars to late-night jazz clubs. Guinness and Heineken are the most popular imported beers on the island, but be sure to try the local varieties, including Spinnaker and Half-Moon, which are quite good and less expensive.

To take liquor back duty-free, visit one of the larger shops and arrange for your purchases to be delivered to the airport or your cruise ship at no extra charge. There are good savings, with liters of rum costing approximately $10 duty-free (it's about $20 for regular purchases). Make sure you leave enough time for the shop to make the delivery (one to two days is ideal).

GAY & LESBIAN TRAVEL

Bermuda remains socially conservative in many respects, so same-sex couples may encounter some stares and whispers. However, discriminating against anyone based on sexual orientation is against the law.

➤ GAY- & LESBIAN-FRIENDLY TRAVEL AGENCIES: **Different Roads Travel** (✉

8383 Wilshire Blvd., Suite 902, Beverly Hills, CA 90211, ☎ 323/651–5557 or 800/429–8747, FAX 323/651–3678, leigh@west.tzell.com). **Kennedy Travel** (✉ 314 Jericho Turnpike, Floral Park, NY 11001, ☎ 516/352–4888 or 800/237–7433, FAX 516/354–8849, main@kennedytravel.com, www.kennedytravel.com). **Now Voyager** (✉ 4406 18th St., San Francisco, CA 94114, ☎ 415/626–1169 or 800/255–6951, FAX 415/626–8626, www.nowvoyager.com). **Skylink Travel and Tour** (✉ 1006 Mendocino Ave., Santa Rosa, CA 95401, ☎ 707/546–9888 or 800/225–5759, FAX 707/546–9891, skylinktvl@aol.com, www.skylinktravel.com), serving lesbian travelers.

HEALTH

Sunburn and sunstroke are legitimate concerns if you're traveling to Bermuda in the summer. On hot, sunny days, wear a hat, a beach cover-up, and lots of sunblock. These are essential for a day on a boat, but are also advisable for midday at the beach. Drink plenty of water and, above all, **limit the amount of time you spend in the sun** until you become acclimated.

The Portuguese man-of-war occasionally visits Bermuda's waters, so **be alert when swimming,** especially in summer or whenever the water is particularly warm. This creature is recognizable by a purple, balloonlike float sack of perhaps 8 inches in diameter, below which dangle 20- to 60-inch tentacles armed with powerful stinging cells. Contact with the stinging cells causes immediate and severe pain. Seek medical attention immediately, even if you don't think the sting is severe. A serious sting can send a person into shock. In the meantime—or if getting to a doctor will take a while—treat the affected area liberally with ammonia. Although usually encountered in the water, Portuguese men-of-war may also wash up on shore. If you spot one on the sand, steer clear, as the sting is just as severe out of the water.

DIVERS' ALERT

Do not fly within 24 hours of scuba diving.

MEDICAL PLANS

No one plans to get sick while traveling, but it happens, so **consider signing up with a medical-assistance company.** Members get doctor referrals, emergency evacuation or repatriation, hot lines for medical consultation, cash for emergencies, and other assistance.

➤ MEDICAL-ASSISTANCE COMPANIES: **International SOS Assistance** (✉ 8 Neshaminy Interplex, Suite 207, Trevose, PA 19053, ☎ 215/245–4707 or 800/523–6586, FAX 215/244–9617, www.internationalsos.com; ✉ 12 Chemin Riantbosson, 1217 Meyrin 1, Geneva, Switzerland, ☎ 4122/785–6464, FAX 4122/785–6424, www.internationalsos.com; ✉ 331 N. Bridge Rd., 17-00, Odeon Towers, Singapore 188720, ☎ 65/338–7800, FAX 65/338–7611, www.internationalsos.com).

HOLIDAYS

On Sundays and national public holidays, all shops, businesses, and many restaurants in Bermuda close. Buses and ferries run on limited schedules. Most entertainment venues, sights, and sports outfitters remain open. When holidays fall on a Saturday, government and commercial offices close the following Monday, but restaurants and shops remain open. National public holidays are New Year's Day, Good Friday (Apr. 13 in 2001), Bermuda Day (May 24), Queen's Birthday (June 11 in 2001), Cup Match/Somers Day (Aug. 2–3 in 2001), Labour Day (Sept. 3 in 2001), Remembrance Day (Nov. 11), Christmas, and Boxing Day (Dec. 26).

INSURANCE

The most useful travel insurance plan is a comprehensive policy that includes coverage for trip cancellation and interruption, default, trip delay, and medical expenses (with a waiver for preexisting conditions).

Without insurance you will lose all or most of your money if you cancel your trip, regardless of the reason. Default insurance covers you if your tour operator, airline, or cruise line goes out of business. Trip-delay covers expenses that arise because of bad weather or mechanical delays. Study the fine print when comparing policies.

If you're traveling internationally, a key component of travel insurance is coverage for medical bills incurred if you get sick on the road. Such expenses are not generally covered by Medicare or private policies. U.K. residents can buy a travel insurance policy valid for most vacations taken during the year in which it's purchased (but check preexisting-condition coverage). British and Australian citizens need extra medical coverage when traveling overseas.

Always **buy travel policies directly from the insurance company.** If you buy them from a cruise line, airline, or tour operator that goes out of business you probably will not be covered for the agency or operator's default, a major risk. Before making any purchase, **review your existing health and homeowner's policies** to find what they cover away from home.

➤ INSURANCE INFORMATION: In the U.K.: **Association of British Insurers** (✉ 51–55 Gresham St., London EC2V 7HQ, ☎ 020/7600–3333, FAX 020/7696–8999, info@abi.org.uk, www.abi.org.uk). In Australia: **Insurance Council of Australia** (☎ 03/9614–1077, FAX 03/9614–7924).

➤ TRAVEL INSURERS: In the U.S.: **Access America** (✉ 6600 W. Broad St., Richmond, VA 23230, ☎ 804/285–3300 or 800/284–8300, FAX 804/673–1583, www.previewtravel.com), **Travel Guard International** (✉ 1145 Clark St., Stevens Point, WI 54481, ☎ 715/345–0505 or 800/826–1300, FAX 800/955–8785, www.noelgroup.com). In Canada: **Voyager Insurance** (✉ 44 Peel Center Dr., Brampton, Ontario L6T 4M8, ☎ 905/791–8700; 800/668–4342 in Canada).

LODGING

Bermuda's most ubiquitous lodging is the cottage colony—a cluster of freestanding cottages situated around a main building usually housing check-in, activities desk, one or more restaurants, and a lounge area. That said, you'll find innumerable other options, from large hotels and luxury resorts to guest houses. The lodgings we list are the cream of the crop in each price category. We always list the facilities that are available, but we don't specify whether they cost extra. When pricing accommodations, **always ask what's included and what costs extra.** All accommodations we list have private bathrooms unless stated otherwise.

Assume that hotels operate on the **European Plan** (EP, with no meals) unless we specify that they use the **Continental Plan** (CP, with a Continental breakfast), **Breakfast Plan** (BP, with a full breakfast), **Modified American Plan** (MAP, with breakfast and dinner), or the **Full American Plan** (FAP, with all meals).

APARTMENT & VILLA RENTALS

If you want a home base that's roomy enough for a family and comes with cooking facilities, **consider a furnished rental.** These can save you money, especially if you're traveling with a group. Home-exchange directories sometimes list rentals as well as exchanges.

➤ INTERNATIONAL AGENTS: **Europa-Let/Tropical Inn-Let** (✉ 92 N. Main St., Ashland, OR 97520, ☎ 541/482–5806 or 800/462–4486, ℻ 541/482–0660). **Villas International** (✉ 950 Northgate Dr., Suite 206, San Rafael, CA 94903, ☎ 415/499–9490 or 800/221–2260, ℻ 415/499–9491, villas@best.com, www.villasintl.com).

➤ LOCAL AGENTS: **C.R.E. Properties, Ltd.** (Washington Mall, Church St., Hamilton, Bermuda, ☎ 441/295–5487, ℻ 441/295–8158, creprop@ibl.bm). **Kitson & Company Ltd.** (Reid St., Hamilton, Bermuda, ☎ 441/295–2525, ℻ 441/295–0814, brenda@kitson.bm).

➤ RESERVATION SERVICES: **Small Properties Ltd.** (☎ 800/637–4116, ℻ 441/236–1662, reservation@bspl.bm, www.bermudareservation.net) is a group of small hotels and guest houses that share a toll-free information and reservations line and a fax number.

HOME EXCHANGES

If you would like to exchange your home for someone else's, **join a home-exchange organization,** which will send you its updated listings of available exchanges for a year and will include your own listing in at least one of them. It's up to you to make specific arrangements.

➤ EXCHANGE CLUBS: **HomeLink International** ($98 per year; ✉ Box 650, Key West, FL 33041, ☎ 305/294–7766 or 800/638–3841, ℻ 305/294–1448, usa@homelink.org, www.homelink.org).

HOSTELS

There are no youth hostels, YMCAs, or YWCAs on the island. During Bermuda Spring Break Sports Week (☞ Festivals and Seasonal Events *in* Chapter 1), however, special student rates are offered at some hotels and guest houses, restaurants, pubs, and nightclubs.

MAIL & SHIPPING

Allow seven to ten days for mail from Bermuda to reach the United States, Canada, or the United Kingdom, and about two weeks to arrive in Australia or New Zealand.

OVERNIGHT SERVICES

Overnight courier service is available to or from the continental United States through several companies. Service between Bermuda and Canada takes one or two business days, depending on the part of Canada; between Bermuda and the United Kingdom, generally two business days; and between Bermuda and Australia or New Zealand, usually three.

In Bermuda, rates include pickup from anywhere on the island. Prices for a document up to the first pound start at about $26 to the United States, $32 to Canada, and $34 to the United Kingdom, Australia, or New Zealand. For the fastest delivery, your pickup request must be made before about 10 AM. Note that pickups (and drop-off locations) are limited on Saturdays, and there is no service on Sunday. Also, nondocuments sent to Bermuda may take a day longer than documents.

➤ MAJOR SERVICES: **Federal Express** (☎ 441/295–3854). **International Bonded Couriers** (☎ 441/295–2467).

United Parcel Service (☎ 441/292–6760).

POSTAL RATES

Airmail postcards to the United States and Canada cost 60¢, letters 65¢ for the first 10 grams. Postcards to the United Kingdom cost 75¢, letters 80¢ for the first 10 grams. Postcards to Australia and New Zealand cost 85¢, letters 90¢ for the first 10 grams.

RECEIVING MAIL

If you have no address in Bermuda, you can **have mail sent care of General Delivery,** General Post Office, Hamilton HM GD, Bermuda.

SHIPPING PARCELS

Through Parcel Post at Bermuda's post office, you can send packages either International Data Express (which takes two to five business days to the United States, Canada, the United Kingdom, Australia, and New Zealand) or Air Parcel Post (which takes five to ten business days to the U.S., Canada, and the U.K., or two weeks to Australia and New Zealand). For additional information, *see* Overnight Services, *above.*

For the first 500 grams, International Data Express rates are $22 to the U.S. and Canada, $28 to the U.K., and $35 to Australia or New Zealand. Air Parcel Post rates run $5.65 for the first 500 grams to the U.S., $9.10 to Canada, $11.75 to the U.K., and $14.75 to Australia or New Zealand.

Most of Bermuda's largest stores offer shipping of purchases. Some may ask you either to buy insurance or to sign a waiver absolving them of any responsibility for potential loss or damage.

➤ POST OFFICE: **Parcel Post** (☎ 441/295–5151).

MEDIA

NEWSPAPERS & MAGAZINES

The Royal Gazette, Bermuda's only daily newspaper, is considered the paper of record. Established in 1828, it is published Monday–Saturday, and offers a comprehensive mix of international hard news along with sports, business, and features. You can find it on the Web at www.accessbda.bm/gazette.htm. Its weekly sister paper,

The Mid-Ocean News, is more community oriented, with extensive coverage of local arts, theater, politics, and overseas travel. Published twice a week, **The Bermuda Sun** (www.bermudasun.org) also focuses on local politics, trends, and events.

Appearing monthly in **The Royal Gazette, RG** magazine is a high-quality glossy, with topical features. **The Bermudian,** the island's oldest monthly, is another glossy, showcasing local lifestyles, personalities, history, arts, and social events. Distributed in 80 countries, **Bermuda,** a quarterly, keeps Bermudaphiles up-to-date on local cultural, political, and social trends.

Two quarterlies, **Bottom Line** and **Bermudian Business,** provide comprehensive coverage of local and international money-making, from banking, financial services, and insurance to new technologies.

RADIO & TELEVISION

Dial **Mix 106** (106.1 FM) for calypso, reggae, and soca, plus R&B, adult contemporary, local jazz, and European classical. For country music, listen to **1450 Country** (1450 AM), which also features a midday call-in talk show covering hot local issues. **Z2** (1340 AM) surrounds its talk shows with Billboard Top 100 and country-and-western tunes. You can hear more Top 100 rock, R&B, hip–hop, and reggae on **Power 95** (94.9 FM). Gospel, easy listening, and religious talk are the sounds on **ZFB 1230 AM.**

In addition to a slew of cable television stations (mainly from the U.S.), Bermudian sets can be tuned in to **ZBM** ("Zed BM"), the CBS affiliate, on TV channel 9 or cable 3; **ZFB** ("Zed FB"), the ABC affiliate, on TV channel 7 or cable 2; and **VSB,** the NBC affiliate, on TV channel 11 or cable 4. Along with the nightly news, local programming, which is interspersed with the networks' offerings, might include a cooking show, a cricket or football (soccer) match, or a program on health awareness.

MONEY MATTERS

Since Bermuda imports everything from cars to cardigans, prices are very high. At an upscale restaurant, for example, you're bound to pay as much for a meal as you would in New York, London, or Paris: on average, $60 to $80 per person, $120 with drinks and wine. There are other options, of course; the island is full of coffee shops, where you can eat hamburgers and french fries with locals for about $7. The same meal at a restaurant costs about $15.

A cup of coffee costs between $1.50 and $3; a mixed drink from $4 to $6; a bottle of beer from $2.25 to $6; and a can of soda about $1.50. A 15-minute cab ride will set you back about $25 including tip. A 36-exposure roll of 35mm 100 ASA print film costs $6 to $8. A pack of cigarettes costs between $5 and $7.

Prices throughout this guide are given for adults. Substantially reduced fees are almost always available for children, students, and senior citizens. For information on taxes, *see* Taxes, *below*.

ATMS

ATMs are found all over Bermuda, in shops, arcades, supermarkets, the airport, and two of the island's banks. Both **The Bank of Bermuda** and **The Bank of Butterfield** are affiliated with the Cirrus and Plus networks. Note that the personal identification number (PIN) you use with Bank of Bermuda ATMs must be four digits, while Bank of Butterfield ATMs accept PINs with four to sixteen digits.

➤ ATM LOCATIONS: **Cirrus** (☎ 800/424–7787). **Plus** (☎ 800/843–7587) for locations in the U.S. and Canada, or visit your local bank.

CREDIT CARDS

In Bermuda, most shops and restaurants accept credit and debit cards, but some hotels insist on cash or traveler's checks, so **check in advance whether your hotel takes credit cards.** The most widely accepted cards are **MasterCard, Visa,** and **American Express. Discover** and **Diner's Club** are welcomed to a much lesser degree.

Throughout this guide, the following abbreviations are used: AE, American Express; DC, Diner's Club; MC, MasterCard; and V, Visa.

➤ REPORTING LOST CARDS: **American Express** (☎ 800/327–1267). **Diner's Club** (☎ 702/234–6377; call collect). **Discover** (☎ 800/347–2683). **MasterCard** (☎ 800/307–7309). **Visa** (☎ 800/847–2911).

CURRENCY

The Bermudian dollar is on par with the U.S. dollar, and the two currencies are used interchangeably. (Other non-Bermudian currency must be converted.) You can use American money anywhere, but change is often given in Bermudian currency. Try to **avoid accumulating large amounts of local money,** which is difficult to exchange for U.S. dollars in Bermuda and expensive to exchange in the United States.

CURRENCY EXCHANGE

If you need to exchange Canadian dollars, British pounds, or other currencies, for the most favorable rates **change money through banks.** Although ATM transaction fees may be higher abroad than at home, ATM rates are excellent because they are based on wholesale rates offered only by major banks. You won't do as well at exchange booths in airports or rail and bus stations, in hotels, in restaurants, or in stores. To avoid lines at airport exchange booths, **get a bit of local currency before you leave home.**

➤ EXCHANGE SERVICES: **International Currency Express** (☎ 888/278–6628 for orders, www.foreignmoney.com). **Thomas Cook Currency Services** (☎ 800/287–7362 for telephone orders and retail locations, www.us.thomascook.com).

TRAVELER'S CHECKS

Traveler's checks are widely accepted throughout Bermuda. Lost or stolen, they can usually be replaced within 24 hours. To ensure a speedy refund, buy your own traveler's checks. Don't let someone else pay for them, as irregularities like this can cause delays. The person who bought the checks should make the call to request a refund.

Some hotels take personal checks by prior arrangement (a letter from your bank is sometimes requested).

MOPED & SCOOTER RENTAL

Because car rentals are not allowed in Bermuda, you might decide to get around by moped or scooter. Bermudians routinely use the words "moped" and "scooter" interchangeably, even though they are different. You must pedal to start a moped, and it carries only one person. A scooter, on the other hand, which starts when you put the key in the ignition, is more powerful and holds one or two passengers.

Riding a moped is not without hazards, especially for first-time riders and those not accustomed to driving on the left. Roads are narrow, winding, and full of blind curves. Whether driving cars or scooters, Bermudians tend to be quite cautious around less experienced visiting riders. However, it's still wise to **think twice before renting a moped,** as accidents occur frequently and are sometimes fatal. The best ways to avoid mishaps are to drive defensively, obey the 20-mph (35-kph) speed limit, remember to **stay on the left-hand side of the road**—especially at traffic circles—and avoid riding in the rain and at night.

Helmets are required by law. Single- or double-seat mopeds and scooters can be rented from cycle liveries by the hour, the day, or the week. The liveries will show first-time riders how to operate the vehicles. Rates vary, but single-seat mopeds cost about $32 per day or $113 per week (plus the mandatory $15 insurance and repair waiver). The fee includes third-party insurance, breakdown service, pickup and delivery, and a tank of gas. A $20–$50 deposit is required for the lock, key, and helmet, and you must be at least 16 and have a valid driver's license to rent. Major hotels have their own cycle liveries, and all hotels and guest houses will make rental arrangements. Many gas stations are open daily 7–7, and a few stay open until midnight. Gas for cycles runs $3–$4 per liter, but you can cover a great deal of ground on the full tank that comes with the wheels.

➤ RENTAL COMPANIES: **Oleander Cycles** (✉ Valley Rd., Paget, ☎ 441/236–5235; ✉ Gorham Rd., Hamilton, ☎ 441/295–0919; ✉ Middle Rd., Southampton, ☎ 441/234–0629; ✉ The Reefs, Southampton, ☎ 441/238–0222; ✉ Dockyard, Sandys, ☎ 441/234–2764). **Eve's Cycle Livery** (✉ Middle Rd., Paget, ☎ 441/236–6247). **Wheels Cycles** (✉ 117 Front Street, Hamilton, ☎ 441/292–2245 or 441/295–0112).

PACKING

Bermudians dress more formally than most Americans. Although attire tends to be casual during the day—Bermuda shorts are acceptable even for businessmen—cutoffs, short shorts, and halter tops are inappropriate. Swimsuits should not be worn outside pool areas or off the beach. You'll need a cover-up in your hotel's common areas. Joggers may wear standard jogging shorts but should avoid appearing on public streets without a shirt. In the evening, many restaurants and hotel dining rooms require men to wear a jacket and tie and women to dress comparably, so **it's best to bring a few dressy outfits.** Some hotels have begun setting aside one or two nights a week for "smart casual" attire, when jacket-and-tie restrictions are loosened. In this case, women should be fine with tailored slacks and a dressy blouse or sweater (though most Bermudian women wear dresses or skirts and blouses). Bermudian men often wear Bermuda shorts (and proper knee socks) with a jacket and tie.

During the **cooler months, you should bring lightweight woolens or cottons** that you can wear in layers, depending on the vagaries of the weather. A few sweaters and a lightweight jacket are always a good idea. Regardless of the season, you should **pack a swimsuit, a cover-up, sunscreen, and sunglasses** as well as an umbrella and raincoat. Comfortable walking shoes and a bag for carrying maps and cameras are a must. If you plan to play tennis, be aware that many courts require proper whites and that tennis balls in Bermuda are extremely expensive. Bring your own if possible.

In your carry-on luggage, **pack an extra pair of eyeglasses or contact lenses** and **enough of any medication you take** to last the entire trip. You may also ask your doctor to write a spare prescription using the drug's generic name, since brand names may vary from country to country. In luggage to be checked, **never pack prescription drugs or valuables.** To avoid customs delays, carry medications in their original packaging. And don't forget to carry with you the addresses of offices that handle refunds of lost traveler's checks.

CHECKING LUGGAGE

How many carry-on bags you can bring with you is up to the airline. Most allow two, but not always, so make sure that everything you carry aboard will fit under your seat or in the overhead bin, and get to the gate early. Note that if you have a seat at the back of the plane, you'll probably board first, while the overhead bins are still empty.

If you are flying internationally, note that baggage allowances may be determined not by piece but by weight—generally 88 pounds (40 kilograms) in first class, 66 pounds (30 kilograms) in business class, and 44 pounds (20 kilograms) in economy.

Airline liability for baggage is limited to $1,250 per person on flights within the United States. On international flights it amounts to $9.07 per pound or $20 per kilogram for checked baggage (roughly $640 per 70-pound bag) and $400 per passenger for unchecked baggage. You can buy additional coverage at check-in for about $10 per $1,000 of coverage, but it excludes a rather extensive list of items, shown on your airline ticket.

Before departure, **itemize your bags' contents** and their worth, and label the bags with your name, address, and phone number. (If you use your home address, cover it so potential thieves can't see it readily.) Inside each bag, **pack a copy of your itinerary.** At check-in, **make sure that each bag is correctly tagged** with the destination airport's three-letter code. If your bags arrive damaged or fail to arrive at all, file a written report with the airline before leaving the airport.

PASSPORTS & VISAS

When traveling internationally, **carry your passport even if you don't need one** (it's always the best form of ID) and **make two photocopies of the**

data page (one for someone at home and another for you, carried separately from your passport). If you lose your passport, promptly call the nearest embassy or consulate and the local police.

ENTERING BERMUDA

➤ U.S. CITIZENS: **Bring your passport to ensure quick passage through immigration and customs.** You do not need a passport to enter Bermuda if you plan to stay less than six months, but you must have onward or return tickets and proof of identity (original or certified copy of your birth certificate with raised seal, a U.S. Naturalization Certificate, a U.S. Alien Registration Card, or a U.S. Reentry Permit).

➤ CANADIANS: Canadians do not need a passport to enter Bermuda, though a passport is helpful to ensure quick passage through customs and immigration. A birth certificate or a certificate of citizenship is required, along with a photo ID.

➤ OTHER CITIZENS: Citizens of the United Kingdom and other countries must have a valid passport to enter Bermuda.

PASSPORT OFFICES

The best time to apply for a passport or to renew is in fall and winter. Before any trip, check your passport's expiration date, and if necessary, renew it as soon as possible.

➤ AUSTRALIAN CITIZENS: **Australian Passport Office** (☎ 131–232, www.dfat.gov.au/passports).

➤ CANADIAN CITIZENS: **Passport Office** (☎ 819/994–3500 or 800/567–6868, www.dfait-maeci.gc.ca/passport).

➤ NEW ZEALAND CITIZENS: **New Zealand Passport Office** (☎ 04/494–0700, www.passports.govt.nz).

➤ U.K. CITIZENS: **London Passport Office** (☎ 0990/210–410) for fees and documentation requirements and to request an emergency passport.

➤ U.S. CITIZENS: **National Passport Information Center** (☎ 900/225–5674. Calls are 35¢ per minute for automated service, $1.05 per minute for operator service).

SAFETY

Bermuda is a small, fairly affluent country, and as a consequence has a very low crime rate. Serious crimes against visitors—or anyone, for that matter—are rare. Still, **exercise the usual precautions with wallets, purses, cameras,** and other valuables, particularly at the beach. Always lock your moped or pedal bike, and store valuables in your hotel's safe. **Remember that vacation is never an excuse to let your guard down,** and everyone—particularly women traveling alone—needs to act with personal safety in mind at all times.

SENIOR-CITIZEN TRAVEL

To qualify for age-related discounts, **mention your senior-citizen status up front** when booking hotel reservations (not when checking out) and before you're seated in restaurants (not when paying the bill).

➤ EDUCATIONAL PROGRAMS: **Elderhostel** (✉ 75 Federal St., 3rd floor, Boston, MA 02110, ☎ 877/426–8056, FAX 877/426–2166, www.elderhostel.org).

SIGHTSEEING TOURS

BOAT TOURS

Bermuda Island Cruises operates a 200-passenger boat that leaves Albuoy's Point in Hamilton at 7 PM on Tuesday, Wednesday, Friday, and Saturday for a "Don't Stop the Carnival Cruise" ($75 including dinner, drinks, and entertainment). Two-hour tours of Sea Gardens ($30) in glass-bottom boats leave twice daily from the ferry terminal in Hamilton. A five-hour island cruise ($65) is also available on Wednesday.

Windjammer Watersports conducts 1¼-hour jet-ski tours ($95 for a single jet ski, $125 for a double).

➤ INFORMATION: **Bermuda Island Cruises** (☎ 441/292–8652, FAX 441/292–5193, bic@ibl.bm, www.bermuda.com). **Windjammer Water Sports** (☎ 441/234–0250).

GARDEN TOURS

In spring, the Garden Club of Bermuda arranges tours to three

different houses each Wednesday between 1 and 4. Admission is $12.

Free 75-minute guided tours of the Botanical Gardens leave at 10:30 AM from the car park by the Berry Hill Road entrance year-round: Tuesday, Wednesday, and Friday from April to October, and Tuesday and Friday from November to March. You can take a tour at another time by special arrangement with the curator of the gardens, in exchange for a donation to the Botanical Society.

➤ INFORMATION: **Visitors Service Bureau** (☎ 441/295–1480). **Botanical Gardens** (☎ 441/236–4201).

HORSE-DRAWN CARRIAGE TOURS

You can hire carriages on Front Street in Hamilton. Rates for a one- or two-horse carriage for up to four passengers are $20 for the first 30 minutes and $20 for each additional 30 minutes. Each adult is charged an additional $5 per half hour when more than five people ride in one carriage.

SNORKELING TOURS

Bermuda's Multihull Sailing Adventures offers two vessels for daily snorkeling trips ($40 for a half day; $75 for a full day with lunch), April–October. Boats depart from various points around the island.

Hayward's Snorkeling and Glass Bottom Boat Cruises has one of the island's best sightseeing-snorkeling excursions ($45, including instruction and gear) aboard the 54-ft glass-bottom *Explorer.* From this boat, access in and out of the water is exceptionally easy. The cruise departs from the dock adjacent to Hamilton's ferry terminal. Special excursions are arranged during the spring migration of the humpback whales; call for prices.

Jessie James Snorkeling & Sightseeing Cruises offers half-day snorkeling cruises ($45 adult; $25 children 5–12) aboard its 40-passenger luxury Chris-Craft *Rambler* from Albuoy's Point in Hamilton and Darrell's Wharf and Belmont dock in Warwick. Cruises depart daily at 9:15 and 2:15.

➤ INFORMATION: **Bermuda's Multihull Sailing Adventures** (☎ 441/234–

1434). **Hayward's Snorkeling & Glass Bottom Boat Cruises** (☎ 441/236–9894, FAX 441/236–2608). **Jesse James Cruises** (☎ 441/295–0460 or 235–0817, FAX 441/296–7099,jessie-james@bermuda-shorts.com, www.jessiejames.bm).

TAXI & MINIBUS TOURS

For an independent tour of Bermuda, a taxi is a good but more expensive alternative to a group tour. A blue flag on the hood of a cab indicates that the driver is a qualified tour guide. These cabs can be difficult to find, but most of their drivers are friendly, entertaining—they sometimes bend the truth for a good yarn—and well informed about the island and its history. Ask your hotel to arrange a tour with a knowledgeable driver.

Cabs seat four or six, and the legal rate for island tours (minimum three hours) is $30 per hour for one to four passengers and $42 per hour for five or six passengers. Two children under 12 equal an adult.

➤ OPERATORS: **Bee-Line Transport Ltd.** (✉ Box HM 2270, Hamilton HM, ☎ 441/293–0303, FAX 441/293–8015). **Bermuda Hosts Ltd.** (✉ Box CR 46, Crawl, Hamilton CR, ☎ 441/293–1334, FAX 441/293–1335). **Destination Bermuda Ltd.** (✉ Box HM 1822, Hamilton HM HX, ☎ 441/292–2325, FAX 441/292–2252).

WALKING TOURS

The Bermuda Department of Tourism publishes brochures with self-guided tours of Hamilton, St. George's, the West End, and the Railway Trail. "The Bermuda Nature Guide," also issued by the Bermuda Department of Tourism, has details on the island's flora, fauna, and pink-coral sand. Available free at all Visitor Service Bureaus and at hotels and guest houses, the brochures also contain detailed directions for walkers and cyclists, and historical notes and anecdotes.

From November through March, the Bermuda Department of Tourism coordinates walking tours of Hamilton, St. George's, Spittal Pond Nature Reserve, the Royal Naval Dockyard, and Somerset. The tours of Hamilton and St. George's, as well as most of the Royal Naval Dockyard tours, take in historic buildings, while the Spittal Pond and Somerset tours focus on the island's flora.

The enjoyable walking tours organized by Native Adventures allow visitors to experience Bermuda's natural beauty and remote corners through the eyes of a professional photographer. Tailoring routes (and photography tips) to the desires of participants, Tamell Simons limits his guided ambles to six people. The 2 ½-hour tour costs $65, while the five-hour sunrise or afternoon trip with a picnic lunch is $100.

Out & About Bermuda leads walking tours through some of Bermuda's most scenic nature reserves, parks, residential neighborhoods, and historic areas. Rates begin at $20 per person.

Finally, the Walking Club of Bermuda sponsors walks around sundry areas of interest on the island.

➤ INFORMATION: **Bermuda Department of Tourism** (☎ 441/292–0023). **Native Adventures** (☎ 441/295–2957 or 441/235–6515). **Out & About Bermuda** (☎ 441/295–2595). **Walking Club of Bermuda** (☎ 441/295–0008 days; 441/295–4148 evenings); www.bermudatourism.com.

STUDENTS IN BERMUDA

Like other travelers, students arriving in Bermuda must have confirmation of hotel reservations, a return plane ticket, a photo ID, and proof of citizenship, such as a passport, birth certificate, or a signed voter-registration card. There are no youth hostels, YMCAs, or YWCAs on the island. During Bermuda Spring Break Sports Week (☞ Festivals and Seasonal Events *in* Chapter 1), however, special student rates are offered at some hotels and guest houses, restaurants, pubs, and nightclubs.

➤ IDs & SERVICES: **Council Travel** (CIEE; ✉ 205 E. 42nd St., 14th floor, New York, NY 10017, ☎ 212/822–2700 or 888/268–6245, FAX 212/822–2699, info@councilexchanges.org, www.councilexchanges.org) for mail orders only, in the U.S. **Travel Cuts** (✉ 187 College St., Toronto, Ontario M5T 1P7, ☎ 416/979–2406 or 800/ 667–2887, www.travelcuts.com) in Canada.

TAXES

Hotels add a 7.25% government tax to the bill, and most add a 10% service charge or a per diem dollar equivalent in lieu of tips. Other extra charges sometimes include a 5% "energy surcharge" (at small guest houses) and a 15% service charge (at most restaurants).

A $20 airport departure tax is built into the price of your ticket.

TAXIS

Taxis are the fastest and easiest way around the island—and also the most costly. Four-seater taxis charge $3.12 for the first quarter mile and 24¢ for each subsequent quarter mile. Between midnight and 6 AM, and on Sunday, a 25% surcharge is added to the fare. There is a 25¢ charge for each piece of luggage stored in the trunk or on the roof. For a personalized taxi tour of the island, the minimum duration is three hours, at $30 per hour for one to four people and $42 an hour for five or six, excluding tip.

For information on taxi tours, *see* Sightseeing Tours, *above.*

➤ CAB COMPANIES: **Bermuda Taxi Operators Company** (☎ 441/292–4175). **Bermuda Taxi Radio Cabs** (☎ 441/295–4141). **The Co-op Taxi Service** (☎ 441/292–4476). **Sandys Taxi Service** (☎ 441/234–2344).

TELEPHONES

AREA & COUNTRY CODES

The country code for Bermuda is 441. When dialing a Bermuda number from abroad, drop the initial 0 from the local area code. The country code is 1 for the United States and Canada, 61 for Australia, 64 for New Zealand, and 44 for the U.K.

DIRECTORY & OPERATOR ASSISTANCE

When in Bermuda, call 411 for local phone numbers. To reach directory assistance from outside the country, call 441/555–1212.

INTERNATIONAL CALLS

You can dial direct from anywhere on the island. Most hotels impose a surcharge for long-distance calls, even those made collect or with a phone card or credit card. Many small guest houses and apartments have no central switchboard. So if you have a phone in your room, it's a private line from which you can make only collect, credit-card, or local calls. Some small hotels have a telephone room or kiosk where you can make long-distance calls.

You'll find specially marked AT&T USADirect phones at the airport, the cruise-ship dock in Hamilton, and King's Square and Ordnance Island in St. George's. You can also make international calls with a calling card from the main post office. You can make prepaid international calls from the Cable & Wireless Office, which also has international telex, cable, and fax services Monday–Saturday 9–5.

To call the United States, Canada, and most Caribbean countries, simply dial 1 (or 0 if you need an operator's assistance), then the area code and the number. For all other countries, dial 011 (or 0 for an operator), the country code, the area code, and the number. Using an operator for an overseas call is more expensive than dialing direct. For calls to the United States, rates are highest from 10 AM to 7 PM and discounted from 7 PM to 11 PM. The lowest rates are from 11 PM to 7 AM. Calls to Alaska and Hawaii are not discounted. Calls to Canada are cheapest from 9 PM to 7 AM; to the United Kingdom, from 6 PM to 7 AM.

➤ TO OBTAIN ACCESS CODES: **AT&T USADirect** (☎ 800/874–4000). **MCI Call USA** (☎ 800/444–4444). **Sprint Express** (☎ 800/793–1153).

➤ INTERNATIONAL CALLS: **Main post office** (Church and Parliament Sts., Hamilton, ☎ 441/295–5151). **Cable & Wireless Office** (20 Church St., opposite City Hall, Hamilton, ☎ 441/297–7000).

LONG-DISTANCE SERVICES

AT&T, MCI, and Sprint access codes make calling long distance relatively convenient, but you may find the local access number blocked in many hotel rooms. First ask the hotel operator to connect you. If the hotel operator balks, ask for an international operator, or dial the international operator yourself. One way to improve your odds of getting connected to your long-distance carrier is to travel with more than one company's calling card (a hotel may block Sprint, for example, but not MCI). If all else fails, call from a pay phone.

➤ ACCESS CODES: **AT&T Direct** (☎ 800/872–2881). **MCI WorldPhone** (☎ 800/888–8000). **Sprint International Access** (☎ 800/623–0877).

PHONE CARDS

Phone cards can be used with any Touch-Tone phone in Bermuda. However, some hotels will charge you for making the call to your card's 800 number.

Bermuda's prepaid phone cards are available at pharmacies, shops, restaurants, and hotels. You can use them from any Touch-Tone phone, but they are for calls outside Bermuda only. Both **TeleBermuda** and **Cable & Wireless** sell the cards in denominations of $10, $25, and $50.

You can use any balances remaining on the TeleBermuda cards when you return to the United States, Canada, or the United Kingdom. With Cable & Wireless cards, only balances on Truly Global cards (costing $50, $75, or $100) can be used when you are outside of Bermuda.

➤ PHONE CARD COMPANIES: **Cable & Wireless** (☎ 441/297–7022). **TeleBermuda** (☎ 441/292–7283).

PUBLIC PHONES

You'll find pay phones similar to those in the United States on the streets of Hamilton, St. George's, and Somerset as well as at ferry landings, some bus stops, and public beaches. Deposit 20¢ (U.S. or Bermudian) in the meter as soon as your party answers. (You can also deposit a U.S. or Bermudian quarter, but you won't receive the 5¢ change.) Most hotels charge 20¢–$1 for local calls.

TIME

Bermuda, in the Atlantic Time Zone, is on Greenwich Mean Time, minus four hours (which means that it is four hours later in London than in Bermuda). Because, like the United States, the island observes Daylight Saving Time (from the first Sunday in April to the last Sunday in October), it is always one hour ahead of U.S. Eastern Standard Time. Thus, for instance, when it is 5 PM in Bermuda, it is 4 PM in New York, 3 PM in Chicago, and 1 PM in Los Angeles. Sydney is 14 hours ahead of Bermuda, so when it is 5 PM in Bermuda, it is 8 AM the next morning in Sydney.

TIPPING

A service charge of 10% (or an equivalent per-diem amount), which covers everything from baggage handling to maid service, is added to your hotel bill. Most restaurants tack on a 15% service charge; if not, a 15% tip is customary (more for exceptional service). Porters at the airport expect about a dollar a bag, while taxi drivers usually receive 15% of the fare.

TOURS & PACKAGES

Because everything is prearranged on a prepackaged tour or independent vacation, you'll spend less time planning—and often get it all at a good price.

BOOKING WITH AN AGENT

Travel agents are excellent resources. But it's a good idea to collect brochures from several agencies as some agents' suggestions may be influenced by relationships with tour and package firms that reward them for volume sales. If you have a special interest, **find an agent with expertise in that area.** ASTA (☞ Travel Agencies, *below*) has a database of specialists worldwide.

Make sure your travel agent knows the accommodations and other services of the place they're recommending. Ask about the hotel's location, room size, beds, and whether it has a pool, room service, or programs for children, if you care about these. Has your agent been there in person or sent others whom you can contact?

Do some homework on your own, too. Local tourism boards can provide information about lesser-known and small-niche operators, some of which may sell only direct.

BUYER BEWARE

Each year consumers are stranded or lose their money when tour operators—even large ones with excellent reputations—go out of business. So **check out the operator.** Ask several travel agents about its reputation, and try to **book with a company that has a consumer-protection program.** (Look for information in the company's brochure.) In the United States, members of the National Tour Association and the United States Tour Operators Association are required to set aside funds to cover your payments and travel arrangements in the event that the company defaults. It's also a good idea to choose a company that participates in the American Society of Travel Agents' Tour Operator Program (TOP). ASTA will act as mediator in any disputes between you and your tour operator.

Remember that the more your package or tour includes the better you can predict the ultimate cost of your vacation. Make sure you know exactly what is covered, and **beware of hidden costs.** Are taxes, tips, and transfers included? Entertainment and excursions? These can add up.

➤ TOUR-OPERATOR RECOMMENDATIONS: **American Society of Travel Agents** (☞ Travel Agencies, *below*). **National Tour Association** (NTA; ⊠ 546 E. Main St., Lexington, KY 40508, ☎ 606/226–4444 or 800/682–8886, www.ntaonline.com). **United States Tour Operators Association** (USTOA; ⊠ 342 Madison Ave., Suite 1522, New York, NY 10173, ☎ 212/599–6599 or 800/468–7862, FAX 212/599–6744, ustoa@aol.com, www.ustoa.com).

THEME TRIPS

➤ FISHING: **Fishing International** (⊠ Box 2132, Santa Rosa, CA 95405, ☎ 707/539–3366 or 800/950–4242, FAX 707/539–1320).

➤ GOLF: **Stine's Golftrips** (⊠ 193 Towne Center Dr., Kissimmee, FL 34759, ☎ 407/933–0032 or 800/428–1940, FAX 407/933–8857).

➤ SPAS: **Spa-Finders** (⊠ 91 5th Ave., #301, New York, NY 10003-3039, ☎ 212/924–6800 or 800/255–7727).

TRANSPORTATION AROUND BERMUDA

Despite its small size, Bermuda does pose some transportation problems. Because rental cars are not allowed, you'll have to **travel by bus, taxi, ferry, moped, bike, or on foot.** More than 1,200 mi of narrow, winding roads and a 20-mph speed limit make moving around the island a time-consuming process. Though the island was once famous for its "mopeds" (motorized pedal cycles), the island's rapidly increasing number of cars and overall congestion can make this mode of travel somewhat stressful, if not dangerous. Ferries, on the other hand, offer clean, relaxing jaunts and are an inexpensive way to see the island from the water. Traveling the length of this long, skinny island by bus takes a long time. The trip from St. George's to Hamilton takes an hour, and the journey onward to the West End takes another hour, though an express bus from Hamilton to the West End takes only 40 minutes. Hiring a taxi can cut down the amount of time you spend on the road, but it costs significantly more. Fortunately, Hamilton, St. George's, and Somerset are all manageable on foot.

TRAVEL AGENCIES

A good travel agent puts your needs first. Look for an agency that has been in business at least five years, emphasizes customer service, and has someone on staff who specializes in your destination. In addition, **make sure the agency belongs to a professional trade organization.** The American Society of Travel Agents (ASTA), with 27,000 agents in some 170 countries, is the largest and most influential in the field. Operating under the motto "Integrity in Travel," it maintains and enforces a strict code of ethics and will step in to help mediate any agent-client disputes if necessary. ASTA also maintains a Web site that includes a directory of agents. If a travel agency is also acting as your tour operator, *see* Buyer Beware *in* Tours & Packages, *above*.

➤ LOCAL AGENT REFERRALS: American Society of Travel Agents (ASTA; ☎ 800/965–2782 24-hr hot line, FAX 703/684–8319, www.astanet.com). Association of British Travel Agents (✉ 68–71 Newman St., London W1P 4AH, ☎ 020/7637–2444, FAX 020/7637–0713, abta.co.uk, www.ab-tanet.com). Association of Canadian Travel Agents (✉ 1729 Bank St., Suite 201, Ottawa, Ontario K1V 7Z5, ☎ 613/521–0474, FAX 613/521–0805, acta.ntl@sympatico.ca). Australian Federation of Travel Agents (✉ Level 3, 309 Pitt St., Sydney 2000, ☎ 02/9264–3299, FAX 02/9264–1085, www.afta.com.au). Travel Agents' Association of New Zealand (✉ Box 1888, Wellington 10033, ☎ 04/499–0104, FAX 04/499–0827, taanz@tias-net.co.nz).

VISITOR INFORMATION

➤ BERMUDA DEPARTMENT OF TOURISM: Hamilton (✉ Global House, 43 Church St., ☎ 441/292–0023; ✉ ferry terminal, Front St., ☎ 441/295–1480). St. George's (✉ King's Sq., ☎ 441/297–1682, www.bermudatourism.com).

U.S. nationwide (✉ 310 Madison Ave., Suite 201, New York, NY 10017-6083, ☎ 212/818–9800 or 800/223–6106, FAX 212/983–5289). Brochures nationwide (☎ 800/237–6832). Atlanta (✉ 245 Peachtree Center Ave. NE, Suite 803, Atlanta, GA 30303-1223, ☎ 404/524–1541, FAX 404/586–9933). Boston (✉ 44 School St., Suite 1010, Boston, MA 02108, ☎ 617/742–0405, FAX 617/723–7786). Canada (✉ 1200 Bay St., Suite 1004, Toronto, Ontario M5R 2A5, ☎ 416/923–9600, FAX 416/923–4840). U.K. (✉ BCB Ltd., 1 Battersea Church Rd., London SW11 3LY, ☎ 020/7771–7001, FAX 020/7771–7037).

➤ U.S. GOVERNMENT ADVISORIES: U.S. Department of State (✉ Overseas Citizens Services Office, Room 4811 N.S., 2201 C St. NW, Washington, DC 20520, ☎ 202/647–5225 for interactive hot line; 301/946–4400 for computer bulletin board; FAX 202/647–3000 for interactive hot line).

Enclose a self-addressed, stamped, business-size envelope.

WEB SITES

Do check out the World Wide Web when you're planning. You'll find everything from current weather forecasts to virtual tours of famous cities. Fodor's Web site, www.fodors.com, is a great place to start your on-line travels. When you see a ✺ in this book, go to www.fodors.com/urls for an up-to-date link to that destination's site.

WHEN TO GO

In the summer, Bermuda teems with activity. Hotel barbecues and evening dances complement daytime sightseeing trips, and public beaches never close. The pace slows considerably in the off season (November to March). A few hotels and restaurants close, some of the sightseeing, dive, snorkeling, and water-skiing boats are dry-docked, and only taxis and the St. George's minibus operate tours of the island. Most hotels remain open, however, and slash their rates by as much as 40%. The weather at this time of year is often perfect for golf and tennis, and you can still rent boats, tour the island, and take advantage of special events and walking tours.

CLIMATE

Bermuda has a remarkably mild climate that seldom sees extremes of either heat or cold. In the winter (December–March), temperatures range from around 55°F at night to 70°F in the early afternoon. High, blustery winds can make the air feel cooler, however, as can Bermuda's high humidity. The hottest part of the year is between May and mid-October, when temperatures range from 75°F to 85°F. 90°F is not uncommon in July and August. The summer months are somewhat drier, but rainfall is spread fairly evenly throughout the year. Bermuda depends solely on rain for its supply of fresh water, so residents usually welcome the brief storms. In August and September, hurricanes moving northward from the Caribbean sometimes batter the island.

THE GOLD GUIDE / SMART TRAVEL TIPS

The following chart lists average daily maximum and minimum temperatures for Bermuda.

Jan.	68F	20C	May	76F	24C	Sept.	85F	29C
	58	14		65	18		72	22
Feb.	68F	20C	June	81F	27C	Oct.	79F	26C
	58	14		70	21		70	21
Mar.	68F	20C	July	85F	29C	Nov.	74F	23C
	58	14		74	23		63	17
Apr.	72F	22C	Aug.	86F	30C	Dec.	70F	21C
	59	15		76	24		61	16

➤ FORECASTS: **Weather Channel Connection** (☎ 900/932–8437), 95¢ per minute from a Touch-Tone phone.

1 DESTINATION: BERMUDA

A TROPICAL COCKTAIL OF CULTURES

BASKING IN THE ATLANTIC, 508 mi due east of Cape Hatteras, North Carolina, Bermuda is one of the wealthiest countries in the world—average per capita income is $36,500. Bermuda has no income tax, no sales tax, no slums, no unemployment, and no major crime problem. Don't come to Bermuda expecting a tropical paradise where laid-back locals wander around barefoot drinking piña coladas. On Bermuda's 22 square mi, you will find neither towering mountains, glorious rain forests, nor exotic volcanoes. Instead, pastel cottages, quaint shops, and manicured gardens betray a more staid, suburban way of life. A British diplomat once said, "Bermuda is terribly middle-aged"—and in many ways he was right. Most of the island is residential, the speed limit is 20 mph (although many drivers go faster), golf and tennis are popular pastimes, most visitors are over 40 years old despite a recent tourism drive to attract younger vacationers, restaurants and shops are expensive, and casual attire in public is frowned upon.

The population of 58,000 is 61% black and 39% white. A few Bermudians still speak the Queen's English but the majority have their own unique accent, which reflects the country's diverse English, American, and African influences. White Bermudians have striven to create a middle-class England of their own. And as in so many colonies, the Bermudian version is more insular, more conservative, and more English than the original. Pubs, cricket, and an obsession with protocol are reminders of a distant loyalty to Britain and everything it used to represent. A self-governing British colony since 1968, with a parliament that dates from 1620, Bermuda loves pomp and circumstance. But the British apron strings are wearing thin. The first pro-independence Government—the Progressive Labour Party (PLP)—was elected in 1998 taking Bermudian identity and autonomy to a new high. Nevertheless, great ceremony still attends the convening of Parliament. Marching bands parade through the capital in honor of the Queen's official birthday, a public holiday. Regimental bands and bagpipers reenact centuries-old ceremonies. And tea is served each afternoon.

Bermuda wears its history like a comfortable old coat. Land is too valuable to permit the island's legacy to be cordoned off for mere display. A traveler need only wander through the 17th-century buildings of St. George's, now home to shops and private homes, to realize that Bermudian history remains part of the fabric of life, with each successive generation adding its own thread of achievement and color. Indeed, the island's isolation and diminutive size have forged a continuity of place and tradition almost totally missing in the United States. Walk into Trimingham's or A. S. Cooper & Son department store, and you are likely to be helped by a descendant of the original founders. The same names keep cropping up— Tucker, Carter, Trott—and a single lane in St. George's can conjure up centuries of memories and events. Even today, the brief love affair in 1804 between Irish poet Thomas Moore and the married Hester Tucker—the "Nea" of his odes—is gossiped about with a zeal usually reserved for the transgressions of a current neighbor. Bermuda's attachment to its history is more than a product of its size, however. It is through its past that Bermuda creates its own unique identity, drawing on its British roots 3,500 mi away and mixing those memories with the cultural influences of its giant American neighbor.

Since the very beginning, the fate of this small colony in the Atlantic has been linked to that of the United States. The crew of the *Sea Venture,* whose wreck on Bermuda during a hurricane in 1609 began the settlement of the island, was actually on its way to Jamestown, Virginia. Indeed, the passenger list of the *Sea Venture* reads like a "Who's Who" of early American history. On board were Sir Thomas Gates, deputy governor of Jamestown; Christopher Newport, who had led the first expedition to Jamestown; and John Rolfe, whose second wife was the Native American Pocahontas. In the centuries since then, Bermuda has been a remarkable barometer of the evolving relationship between the United States and Britain. In 1775, Bermuda was secretly persuaded to give gunpowder to George Washington in return for the lifting of a trade blockade that threatened the island with starvation. In the War of 1812, Bermuda was the staging post for the British fleet's attack on Washington, D.C. When Britain faced a national crisis in 1940, it gave the United States land on Bermuda to build a Naval Air Station in exchange for ships and supplies. In 1990, Prime Minister Thatcher and President Bush held talks on the island.

The fact that Bermuda—just two hours by air from New York—has maintained some of its English character through the years is obviously part of its appeal for the half million–plus Americans (more than 90% of all visitors) who flock here each year. More important, however, Bermuda means sun, sea, and sand. It boasts a year-round mild climate, pink beaches, turquoise waters, coral reefs, 17th-century architecture, and splendid golf courses. Indeed, Bermuda has more golf courses per square mile than anywhere else in the world, and there are even more in the planning stages.

Bermuda did not always seem so attractive. After all, more than 300 wrecks lie submerged on the same reefs where divers now frolic. William Strachey, secretary-elect for Virginia and a passenger on the *Sea Venture*, wrote that Bermuda was "a place so terrible to all that ever touched on them. Such tempests, thunders and other fearful objects are seen and heard about those islands that they are called The Devills Islands, feared and avoided by all sea travelers above any place in the world." For the crew of the *Sea Venture*, however, the 181 small islands that compose Bermuda meant salvation. Contrary to rumor, the islands proved to be unusually fertile and hospitable, supporting the crew during the construction of two new ships, in which they departed for Jamestown on May 10, 1610.

Shakespeare drew on the accounts of these survivors in *The Tempest,* written in 1611. The wreck of the *Sea Venture* on harsh yet beneficent Bermuda—"these infortunate (yet fortunate) islands," as one survivor described them—contained all the elements of Shakespearean tragicomedy: that out of loss something greater is often born. Just as Prospero loses the duchy of Milan only to regain it and secure the kingdom of Naples for his daughter, Admiral Sir George Somers lost a ship but gained an island. Today, Bermuda's motto is *Quo Fata Ferunt* (Whither the Fates Carry Us), an expression of sublime confidence in the same providence that carried the *Sea Venture* safely to shore.

That confidence has largely been justified over the years, but Bermudians have recently raised concerns about congestion, overfishing, reef damage, and a declining quality of life. The island's nearly 600,000 visitors a year are the golden eggs that many residents feel are now killing the goose. Despite a recent decline in tourism, the summer influx of visitors is still an irritant to many locals and the behavior of some service employees, particularly bus drivers and store clerks, has become sullen and rude. Traffic jams leading into Hamilton, the island's capital, are no longer uncommon, despite the facts that each resident family can have only one car and car rentals are prohibited. In 1990, the government restricted the number of cruise-ship visits to four a week, citing the large numbers of passengers who add to congestion but contribute little to the island's coffers. A drop in visitor numbers during the 1990s has caused increasing concern resulting in a recent drive to save tourism from further decline. Last year saw cruise passengers disembarking at weekends for the first time (cruise ships were previously allowed in only on weekdays). Hotel and retail initiatives have been launched to improve customer service and the Bermuda Department of Tourism is trying to attract a younger, livelier mix of tourists in an effort to change its image as a stodgy place.

When all is said and done, however, Bermuda's problems stem from a surfeit of advantages rather than a dearth, and almost any island nation would gladly inherit them. The "still-vexed Bermoothes" is how Shakespeare described this Atlantic pearl, but he might have changed his tune had he found a chance to swim at Horseshoe Bay, or hit a mashie-niblick to the 15th green at Port Royal. Who knows? Instead of referring to a storm-wracked island, *The Tempest* might have been Shakespeare's reaction to a missed putt on the 18th.

–Honey Naylor

–Updated by Vivienne Sheath

NEW AND NOTEWORTHY

Visitors will be happy to know that Bermuda's airport now has **duty-free shops,** one in the international departures lounge and another adjacent to the U.S. departures lounge. While duty-free items are pretty much limited to liquor, cigarettes, and perfume, this is more convenient than when travelers had to purchase goods a day or two in advance and have them delivered to the airport (although you still, if you prefer, have this option). **The Long-bird Club**—an executive lounge on the upper level of the airport—was introduced in 1999. It provides concierge service, refreshments, a boardroom, and workstations with Internet, fax, and phone. Club membership starts at $275 per year.

The first major hotel development in over 25 years gained approval from the Environmental Ministry in 1999, and the groundbreaking **Daniel's Head Village Resort,** on the West End of the island was under construction at press time. The $8 million project comprises 96 400-square-ft "eco-tents"—cloth-covered wooden frames—built on the Daniel's Head site. Seventeen will be over water with glass viewing panels in the floor. But while the emphasis is on getting back to nature, the interiors of the units are described as more like large hotel rooms than tents, with queen bed, sitting room, bathroom, veranda, and ceiling fans, but no air conditioning. The rate is expected to be about $125 nightly for double occupancy.

In other hotel news, the south shore's **Fairmont Southampton Princess** and the capital's **Fairmont Hamilton Princess** are both set to benefit from a $30 million–plus investment pledge this year. Changes will include guest room improvements and the creation of a world-class spa—the Solace Spa—at the Southampton Princess by October 2001. One of Bermuda's most established hotels, the **Newstead,** is building up its business-traveler base after recent improvements. In addition to the redecoration of rooms, guests will find four new business suites, two conference centers, a new sauna and gym, new outside dining area and bar, and high-speed Internet links to each guest room.

The huge **Marriott's Castle Harbour Resort,** in Tucker's Town, has closed, and at press time a new developer was said to be interested in buying the site to create another resort. The adjacent 18-hole Castle Harbour Golf Course—one of the best on the island—is still open.

The Blue Water Divers operation (based at the Elbow Beach Hotel) has added something special for scuba divers: underwater scooters. Called **DPVs (diver propulsion vehicles),** these new toys carry one passenger each through caves and canyons and around shipwrecks.

WHAT'S WHERE

Hamilton

As the capital of Bermuda since 1815, Hamilton is the home of most of the island's government buildings. Here travelers can watch Parliament in session or visit the grand City Hall, home to two major art galleries. The soaring Cathedral of the Most Holy Trinity, seat of the Anglican Church of Bermuda, is in Hamilton, as is Fort Hamilton, a moated fortress with underground passageways. But most people know Hamilton as the hub of shopping and dining, with colorful Front Street as the main thoroughfare. The departure point for ferries heading to other parts of the island, Hamilton is one of the smallest yet busiest port cities in the world.

St. George's

Bermuda's original capital (from the early 17th century until 1815) is steeped in history. Settled in 1609, it was the second English settlement in the New World (after Jamestown, Virginia). Today its alleys and walled lanes are packed with small museums and historic sights, starting with King's Square, where cedar replicas of the stocks, pillory, and ducking stool once used to punish criminals serve as props.

The West End

The West End of Bermuda, encompassing Somerset and Ireland islands, is a bucolic area of nature reserves, wooded areas, and beautiful bays and harbors. In addition to its natural beauty, the area's big attraction is the Royal Naval Dockyard, a former bastion of the Royal British Navy, now a major tourist center with a maritime museum and a shopping arcade. For those who love arts and crafts, Dockyard has much to offer. Within part of the old Cooperage building is a flourishing crafts market. On most days you can see artisans at work on their crafts—quilts, candles, banana leaf dolls, miniature furniture, hand-painted fabrics, and more. There's also the nearby Bermuda Arts Center and Bermuda Clayworks Pottery, and a number of charming restaurants and pubs.

The Parishes

Bermuda's many other parishes have diverse attractions, from the historic smugglers' town of Flatts Village to the coveted beaches of Paget. Scattered across the island, the parishes of Southampton, Warwick, Paget, Pembroke, Devonshire, Smith's, and Tucker's Town are best visited by bicycle or moped. Just don't try to see them all in one day.

THE WESTERN PARISHES

The Western Parishes are actually four islands connected not only by bridges, but also by history. When you cross over Somerset Bridge, you are, as Bermudians say, "up the country." It is a rural area of small farms and open space, craggy coastlines, gentle beaches, and parks and nature preserves. Picturesque Somerset Village looks much as it did in 1962 when it was featured in *A Touch of Mink,* starring Doris Day and Cary Grant—a town of quiet streets and charming old buildings skirting lovely Mangrove Bay.

THE EASTERN PARISHES

Like their counterparts at the opposite end of the island, the Eastern Parishes couldn't be called lively, although the international airport is here and a number of large resorts call the area around Harrington Sound home. This is a historic area, and the attractions and landscape here tell the complex story of Bermuda's founding and settlement.

PLEASURES AND PASTIMES

Beaches

The fine, pink sand of Bermuda's beaches—a result of shell particles, calcium carbonate, and bits of crushed coral mixed with sand—is an island trademark. This unique mixture also provides Bermuda's beaches with a startling characteristic—even during the summer months, the sand doesn't get hot. Add to this the beaches' picturesque surroundings, which include dramatic cliff formations, coconut palms, and gently rolling dunes sloping into crystal-clear waters. The island's 34 beaches range from long, unbroken expanses of shoreline, such as that at Warwick Long Bay, to small, secluded coves divided by rock cliffs, such as those at Whale Bay Beach and Jobson's Cove.

Cricket

For Americans, the popularity of cricket in Bermuda begins to sink in only when you consider that the annual Cup Match Cricket Festival, a two-day event that pits the west side of the island against the east, is a national holiday. Traditionally held the Thursday and Friday before the first Monday in August, Cup Match draws an average of 12,000 spectators, including zealous supporters who "decorate" the batsman by running out onto the field and slipping a little cash in his pocket. The event is also home to the Crown & Anchor tent packed with gambling tables, the only legal betting event on Bermuda's calendar. Other cricket games are held throughout the summer, from April through September.

Shopping

For shoppers, Bermuda has everything from sophisticated department stores and top-quality boutiques to art galleries with works by local artists, as well as such fun products as Outerbridge's Sherry Peppers and Bermuda rum. On the high end, European-made crystal and china, British-made clothing (especially woolen sweaters), and fine jewelry are popular products.

Duty-free gold items, particularly watches, can sell for up to 20% less than in the U.S. On the arty side, galleries throughout the island sell sculptures and paintings, hand-blown glass, handmade dolls, and other works by Bermudian artists and artisans.

Snorkeling and Diving

Reefs, shipwrecks, underwater caves, a variety of coral and marine life, and warm, clear water combine to make Bermuda an ideal place for underwater exploration. The many sheltering reefs hide parrot fish, angelfish, trumpet fish, and grouper, and divers can enjoy a visibility range of 70 ft–150 ft, the longest in the western Atlantic. The numerous shipwrecks around the island also make great dive sites.

Tennis

With more than 80 tennis courts in its 22 square mi, Bermuda has been a tennis capital since 1873. That was the year when Sir Bronlow Gray, the island's chief justice, introduced the game and built a grass tennis court at his Paget Parish home. The court still stands today. Bermuda is still a perfect place to play tennis year-round, day or night (many courts are lit).

FODOR'S CHOICE

Beaches

☆ The tiny beaches on **Chaplin Bay,** which almost disappear at high tide, are blissfully secluded.

☆ Fine pink sand, clear water, and a vibrant social scene make **Horseshoe Bay** a favorite.

☆ The quiet, low-key **Somerset Long Bay** is shielded by undeveloped parkland, grass, and brush.

☆ **Warwick Long Bay,** the island's longest beach, has a beautiful sculpted coral outcropping that seems to balance on the surface of the water.

Comforts

☆ The island's original cottage colony, 100-year-old **Cambridge Beaches,** remains a favorite among royalty and commoners alike. *$$$$*

☆ The traditional, slightly formal **Fairmont Hamilton Princess,** in business since 1884, is regarded as the mother of Bermuda's tourist industry. *$$$$*

☆ The Relais & Châteaux **Horizons & Cottages** has the elegant feel of an 18th-century home—which, in fact, it once was. *$$$$*

☆ The pink lanais of **The Reefs,** a small, casually elegant resort, are set in cliffs above Christian Bay. *$$$$*

☆ **Waterloo House,** another Relais & Châteaux property, is in an early 19th-century white-column house facing Hamilton Harbour. *$$$–$$$$*

☆ Smack on Harrington Sound, the cottages of **Angel's Grotto** contain attractively furnished efficiency apartments, complete with full kitchens. *$$–$$$*

☆ Charming **Aunt Nea's Inn** offers a great value romantic getaway. With its four-poster beds and beautiful guest rooms you are guaranteed to feel pampered and leave happier than you arrived. *$$–$$$*

☆ In a quiet residential area near Hamilton Harbour, the **Little Pomander Guest House** is a find for budget travelers. *$$*

☆ The cozy **Salt Kettle House,** with its water views, fireside lounge, and hearty English breakfast, attracts repeat visitors year after year. *$*

Favorite Outdoor Activities

☆ Hiring a **Boston Whaler** power boat for a leisurely afternoon is the ideal way to glimpse some of Bermuda's exclusive beachfront homes and enjoy the turquoise waters.

☆ The hard-packed trails that wind through **the dunes in South Shore Park** are a great place to run and ride horses.

☆ **Offshore wreck diving** is a dramatic way to contemplate Bermuda's storm-tossed past. More than 300 wrecks lie under these waters.

☆ **The Port Royal Golf & Country Club's 16th hole** sits on a treeless promontory overlooking the waters of Whale Bay.

☆ For a leisurely tour of the nooks and crannies of a coral-cliff wall, try **snorkeling in Church Bay.**

Flavors

★ **Horizons** was awarded its gold plaque in 2000 from Relais & Châteaux, not least for its consistently exceptional cuisine. *$$$$*

★ Superior French cuisine and a 1670 manor-house setting combine to make the **Waterlot Inn** one of the island's finest restaurants. *$$$$*

★ **Cafe Lido,** with its romantic ocean-front terrace, serves delicious homemade pastas and imaginatively prepared seafood. *$$$*

★ **Black Horse Tavern** is the place to try curried conch stew, Bermuda lobster, amberjack, rockfish, and—a true Bermuda original—shark hash. *$$*

★ At **Dennis's Hideaway,** you'll find the eccentric Dennis Lamb offering everything from conch fritters to mussel pie to bread-and-butter pudding, amid homemade picnic tables and a yapping dog or two. *$$*

★ Cheerful, Mediterranean **Monte Carlo,** in Hamilton, offers excellent crepes and well-seasoned fish and shellfish dishes at surprisingly reasonable prices. *$–$$*

★ Family-run **Jamaican Grill** brings lively Caribbean cooking to Bermuda in the form of peppery jerk chicken, curried goat, or ackee and salt fish. *$*

Special Moments

★ **Riding the ferry from Hamilton to Somerset,** which gives you one of the finest views of Bermuda.

★ **Exploring the parishes on a moped,** feeling like a real onion—that is, a Bermudian—on wheels.

★ **Browsing through the Bermuda Book Store,** a musty old place with stacks of books about the island.

★ **Watching the colorfully costumed Gombey Dancers,** a troupe whose tradition blends African, West Indian, and Caribbean influences.

★ **Stargazing underneath Gibbs Hill Lighthouse.** Beaming through the dead of night this stately beacon and its steady whirr are hypnotizing.

FESTIVALS AND SEASONAL EVENTS

Precise dates and information about the events listed below are available from the Bermuda Department of Tourism (☞ Visitor Information *in* Smart Travel Tips A to Z).

✑ *following the text of a review is your signal that the property has a Web site, where you will find details and, usually, images; for a link, visit www.fodors.com/urls.*

➤ DEC.: The **Hamilton Jaycees Santa Claus Parade** brings Father Christmas to Front Street, along with bands, floats, and other seasonal festivities. The **Bermuda Aquarium, Natural History Museum & Zoo** also has an annual yuletide 'do, with children's games, a crafts workshop, and a visit with Santa in the Zoo Garden (☎ 441/293–2727).

The **Bermuda National Trust Annual Christmas Walkabout in St. George's,** a festive early evening open-house event, features traditional Christmas decorations, musicals in the State House, monologues at the Globe Hotel, and historic readings at the Town Hall. Contact the Trust (☎ 441/236–6483).

➤ DEC. 24–26: **Christmas Eve** is celebrated with midnight candlelight services in churches of all denominations. **Christmas** is a public holiday. **Boxing Day** (Dec. 26) is also a public holiday, traditionally for visiting friends and family. You'll find a variety of sports events, and the Bermuda Gombey Dancers perform around town.

➤ DEC. 31: **St. George's New Year's Eve Celebration** in King's Square and Ordnance Island has food stalls, rides for children, and continuous entertainment by local musicians. A midnight countdown and dropping of the "onion" are followed by fireworks. Contact the Corporation of St. George's (☎ 441/297–1532).

➤ JAN. 1: **New Year's Day** is a public holiday. All sightseeing attractions and restaurants remain open.

➤ JAN. 12–14: **Bermuda International Race Weekend** includes marathon and half-marathon races and a fitness-and-charity 10-km walk. Most races are open to all. Top international runners participate. Contact the Race Committee (✉ Box DV 397, Devonshire DV BX, ☎ 441/236–6086, ✑).

The **Annual Regional Bridge Tournament,** sponsored by the Bermuda Unit of the American Contract Bridge League, is held at a major hotel this month. Contact the tournament chairman (☎ 441/295–5161).

The **Annual Photographic Exhibition,** the third week of the month, features the work of local amateur and professional photographers and includes many underwater shots. It's displayed in the Bermuda Society of Arts' City Hall gallery (☎ 441/292–3824).

➤ JAN.–MAR.: The **Bermuda Festival** attracts internationally known artists for concerts, dance, and theater (☞ Chapter 6).

Regimental Musical Display is a captivating recreation of a retreat ceremony, performed in Hamilton by the Bermuda Regiment Band and the Bermuda Islands Pipe Band with Dancers. It lures both locals and travelers. Contact the Regimental Band (☎ 441/238–2470).

The island hosts various **horse shows,** including harness racing and dressage events. For dates and times contact Annie Sousa, **Bermuda Horse & Pony Association** (☎ 441/232–2162); Michael DiCosta, **Horse & Pony Driving Club** (☎ 441/293–4964); Eve Redford, **Saddle Club of Bermuda** (☎ 441/236–4093); Virginia McKey, **Bermuda Dressage Group** (☎ 441/297–4203); or Michael Cherry, **Bermuda Equestrian Federation** (☎ 441/234–0485).

➤ FEB.: The **Bermuda International Open Chess Tournament,** is open to both residents and visitors. Contact the Bermuda Chess Association (✉ Box HM 1705, Hamilton HM GX, ☎ 441/238–2313, 𝔽𝔸𝕏 441/238–8699).

The annual **Lobster Pot Pro-Amateur Golf Tournament** is played at one of the island's top courses. Contact the Tournament Director (✉ Box HM 1154, Hamilton HMEX, ☎ 441/292–8822, 𝔽𝔸𝕏 441/292–0008).

The **Annual Bermuda Rendezvous Bowling Tournament,** open to all bowlers, is sanctioned by the ABC and WIBC. Cash prizes are awarded. Contact Warwick Lanes (✉ Box WK 128, Warwick WK BX, ☎ 441/236–5290).

SPRING

➤ MAR.: The **Bermuda All Breed Championship Dog Shows and Obedience Trials** draw dog lovers from far and wide to the Botanical Gardens in Paget. It happens again in November. Contact the Bermuda All Breed Club (✉ Box HM 23, Hamilton HM AX, ☎ 441/291–1426).

The **Bermuda Super Senior Invitational Tennis Tournament** is a USTA-sanctioned event held at the Coral Beach & Tennis Club in Paget. Contact the Bermuda Lawn Tennis Association (✉ Box HM 341, Hamilton HM BX, ☎ 441/296–0834, FAX 441/295–3056).

See a range of equestrian events at the **Bermuda Horse & Pony Association Spring Show Horse Trials,** including dressage, jumping, Western, and driving classes at National Equestrian Centre (✉ Vesey St., Devonshire; contact Michael Cherry, ☎ 441/234–0485).The **Bermuda Men's Amateur Golf Championship** is played at the Mid Ocean Club in Tucker's Town. Contact Bermuda Golf Association (✉ Box HM 433, Hamilton HM BX, ☎ 441/238–1367, FAX 441/238–0983).

The **Bermuda Cat Fanciers Association Championship Cat Show** features pedigree felines and household pets judged at various locations. Contact Morag Smith, **Bermuda Cat Fanciers Association** (✉ Box HM 1306, Hamilton HM FX, ☎ 441/238–0112) or Diana Plested (☎ 441/295–5723).

➤ MAR.–APR.: The **Palm Sunday Walk** is an annual 6–8 mi stroll. Contact the Bermuda National Trust (☎ 441/236–6483).

Good Friday is a public holiday and traditionally a kite-flying day. Enjoy a spectacular display of locally made kites at the **Bermuda Kite Festival,** Horseshoe Bay, Southampton. Contact United Bermuda Party (☎ 441/295–0729).

Started in 1994, **Bermuda Spring Break Programme** targets American college students and replaced the decades-old, party-oriented College Weeks. Spring Break Sports is an organized program of lacrosse, golf, tennis, watersports, and rugby. Spring Break Arts offers gallery tours, arts classes, and meet-the-artist events. Contact Bermuda Department of Tourism (✉ Global House, 43 Church St., Hamilton HM 12, ☎ 441/292–0023).

Harvard's Hasty Pudding Club has presented its satirical theatricals in Bermuda for more than 30 years. It's the club's only performance site outside the United States. Call City Hall Theatre in Hamilton (☎ 441/295–1727).

➤ MAR.–OCT.: The **Ceremony** is usually performed twice monthly by the Bermuda Regiment Band, the Bermuda Islands Pipe Band with Dancers, and members of the Bermuda Pipe Band. The historic ceremony is performed alternately on Front Street in Hamilton, King's Square in St. George's, and Dockyard in the West End. No performances in August.

➤ APR.: The **Agricultural Exhibition,** similar to a county or state fair, features entertainment, exhibits, and plays at the Botanical Gardens in Paget (☎ 441/236–4201).

The **Peppercorn Ceremony** celebrates—amid great pomp and circumstance—the payment of one peppercorn in rent to the government by the Masonic Lodge of St. George No. 200 of the Grand Lodge of Scotland for its headquarters in the Old State House in St. George's. Contact the Bermuda Department of Tourism.

The **Bermuda Open Tennis Classic** is an ATP Tour, USTA-sanctioned event of the world's top professionals. Tickets are available in advance through the Bermuda Tennis Foundation, whose office is open November through April. (✉ Box HM 3073, Hamilton, HM NX, ☎ 441/296–2554, FAX 441/296–2551).

The **Annual Fun Run/Walk Around Harrington Sound** invites walkers, joggers, runners, bikers, rollerbladers—whatever—to go the 7- to 8-mi distance around the sound. Contact Donna Heslop (✉ Bermuda Zoological Society, ☎ 441/293–7074).

The seven-day **Bermuda International Film Festival** (✉ Box HM 2963,

Hamilton HM MX, ☎ 441/293–3456, FAX 441/293–7769) screens independent films in three theaters. Filmmakers are on hand to answer questions.

➤ APR.–MAY: The open houses and garden tours allow you to walk through some of Bermuda's private houses and gardens. Contact Joyce Zuill at the **Garden Club of Bermuda** (☎ 441/295–9155, FAX 441/295–2694).

International Race Week pits Bermudians against sailors from around the world in a series of races on the Great Sound. Contact the Sailing Secretary of the Royal Bermuda Yacht Club (☎ 441/295–2214).

➤ MAY: The **Bermuda Heritage Month** features a host of commemorative, cultural, and sporting activities. The climax is Bermuda Day (May 24), a public holiday that includes a parade at Bernard Park, a cycling race, a half-marathon (13 mi) for Bermuda residents only, and Bermuda dinghy races in St. George's Harbour. Contact the Department of Cultural Affairs (☎ 441/292–9447).

The **Bermuda End-to-End Scenic Railway Trail Walk for Charities** is a terrific way to see the island and meet active residents. The 26-mi course begins in King's Square, St. George's, and finishes with a range of festivities at the Royal Naval Dockyard. An alternative, 15-mi course begins at Albouy's Point, Hamilton. Visitors can sign up 30 minutes before either starting point. Contact Bermuda End-to-End (☎ 441/299–8821).

The **Bermuda Senior Amateur Championships for Men and Ladies** are played on a different course each year. Women must be at least 50 years old, men at least 55. Contact Tom Smith, of the Bermuda Golf Association (✉ Box HM 433, Hamilton HM BX, ☎ 441/238–1367, FAX 441/238–0983).

ZooDoo Day, at the Bermuda Aquarium, Natural History Museum & Zoo, has free admission, fun, games, and gift stalls. Contact Donna Heslop (✉ Bermuda Zoological Society, ☎ 441/293–7074).

SUMMER

➤ JUNE: For **Queen Elizabeth II's Birthday,** a public holiday in mid-June, military marching bands parade down Hamilton's Front Street.

The **Bermuda Angler's Club International Light Tackle Tournament,** organized by the Bermuda Anglers' Club and played out the first or second week of the month, draws a large crowd to its 5 PM weigh-in. Contact R. Rego, Bermuda Angler's Club (✉ Box HM 754, Hamilton HM CX, ☎ 441/292–5450 days; 441/236–6565 evenings).

The free **Open Air Pops Concerts,** presented by the Bermuda Philharmonic Society at King's Square, St. George's, and Clocktower Centre at the Royal Naval Dockyard, are a great way to meet residents. Contact Sue Blakeley (✉ Bermuda

Philharmonic Society, Box HM 552, Hamilton HM CX, ☎ 441/238–1108 evenings; 441/291–6690 days).

June brings a host of **sailing races.** Races that attract powerhouse yachtsmen during even-numbered years include the spectacular Newport to Bermuda Ocean Yacht Race and the Onion Patch Series (contact the **Royal Bermuda Yacht Club**), as well as the Bermuda Ocean Race from Annapolis, Maryland (contact **St. George's Dinghy & Sports Club**). Events in alternate (odd-numbered) years include the Bermuda 1-2 Single-Handed Race, from Newport to Bermuda and back (contact St. George's Dinghy & Sports Club), the Marion (MA) to Bermuda Cruising Yacht Race (contact the **Royal Hamilton Amateur Dinghy Club**) and the Trans-At Daytona-to-Bermuda Yacht Race (for more information, *see* St. George's Dinghy & Sports Club, *above*).

The **Bermuda Amateur Stroke Play Championship for Men and Ladies** are two simultaneous events played at the Port Royal Golf Course. Men and women play 72- and 54-hole strokes, respectively. Contact Tom Smith, Bermuda Golf Association (✉ Box HM 433, Hamilton HM BX, ☎ 441/238–1367, FAX 441/238–0983).

➤ JULY: **Atlantic International Junior Championships,** played at the Belmont, Mid Ocean, and Port Royal golf courses, is a 72-hole stroke play junior golf tournament. Contact Bermuda Junior Golf Association (✉ Box

WK 127, Warwick WK BX, ☎ 441/238–3118, FAX 441/238–0338).

➤ JULY OR AUG.: The **Cup Match Cricket Festival** is a public holiday, with matches between East and West End cricket clubs. Held at the **Somerset Cricket Club** (✉ Broome St., Sandys, ☎ 441/234–0327) or the **St. George's Cricket Club** (✉ Wellington Slip Rd., St. George's, ☎ 441/297–0374), the match is one of the most festive occasions of the year, attracting thousands of fans who gather to picnic, chat, and dance.

➤ JULY–AUG.: **Sea Horse Anglers' Club Annual Bermuda Billfish Tournament,** contact David Pantry (✉ Sea Horse Anglers Club, Box HM 1847, Hamilton HM HX, ☎ 441/292–7272, FAX 441/292–7830).

➤ AUG.: Landlubbers in homemade contraptions compete in the hilarious **Non-Mariners Race** on Mangrove Bay. Contact the Race Organizer (☎ 441/236–3683).

AUTUMN

➤ SEPT.: **Labour Day,** a public holiday, occasions a range of activities, including a march from Union Square, in Hamilton, to Bernard Park. Local entertainers and food stalls featuring local fare are included in the festivities.

Marine Science Day at the Bermuda Biological Station allows you to learn about marine research. Contact the development

office (✉ Bermuda Biological Station for Research, Inc., 17 Biological Station La., Ferry Reach GE 01, ☎ 441/297–8143, FAX 441/297–1839).

The **Bermuda Mixed Foursomes Amateur Golf Championship** is a 36-stroke play competition for couples at Port Royal Golf Course. Handicap limit: men 24, ladies 36. Contact Bermuda Golf Association (✉ Box HM 433, Hamilton HM BX, ☎ 441/238–1367, FAX 441/238–0983).

The **Annual Bermuda Triathlon** is open to visiting and local teams who compete in a 1-mi swim, 15-mi cycle, and 6-mi run. Contact the Bermuda Triathlon Association (✉ 48 Par-la-Ville Rd., Suite 547, Hamilton HM 11, ☎ 441/293–2765, ✍).

➤ OCT.: On **Columbus Day Regatta Weekend,** sponsored by the Royal Bermuda Yacht Club, keel boats compete in the Great Sound. Contact the Sailing Secretary of the Royal Bermuda Yacht Club (☎ 441/295–2214).

Bermuda International Open Golf Championship for Men, played at Port Royal Golf Course, is open to professional and amateurs with a handicap of 6. Contact Tom Smith at the Bermuda Golf Association (✉ Box HM 433, Hamilton HM BX, ☎ 441/238–1367, FAX 441/238–0983).

The **King Edward VII Gold Cup International Match Race Tournament** is an exciting series of one-on-one yacht races in Hamilton Harbour that attracts top sailors from around the world. Contact the Sailing Secretary of the

Royal Bermuda Yacht Club (☎ 441/295–2214).

➤ LATE OCT.: The **Bermuda Masters International Golf Classic** is played at Port Royal and Castle Harbour. Contact Elegant Vacations (☎ 800/648–1136, FAX 404/983–8270).

➤ NOV.: **Remembrance Day** is a public holiday in memory of Bermuda's and its allies' fallen soldiers. A parade with Bermudian, British, and U.S. military units, the Bermuda Police, and war veterans' organizations begins at Front Street in Hamilton.

The **Convening of Parliament** on the first Friday of each month is preceded by the arrival of His Excellency the Governor, in plumed hat and full regalia, at the Cabinet Building on Front Street in Hamilton. Arrive by 10:30 to secure a place to stand. Contact the House of Assembly (☎ 441/292–7408).

The **Bermuda Four Ball Stroke Play Amateur Championship for Men and Ladies** are two simultaneous events at the Port Royal Golf Course. Contact Tom Smith, Bermuda Golf Association (✉ Box HM 433, Hamilton HM BX, ☎ 441/238–1367, FAX 441/238–0983).

The **World Rugby Classic** pits former international rugby players against the best players from Bermuda in a match at the National Sports Club (Middle Rd., Devonshire). Contact World Rugby Classic Ltd. (✉ Box HM 2267, Hamilton HM JX, ☎ 441/295–6574, ✍).

2 BERMUDA CRUISE PRIMER

With its fabulous beaches, its turquoise seas, and its isolation in the Atlantic, Bermuda has long been a favorite of cruise passengers. It's understandably Britain's most famous resort island—and its oldest colony, due to the wreck of a New World–bound ship in 1609. The isle is more than 500 mi from the United States, with Cape Hatteras, North Carolina, the nearest point on the mainland.

B ERMUDA IS ONLY A TWO-HOUR FLIGHT from most East Coast cities, but nothing quite compares with sailing up to this crown colony. Most ships make seven-night loops from New York, with three nights at sea and four tied up in port. Three Bermuda harbors serve cruise ships: Hamilton (the capital), St. George's, and the Royal Naval Dockyard. With the exception of the *Crown Dynasty*, ships are not allowed in port on weekends, so your cruise will begin and end on a weekend and you'll be in Bermuda midweek.

By M. T.
Schwartzman

BEFORE YOU GO

Tickets, Vouchers, and Other Travel Documents

After you make the final payment to your travel agent, the cruise line will issue your cruise tickets and vouchers for airport-to-ship transfers. Depending on the airline, and whether you have purchased an air-sea package, you may receive your plane tickets or charter-flight vouchers at the same time; you may also receive vouchers for any shore excursions, although most cruise lines issue these aboard ship. Should your travel documents not arrive when promised, contact your travel agent or call the cruise line directly. If you book late, tickets may be delivered directly to the ship.

Passports and Visas

Read your cruise documents carefully to see what you'll need for embarkation. (You don't want to be turned away at the pier!) Most cruise lines that sail to Bermuda require passengers to have a valid passport.

What to Pack

Certain packing rules apply to all cruises: always take along a sweater in case of cool evening breezes or overactive air-conditioning. A rain slicker usually comes in handy, too, and make sure you take at least one pair of comfortable walking shoes for exploring port towns. Men should pack a dark suit, a tuxedo, or a white dinner jacket. Women should pack one long gown or cocktail dress for every two or three formal evenings on board.

Generally speaking, plan on one outfit for every two days of cruising, especially if your wardrobe contains many interchangeable pieces. Ships often have convenient laundry facilities as well. And don't overload your luggage with extra toiletries and sundry items; they are easily available in port and in the ship's gift shop (though usually at a premium price). Soaps, and sometimes shampoos and body lotion, are often placed in your cabin compliments of the cruise line.

Electrical outlets in cabins on all ships sailing weekly to Bermuda are compatible with U.S.–purchased appliances, such as hair dryers and electric shavers.

Take an extra pair of eyeglasses or contact lenses in your carry-on luggage. If you have a health problem that requires a prescription drug, pack enough to last the duration of the trip or have your doctor write a prescription using the drug's generic name (brand names can vary from country to country). Always carry prescription drugs in their original packaging to avoid problems with customs officials. Don't pack them in luggage that you plan to check, in case your bags go astray. Pack a list of the offices that supply refunds for lost or stolen traveler's checks.

Although no two cruises are quite the same, even aboard the same ship, evening dress tends to fall into three categories.

Formal

Formal cruises celebrate the ceremony of cruising. Jackets and ties for men are the rule for dinner, tuxedos are not uncommon, and the dress code is observed faithfully throughout the evening. Bermuda cruises are rarely formal, the exceptions being Cunard's *Queen Elizabeth 2* and the occasional Seabourn and Silversea Bermuda runs.

Semiformal

Semiformal cruises are a bit more relaxed than their formal counterparts. Men tend to wear a jacket and tie to dinner most nights. Of the cruise lines sailing weekly to Bermuda, Celebrity and Princess are good choices for a semiformal experience.

Casual

Casual cruises are the most popular. Shipboard dress and lifestyle are informal. Men dress in sport shirts and slacks for dinner most nights, in jackets and ties only two or three evenings of a typical seven-day sailing. Cruise lines sailing to Bermuda with a more casual evening atmosphere include Norwegian Cruise Line and Royal Caribbean.

ARRIVING AND DEPARTING

If you have purchased an air-sea package, you will be met by a cruise-company representative when your plane lands at the port city and then shuttled directly to the ship in buses or minivans. Some cruise lines arrange to transport your luggage between airport and ship. You don't have to hassle with baggage claim at the start of your cruise or with baggage check-in at the end. If you decide not to buy the air-sea package but still plan to fly, ask your travel agent if you can use the ship's transfer bus anyway. If you do, you may be required to purchase a round-trip transfer voucher (about $20). Otherwise, you will have to take a taxi to the ship.

If you live close to the port of embarkation, bus transportation may be available. This is often the case on cruises to Bermuda for passengers who live on the East Coast. Another option for those who live close to their point of departure is to drive to the ship. The major U.S. cruise ports all have parking facilities.

Embarkation

Check-In

You must check in before boarding your ship. A cruise line official will collect or stamp your ticket, inspect or even retain your passport or other official identification, and give you the keys to your cabin. Seating assignments for the dining room are often handed out at this time, too.

After this you may be required to walk through a metal detector and pass your hand baggage through an X-ray device. These are the same security checks used in airports, so ask to have your photographic film inspected by hand.

Although it takes only five or ten minutes per family to check in, lines are often long, so aim for off-peak hours. The worst time tends to be immediately after the ship begins boarding. The later it is, the less crowded. For example, if boarding begins at 2 PM and continues until 4:30, you might want to arrive after 3:30.

Boarding the Ship

Before you walk up the gangway, the ship's photographer will probably take your picture. There's no charge unless you buy the picture
(usually $6). On board, stewards may serve welcome drinks in sou-
venir glasses, for which you're usually charged between $3 and $5.

You will be escorted to your cabin by a steward, who will carry your
hand luggage. The rest of your bags will either be inside your cabin
when you arrive or will come shortly thereafter. If your bags don't arrive within a half hour of sailing, contact the purser. If you are among
the unlucky few whose luggage doesn't make it to the ship in time, the
purser will trace it and arrange to have it flown to the ship in Bermuda.

ON BOARD

Checking Out Your Cabin

The first thing to do upon arriving at your cabin or suite is to make
sure that everything is in order. If there are two twin beds instead of
the double bed you wanted, or other serious problems, ask to be
moved before the ship departs. Unless the ship is full, you can usually
persuade the chief housekeeper or hotel manager to allow you to
change cabins. It is customary to tip the stewards who assist you in
moving to another cabin.

Because your cabin is your home-away-from-home for a few days or
weeks, everything should be to your satisfaction. Take a good look
around. Is the cabin clean and orderly? Do the toilet, shower, and faucets
work? Check the telephone and television. Again, major problems
should be addressed immediately. Minor concerns, such as a shortage
of bath towels or pillows, can wait until the frenzy of embarkation has
subsided.

Your dining-time and seating-assignment card may be in your cabin if
it wasn't handed to you upon embarkation. Now is the time to check
it and immediately request any changes. The maître d' usually sets up
shop in one of the public rooms specifically for this purpose.

Communications

Shipboard

Cabins have loudspeakers and telephones. Generally, the loudspeakers cannot be switched off because they are needed to broadcast important notices. Telephones are used to call fellow passengers, order
room service, summon a doctor, request a wake-up call, or speak with
any of the ship's officers or departments.

Ship-to-Shore

Satellite facilities make it possible to call anywhere in the world from
cruise ships, which are equipped with direct-dial phones in every cabin
for calls to shore. Be warned, however, that the cost of sending any
message, regardless of the method, can be quite expensive—up to $15
a minute. (On some ships, though, it's much cheaper, costing as little
as $3.95 a minute.)

It's much cheaper to wait until you arrive in Bermuda to call home.
Once ashore you can use your calling card if you have one. If not, prepaid phone cards are a convenient way to make international calls from
a public phone.

Dining

Cruise ships serve food nearly around the clock. There may be up to four breakfast options: early morning coffee and pastries on deck, breakfast in bed through room service, buffet-style breakfast in the cafeteria, and sit-down breakfast in the dining room. There may also be two or three choices for lunch, mid-afternoon hors d'oeuvres, and midnight buffets. You can eat whatever is on the menu, in any quantity, at as many of these meals as you wish. You are also free to order room service at any time.

Restaurants

The chief meals of the day are served in the main dining room, which on most ships can accommodate only half the passengers at once. Meals are therefore usually served in two sittings—early (or main) and late (or second)—usually from 1½ to 2½ hours apart. Early seating for dinner is generally between 6 and 6:30, late seating between 8 and 8:30.

Cruise ships also have a cafeteria-style restaurant, usually near the swimming pool, where you can eat lunch and breakfast (dinner is usually served only in the dining room). Many ships provide self-serve coffee or tea in their cafeteria around the clock, as well as buffets at midnight.

Seatings

When it comes to your dining-table assignment, you should have options on four important points: early or late seating; smoking or no-smoking section (if smoking is allowed in the dining room); a table for two, four, six, or eight; and special dietary needs. When you receive your cruise documents, you will usually receive a card asking for your dining preferences. Fill this out and return it to the cruise line, but remember that you will not get your seating assignment until you board the ship. Check it out immediately, and if your request was not met, see the maître d'. Usually there is a time and place set up for changes in dining assignments.

Seating assignments on some ships apply only for dinner. Several have open seating for breakfast or lunch, which means you may sit anywhere at any time. Smaller or more luxurious ships offer open seating for all meals.

CHANGING TABLES

Dining is a focal point of the cruise experience, and your companions at meals may become your best friends on the cruise. However, if you don't enjoy the company at your table, the maître d' can usually move you to another one if the dining room isn't completely full (a tip helps). He will probably be reluctant to comply with your request after the first full day at sea, however, because the waiters, busboys, and wine steward who have been serving you up to that point won't receive their tips at the end of the cruise. Be persistent if you are truly unhappy.

The Captain's Table

It is both a privilege and a marvelous experience to be invited to dine one evening at the captain's table. Although some seats are given to celebrities, repeat passengers, and passengers in the most expensive suites, other invitations are given at random to ordinary passengers. You can request an invitation from the chief steward or the hotel manager, although there is no guarantee you will be accommodated. The captain's guests always wear suits and ties or dresses, even if the dress code for that evening is casual. On many ships, passengers may also be invited to dine at the other officers' special tables, or officers may visit a different passenger table each evening.

Room Service

Cruise ships sailing to Bermuda offer room service round-the-clock. Oftentimes you can order from the full menu during mealtimes. At other times of the day, room service is restricted to selections from a limited menu, which you'll find in your cabin. Choices may include soup, salad, burgers, and finger sandwiches. There is no charge for room service, other than for beer, wine, or spirits.

Special Diets

With advance notification, many ships can provide a kosher, low-salt, low-cholesterol, sugar-free, vegetarian, or other special menu. However, there's always a chance that the wrong dish will somehow be handed to you. Especially when it comes to soups and desserts, it's a good idea to ask about the ingredients.

Cruise-ship menus usually offer alternative "light" or "spa" dishes based upon American Heart Association guidelines, using less fat, leaner cuts of meat, low-cholesterol or low-sodium preparations, smaller portions, salads, fresh-fruit desserts, and healthy garnishes. Some smaller ships may not be able to accommodate special dietary needs. Vegetarians generally have no trouble finding appropriate selections on ship menus.

Entertainment

Bars, Lounges, and Nightclubs

A ship's bars, whether adjacent to the pool or attached to one of the lounges, tend to be its social centers. Bar drinks, including soft drinks, are not included in the cruise fare. Rather than demand cash after every round, however, most ships allow passengers to charge drinks to their accounts.

The main entertainment lounge or showroom schedules nightly musical revues, magic acts, comedy performances, and variety shows. During the rest of the day the room is used for group activities, such as talks or bingo games. Generally, the larger the ship, the bigger and more impressive the productions.

Other entertainment and ballroom dancing may be found throughout the ship. After the main lounge, the most popular nightspot is usually the disco or cabaret. Piano bars are popular spots for sing-alongs.

Casinos

Once a ship is 12 mi off the U.S. shore it is in international waters and gambling is permitted. (Some "cruises to nowhere," in fact, are little more than sailing casinos.) All ocean liners, as well as many cruise yachts and motor-sailing ships, have casinos. On larger vessels, they usually have poker, baccarat, blackjack, roulette, craps, and slot machines. House stakes are much more modest than those in Las Vegas or Atlantic City. On most ships the maximum bet is $200. Some ships allow $500. Payouts on the slot machines are generally much lower, too. Credit is never extended, but many casinos have handy ATMs that dispense cash (for a hefty fee). Casinos are usually open from early morning to late at night, although you may find only unattended slot machines before evening. By law, casinos are always closed while at port in Bermuda.

Game Rooms

Every cruise ship has a game or card room with card tables and board games. These rooms are for serious players and are often the site of friendly round-robin competitions and tournaments. Most ships furnish everything for free (cards, chips, games, and so forth), but a few charge $1 or more for each deck of cards. Be aware that professional cardsharps and hustlers have been fleecing ship passengers almost as long as there have been ships.

Bingo and Other Games

The daily high-stakes bingo games are even more popular than the casinos. You can play for as little as $1 a card. Most ships have a snowball bingo game with a jackpot that grows throughout the cruise into hundreds or even thousands of dollars.

Another popular cruise pastime is the so-called "horse races." Fictional horses are auctioned off to "owners." Individual passengers can buy a horse or form "syndicates." Bids usually begin at around $25 and can top $1,000 per horse. Races are then "run" according to dice throws or computer-generated random numbers. Audience members bet on their favorites.

Health & Safety at Sea

Crime

Most people never have any problem with crime aboard cruise ships, but you should exercise the same precautions aboard that you would at home. Keep your valuables out of sight. On big ships virtually every cabin has a small safe in the closet. Don't carry too much cash ashore, use credit cards whenever possible, and keep your money in a secure place, such as a front pocket that's harder to pick. Single women traveling with friends should stick together, especially when returning to their cabins late at night. And be careful about whom you befriend, as you would anywhere, whether it's a fellow passenger or a member of the crew. Don't be paranoid, but do be prudent.

Fire Safety

The greatest danger facing cruise-ship passengers is fire. All of the ships reviewed in this book must meet certain international standards for fire safety. Ships must have sprinkler systems, smoke detectors, and other safety features. However, these rules are designed to protect against loss of life. They do not guarantee that a fire will not happen. In fact, fire is a relatively common occurrence on cruise ships. The point here is not to create alarm, but to emphasize the importance of taking fire safety seriously.

Once settled into your cabin, find your life vests and review the emergency instructions posted inside the cabin door or near the life vests. Make sure your vests are in good condition and learn to secure the vest properly. Make certain the ship's purser knows if you or your companion has a physical infirmity that may hamper a speedy exit from your cabin. In case of an emergency, the purser can quickly dispatch a crew member to assist you. If you are traveling with children, be sure that child-size life jackets are placed in your cabin.

Within 24 hours of embarkation you will be asked to attend a mandatory lifeboat drill. Listen carefully. If you have any questions, ask them. If you are unsure how to use your vest, now is the time to ask. Only in the most extreme circumstances will you need to abandon ship, but it has happened. The few minutes you spend learning the right procedure may serve you well in a mishap.

Health Care

Quality medical care at sea is another important safety issue. All big ships are equipped with medical infirmaries to handle minor emergencies. However, these should not be confused with hospitals. There are no international standards governing medical facilities or personnel aboard cruise ships, although the American Medical Association has recommended that such standards be adopted. If you have a preexisting medical condition, discuss your upcoming cruise with your doctor. Pack an extra supply of any medicines you might need. Once aboard, see the ship's doctor and alert him or her to your condition, and discuss treatments or emergency procedures before any problem arises. Passengers with potentially life-threatening conditions should seriously consider signing up with a medical evacuation service, and all passengers should review their health insurance to make sure they are covered while on a cruise.

If you become seriously ill or injured and happen to be near a major city, you may be taken to a medical facility shoreside. But if you're farther afield, you may have to be airlifted off the ship by helicopter and flown either to the nearest American territory or to an airport where you can be taken by charter jet to the United States. Many standard health insurance policies, as well as Medicare, do not cover these or other medical expenses incurred outside the United States. You can, however, buy supplemental health insurance to cover you while you're traveling.

The most common minor medical problems confronting cruise passengers are seasickness and gastrointestinal distress. Modern cruise ships, unlike their transatlantic predecessors, are relatively motion-free vessels with computer-controlled stabilizers, and they usually sail in relatively calm waters. If, however, you do feel queasy, you can always get seasickness pills aboard ship. (Many ships give them out for free at the front desk.)

Outbreaks of food poisoning happen from time to time aboard cruise ships. Episodes are random. They can occur on ships old and new, big and small, budget and luxury. The Centers for Disease Control and Prevention (CDC) monitors cruise-ship hygiene and sanitation procedures, conducting voluntary inspections twice a year of all ships that sail regularly from U.S. ports (this program does not include ships that never visit the United States). For a free listing of the latest ship scores, write the CDC's National Center for Environmental Health (Vessel Sanitation Program, 1015 North America Way, Room 107, Miami, FL 33132). You can also get a copy from the CDC's fax-back service at 888/232–3299. Request publication 510051. Another alternative is to visit the Centers' Web site at www.cdc.gov.

A high score on the CDC report isn't a guarantee that you won't get sick. Outbreaks have taken place on ships that consistently score very highly. Conversely, on some ships that score very poorly passengers never get sick. So use these scores as a guideline and factor them in with other considerations when choosing your ship.

Money Matters Onboard

Shipboard Accounts

Cruise ships operate as cashless societies. Passengers charge onboard purchases and settle their accounts at the end of the cruise with a credit card, traveler's checks, or cash. You can sign for wine at dinner, drinks at the bar, shore excursions, gifts in the shop—virtually any expense you may incur aboard ship. On some lines, an imprint from a major credit card is necessary to open an account. Otherwise, a cash deposit may be required and a positive balance maintained to keep the shipboard account open. Either way, you will want to open a line of credit soon after settling into your cabin if an account was not opened for you at embarkation. This can easily be arranged by visiting the purser's office, located in the central atrium or main lobby.

Tipping

For better or worse, tipping is an integral part of the cruise experience. Most companies pay their cruise staff nominal wages and expect tips to make up the difference. Most cruise lines have recommended tipping guidelines, and on many ships "voluntary" tipping for beverage service has been replaced with a mandatory 15% service charge, which is added to every bar bill.

Shipboard Services

Film Processing and Supplies

Cruise ships carry a supply of film and batteries to fit most recent cameras. However, you're less likely to find slide film, black-and-white film, and batteries for older cameras aboard. Either bring an adequate supply from home or pick up a fresh stock while in Bermuda. Cruise ships can usually process and print your film overnight, again provided you're shooting standard color prints. Otherwise, you'll have to wait until you get home to see your pictures, or have the film processed ashore.

Hair Stylists

Hair salons are a standard feature on all ships sailing to Bermuda. Book your appointment well in advance, especially before such popular events as the farewell dinner.

Laundry and Dry Cleaning

All ships sailing weekly to Bermuda offer valet laundry service and dry cleaning, but none of the weekly ships has self-service laundry machines. Valet laundry service includes cabin pickup and delivery and usually takes 24 hours. If you choose this service, remember that the cost of washing your shirts, shorts, socks, and so forth can add up quickly.

Minibars

More expensive cabins, particularly suites, are equipped with small refrigerators or minibars stocked with snacks and soft drinks (beer, wine, and alcohol must be ordered from room service). Usually you are charged for what you consume.

Photographer

The staff photographer, a near-universal fixture on cruise ships, typically shoots pictures of passengers on the gangway upon embarkation, outside the dining room, and on many shore excursions. The thousands of photos snapped over the course of a cruise are displayed publicly in special cases every morning and are offered for sale, usually for $6 for a 5″ × 7″ color print or $12 for an 8″ × 10″. If you want a special photo or a portrait, the photographer is usually happy to oblige. Many passengers choose to have a formal portrait taken before the captain's farewell dinner, the dressiest evening of the cruise. The ship's photographer usually anticipates this demand by setting up a studio near the dining room entrance.

Religious Services

Your ship may provide nondenominational religious services on Sundays and religious holidays, and a number offer Catholic Masses daily and Jewish services on Friday evenings. The kind of service held depends upon the clergy the cruise line invites on board. Usually religious services are held in the library, the theater, or one of the private lounges, although a few ships have actual chapels.

Sports and Fitness

Exercise and Fitness Rooms

Cruise ships sailing to Bermuda have well-equipped fitness centers, many with massage, saunas, and whirlpools. Exercise rooms are equipped with bodybuilding equipment, stationary bicycles, rowing machines, treadmills, and the like. Aerobics classes are offered several times a day. Beauty salons adjacent to the health club may offer spa treatments such as facials and mud wraps. Celebrity in particular is well-known for its "AquaSpa," an upper-deck fitness center with an airy and sunny view of the sea, plus a full array of exercise equipment and private rooms for the latest European-inspired spa treatments.

Promenade Deck

Certain decks are designated for jogging, and fitness instructors may lead daily walks around the deck. Often, joggers are asked not to run before 8 AM or after 10 PM, so as not to disturb passengers in cabins.

Sun Deck

The top deck on a cruise ship is usually called the Sun Deck or Sports Deck. This is where you'll find the pool and hot tubs. Nearby are volleyball, table tennis, shuffleboard, and other such sports. Often, at twilight or after the sun goes down, the Sun Deck is used for dancing, barbecues, limbo contests, or other social activities.

DISEMBARKATION

The last night of your cruise is full of business. On most ships you must place everything except your hand luggage outside your cabin door, ready to be picked up by midnight. Color-coded tags, distributed to your cabin in a debarkation packet, should be placed on your luggage before the crew collects it. Your designated color will later determine when you leave the ship and help you retrieve your luggage on the pier.

Your shipboard bill is left in your room during the last day; to pay the bill (if you haven't already put it on your credit card) or to settle any questions, you must stand in line at the purser's office. Tips to the cabin steward and dining staff are distributed on the last night.

The next morning, in-room breakfast service is usually not available because stewards are too busy. Most passengers clear out of their cabins as soon as possible, gather their hand luggage, and stake out a chair in one of the public lounges to await the ship's clearance through customs. Be patient. It takes a long time to unload and sort thousands of pieces of luggage. Passengers are disembarked by groups according to the color-coded tags placed on luggage the night before. Those with the earliest flights get off first. If you have a tight connection, notify the purser before the last day, and he or she may be able to arrange faster debarkation for you.

Customs and Duties

U.S. Customs

Before your ship lands, each individual or family must fill out a customs declaration, regardless of whether anything was purchased abroad. If you have less than $1,400 worth of goods, you will not need to itemize purchases. Be prepared to pay whatever duties are owed directly to the customs inspector, with cash or check.

U.S. Customs now preclears a number of ships sailing in and out of Miami and other ports. It's done on the ship before you disembark. In other ports you must collect your luggage from the dock and then stand in line to pass through the inspection point. This can take up to an hour.

DUTIES FOR U.S. CITIZENS

For general customs and duty information, *see* Customs & Duties *in* Smart Travel Tips A to Z. Duties are the same for returning cruise passengers as for all other travelers, with a few exceptions. On certain Caribbean or Panama Canal itineraries that include a visit to Bermuda, you may be entitled to bring back $600 worth of goods duty-free, as opposed to the usual $400. If you're returning from a cruise that called in the U.S. Virgin Islands, the duty-free allowance is even higher: $1,200.

DUTIES FOR NON-U.S. CITIZENS

If you hold a foreign passport and will be returning home within hours of docking, you may be exempt from all U.S. Customs duties. Everything you bring into the United States must leave with you when you return home. When you reach your own country, you will have to pay appropriate duties there.

THE BERMUDA CRUISE FLEET

Concerned about overcrowding, the government of Bermuda limits the number of cruise ships that can visit the island on a weekly basis. At press time, only six ships from five cruise lines were making regular sailings. Choices include Crown Cruise Lines, Celebrity Cruises, Norwegian Cruise Line, Princess Cruises, and Royal Caribbean International. At the end of 1999, Celebrity won the right to staff the sixth ship after Norwegian Cruise Line moved *Norwegian Crown* to a subsidiary company operating in the deep sea. NCL's replacements, *Leeward* and *Norwegian Sea,* were deemed too small, opening the door to *Horizon,* which has a capacity of 1,354. *Horizon* joins sister vessel *Zenith,* two years her senior.

Ships generally call in Bermuda during the week and sail to and from the island on the weekends. While in Bermuda the ship acts as a hotel. Some ships may call at only one port city, such as the capital Hamilton, while others may split their time between Hamilton and St. George's or the West End. In any case, you'll have access to the entire island by taxi, moped, or shore excursion. Departure points for Bermuda cruises run the length of the Eastern Seaboard, including Cape Canaveral, Philadelphia, New York, and Boston. Special departures are sometimes scheduled from other Mid-Atlantic ports, so check with the cruise line or your travel agent. The Bermuda cruise season runs from April through October.

CROWN DYNASTY

The *Crown Dynasty* is unique among ships sailing to Bermuda for several reasons. For one thing, it's the only vessel with a Bermuda-inspired onboard decor, including island artwork, cuisine, and Bermuda-derived names for the ships decks and public rooms. It's also the only ship allowed to be in Bermuda on the weekends. Furthermore, the ship's unusual cruise-stay-fly itinerary allows passengers to enjoy the leisure and luxury of cruising to Bermuda on one leg of their vacation, staying for three days in a hotel on the island, and flying on the return leg of their trip. For passengers torn between cruising and flying, its the best of both worlds. *Built: 1993. Size: 20,000 tons. Capacity: 800 passengers. Cruise style: Casual.* ⊠ *400 Hollywood Blvd., Hollywood, FL 33021,* ☎ *800/832–1122.*

HORIZON

Like its sister ship, *Zenith, Horizon* has been brought up-to-date with the addition of such trademark Celebrity features as a new AquaSpa fitness center, cigar club, specialty-coffee lounge, and martini bar. Ship facilities and decor are almost identical to those of the more senior *Zenith* (☞ below). Both Celebrity ships benefit from outstanding kitchens overseen by chef Michel Roux. *Built: 1990. Size: 46,811 tons. Capacity: 1,354 passengers. Cruise style: Semiformal.* ⊠ *Celebrity Cruise Line, 1050 Caribbean Way, Miami, FL 33132,* ☎ *800/437–3111.*

NORDIC EMPRESS

Of the six ships sailing weekly to Bermuda, the *Nordic Empress* has the most bells and whistles. It has a nine-deck atrium and a three-level casino, the only one of its kind at sea. The ship was designed specifically for short cruises and has unique features, such as a single corridor that runs down just one side of the ship, a feature intended to help passengers get oriented to the vessel quickly. The *Nordic Empress* accomplishes an admirable feat. It delivers the big-ship style that is so popular today without the cavernous feeling sometimes found on the megaliners. *Built: 1990. Size: 48,563 tons. Capacity: 1,600 passengers. Cruise style: Casual.* ⊠ *Royal Caribbean International, 1050 Caribbean Way, Miami, FL 33132,* ☎ *800/327–6700 for reservations, 800/255–4373 for brochures only.*

NORWEGIAN MAJESTY

Technically speaking, the *Norwegian Majesty* is the "newest" ship sailing to Bermuda. That's because in April 1999 the ship was relaunched after a new midsection was inserted. The stretch job lengthened the ship by more than 100 feet and added more than 200 new cabins. Among the new public areas are a second swimming pool, a second dining room, a specialty-coffee lounge, and a new casino. The ship also received Norwegian Cruise Line's signature Le Bistro alternative restaurant, which serves Italian fare every evening by reservation for passengers who want a change of scenery and cuisine from the main dining rooms. Even so, it's still a moderately sized ship carrying fewer than 1,500 guests. *Built: 1992, stretched 1999. Size: 40,876 tons. Capacity: 1,462 passengers. Cruise style: Casual.* ⊠ *Norwegian Cruise Line, 7665 Corporate Center Dr., Miami, FL 33126,* ☎ *305/436–0866 or 800/327–7030.*

PACIFIC PRINCESS

The original "Love Boat" is the smallest ship sailing to Bermuda on a weekly basis. At 20,000 tons and carrying only 620 passengers, it's about half the size of most of its competitors. So it's good if you're seeking something cozier, more intimate, or a bit more traditional. Even so, the *Pacific Princess* does offer some of the latest cruising additions, like bistro-style dining in the buffet restaurant as an alternative to dinner in the main dining room. And while its an older ship, built in the early 1970s, its decor has been kept up-to-date through periodic refurbishments. Passengers may also like the British ambience of the Pacific Princess—most appropriate for sailing to decidedly British Bermuda. *Built: 1972. Size: 20,000 tons. Capacity: 620 passengers. Cruise style: Semiformal.* ⊠ *Princess Cruises, 10100 Santa Monica Blvd., Los Angeles, CA 90067,* ☎ *800/PRINCESS.*

ZENITH

Already one of the newest and most attractive ships sailing to Bermuda, the *Zenith* underwent a major refurbishment in 1999 that brought it up-to-date with such trademark Celebrity features as a new AquaSpa fitness center, cigar club, specialty-coffee lounge, and martini bar. From the outside, the Zenith strikes a handsome profile in port with Celebrity's signature blue-and-white hull. Inside, the ship is equally distinctive with its mix of decor that spans the range, taking its cues from contemporary and classic inspirations. Most of all, however, Celebrity is known for the culinary styling of chef Michel Roux, who designs Celebrity's menus and who has made the line's food a cut above the rest. *Built: 1992. Size: 47,255 tons. Capacity: 1,374 passengers. Cruise style: Semiformal.* ✉ *Celebrity Cruise Line, 1050 Caribbean Way, Miami, FL 33132,* ☎ *800/437–3111.*

SHORE EXCURSIONS

Shore excursions are optional tours organized by the cruise line and sold aboard the ship. Booking these tours saves you time, because the cruise line does the advance research and leg work. You'll pay a bit more for these tours than if you booked them independently but most passengers find that the convenience is worth the price. Of course, you are always free to explore on your own. With its excellent taxi service, Bermuda is a good island for hiring a car and driver. Ships calling in Bermuda pull up along the pier, so you can walk right off the ship to the center of town and major attractions. In Hamilton, for instance, passengers walk off the ship right onto Front Street, with its shops and restaurants.

The following tours are good options. Note that they may not be offered by all cruise lines. All the following tours last between two and three hours, and fees are generally between $30 and $40 per person, although snorkeling and helmet diving cost a bit more.

ISLAND SIGHTS

St. George's Highlight Tour: A quick overview of the area around St. George's includes Fort St. Catherine, Gates Fort, the Unfinished Church, Somers Garden, Tobacco Bay, and other sites. The guide also points out the popular shopping areas.

West End Highlight Tour: Visit Island Pottery, the Bermuda Art Centre, the Craft Market, Maritime Museum, Heydon Trust Chapel, and Gibbs Hill Lighthouse during a drive through Somerset. This tour is highly recommended if you are docked in Hamilton and won't be going to the West End on your own.

UNDERSEA CREATURES

Bermuda Glass-Bottom Boat Cruise: A tame but pleasant cruise through the harbor and over reefs, where you can view sea life from the comfort of a glassed-in viewing area. You can feed fish from the boat.

Helmet Diving: Walk on the bottom of the sea, play with fish, and learn about coral, all without getting your hair wet. Helmets cover your head and feed you air from the surface.

Snorkeling Tour: Equipment, lessons, and an underwater guided tour are included. Underwater cameras are available for an extra charge.

3 EXPLORING BERMUDA

Travel Bermuda's twisting roads past sherbet-color cottages, manicured gardens heavy with tropical scents, and rocky coves embracing sapphire-color waters. The capital of Hamilton has a bustling harbor, shops full of porcelain, museums, and shaded parks. And St. George's, at the island's northeastern end, has several historic sites. On the West End, pick out your favorite deserted beach. Elsewhere on the island are Bermuda's many parishes, where you can wander along quiet streets or lose yourself on soft, pink-sand shores.

B**ERMUDA** is nothing if not colorful. Its streets are lined with hedges of hibiscus and oleander, and its rolling green hills are shaded by tall palms and casuarina trees. The limestone buildings are painted in pretty pastels—pink and white seem to be most popular—and their gleaming white roofs are steeply pitched to channel the rain upon which Bermudians depend, because the island has no freshwater lakes or streams. Many houses also have quaint butteries, miniature cottages that were once used to keep food cool. House numbers are a relatively new phenomenon here. Most houses have names, such as Tranquillity, Struggle, and Last Penny. Bermuda's moon gates are another common architectural feature. You'll find these Chinese-inspired freestanding stone arches, which have been popular since the late 18th century, in gardens all over the island, and Bermudians favor them as backdrops for wedding pictures.

Updated by
Ron Bernthal

Bermuda's early history is closely tied with that of the United States. In 1609 three ships set sail from Plymouth, England, taking passengers and supplies to the beleaguered colony of Jamestown, Virginia. One of the ships, the *Sea Venture,* captained by Sir George Somers, ran into a fierce storm and was wrecked off Bermuda's east end, near the present site of the town of St. George (usually called "St. George's"). Shakespeare's *Tempest* was based on the famous shipwreck. Somers and the *Sea Venture* are legendary on Bermuda, so you'll see many references to the man and his ship.

Hamilton is of primary interest for its harbor, its shops—housed, of course, in small pastel-color buildings—and the government buildings, where you can see Parliament in session. In addition, the town is the major departure point for sightseeing boats, ferries, and the pink-and-blue buses that ramble all over the island. Don't confuse Hamilton town with the parish of the same name. Hamilton town is adjacent to Pembroke Parish.

The island's first capital was the town of St. George, on the island's northeastern end. History mavens will find much of interest in St. George's, including several noteworthy 17th-century buildings. The West End has the sleepy hamlet of Somerset and the Royal Naval Dockyard, a former British naval shipyard that is home to the Maritime Museum and a developing tourist center. The West End is in Sandys Parish, which can be pronounced either "Sandies" or "Sands."

Hamilton, St. George's, and Dockyard can all be explored easily on foot. The other parishes, however—the part of the island Bermudians refer to as "the country"—are best explored by moped, bicycle, or taxi. The parishes date back to 1616, when Bermuda was first surveyed and the island was divided into eight tribes or parishes, each named for an investor in the Bermuda Company, an offshoot of the Virginia Company, which controlled the island until 1684. The parishes are Sandys, Southampton, Warwick, Paget, Smith's, Hamilton, Pembroke, and Devonshire. St. George's, which was considered public land in the early days, is the ninth parish and includes the town of St. George. Bermudians customarily identify sites on the island by the parish in which they're located. A resident will say, "It's in Pembroke" or "It's in Warwick."

The main roads connecting the parishes are self-explanatory: North Shore Road, Middle Road, South Shore Road, and Harbour Road. Almost all traffic traversing the island's 22-mi length uses these roads, although some 1,200 smaller ones crisscross the land. In all, there are more than 400 mi of road on this small island. You'll also see several "tribe roads" that date back to the initial survey of the island. Many are now no more than country lanes, and some are dead ends. As you travel around the island, you'll see small brown-and-white signs that point to the Railway Trail. Built along the route of Bermuda's old railway line, it's now a peaceful route reserved for pedestrians and cyclists.

Hamilton

Bermuda's capital is a small town on Hamilton Harbour, where sight-seeing boats and ferries bob on the water waiting for passengers. Downtown Hamilton rises on hills above the harbor, its busy streets lined with small two- and three-story shops and office buildings painted in the requisite pastels. Many of the buildings have arcades, and narrow alleyways are strung between Front and Reid streets, two of the main drags. Imagine what Front Street was like prior to 1946, when horse-drawn carriages and bicycles were the main modes of transportation, and "Old Rattle and Shake," the narrow-gauge railway that ran from East End to West End, chugged along Hamilton's main street. The town has several important museums and galleries, though for many its main attractions are the plethora of shops selling discounted woolens, jewelry, perfumes, and electronics.

Numbers in the text correspond to numbers in the margin and on the Hamilton, Town of St. George, West End, and Parishes maps.

A Good Walk

Any tour of Hamilton should begin on **Front Street** ①, a pretty thoroughfare lined with small, colorful buildings, many with balconies and arcades. The Visitors Service Bureau in the Ferry Terminal Building on Front Street is an appropriate starting point. Turn left after leaving the bureau and cross Point Pleasant Road to reach the **Bank of Bermuda** ②, which houses displays of old Bermudian coins. For a splendid view of Hamilton Harbour, follow Point Pleasant Road to the waterside park at **Albuoy's Point** ③. From here, retrace your steps and pass the Ferry Terminal Building, where passengers board sightseeing boats to tour the island's waterways. Just beyond the docks is a large pink building called the No. 1 Shed, one of the island's several terminals for the elegant cruise ships that call at Bermuda.

At Heyl's Corner, at Front and Queen streets, you'll see the Birdcage, a traffic box where police occasionally direct traffic. Named for its designer, Michael "Dickey" Bird, the traffic box has been a Hamilton landmark for more than 30 years. The corner itself is named for J. B. Heyl, an American southerner who came to Bermuda in the 19th century and opened an apothecary shop here. Continue up Queen Street to the 19th-century **Perot Post Office** ④, Hamilton's main post office. Just beyond it is the **Museum of the Bermuda Historical Society/Bermuda Public Library** ⑤. Continue up Queen Street, or cut through the Washington Mall, to reach **City Hall** ⑥, which, in addition to administrative offices, houses a theater, the Bermuda National Gallery, and the Bermuda Society of Arts Gallery.

Behind City Hall, on Victoria Street, is **Victoria Park** ⑦, a lush 4-acre oasis with a Victorian bandstand. From the park follow Cedar Avenue one block to see **St. Theresa's Church** ⑧, a dramatic, Spanish Mission–style church not unlike some of those in the western United States. Retrace your steps to Victoria Park and continue walking toward Front Street. At Victoria Street, Cedar Avenue becomes Burnaby Street. Walk past the Central Bus Terminal and turn left on Church Street. On your left you'll see the imposing **Cathedral of the Most Holy Trinity** ⑨. Just beyond the cathedral, at the corner of Church and Parliament streets,

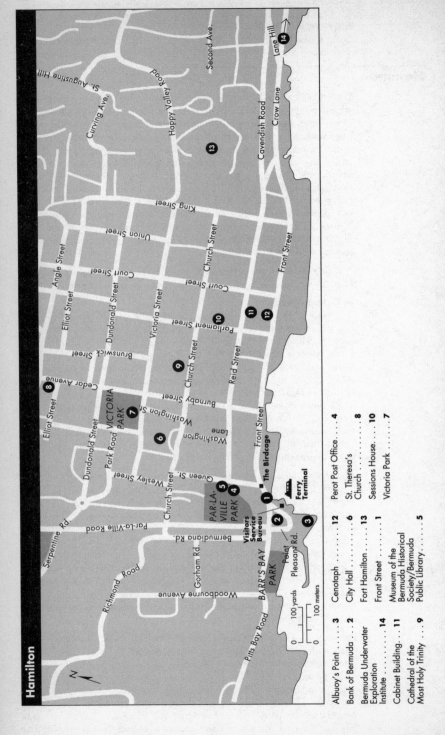

Hamilton

Albuoy's Point **3**
Bank of Bermuda **2**
Bermuda Underwater
Exploration
Institute **14**
Cabinet Building . . . **11**
Cathedral of the
Most Holy Trinity . . . **9**

Cenotaph **12**
City Hall **6**
Fort Hamilton **13**
Front Street **1**
Museum of the
Bermuda Historical
Society/Bermuda
Public Library **5**

Perot Post Office **4**
St. Theresa's
Church **8**
Sessions House . . . **10**
Victoria Park **7**

is **Sessions House** ⑩. Continue down Parliament Street to Front Street to see the **Cabinet Building** ⑪ and, in front of it, the **Cenotaph** ⑫.

Fort Hamilton ⑬, which lies on the eastern outskirts of the capital, is a bit far to walk. It's best reached by taxi or moped. After leaving Fort Hamilton, moped or taxi back down King Street and turn left on Front Street to see the **Bermuda Underwater Exploration Institute** ⑭, located on East Broadway near the traffic circle.

TIMING

You can see Hamilton in less than an hour, but you should allow at least a full day to explore the Bermuda Underwater Exploration Institute along with the museums and galleries. Die-hard shoppers will need two to three days here, and perhaps even longer. Avoid sightseeing during lunch hours, as the streets are thronged with office workers. The streets are also crowded when cruise ships are docked, from late spring to early fall.

Sights to See

⌇ *following the text of a review is your signal that the property has a Web site, where you will find details and, usually, images; for a link, visit www.fodors.com/urls.*

❸ **Albuoy's Point.** Picturesque Hamilton Harbour is dotted with tiny islands, and its blue waters are graced with the white sails of pleasure craft. Ferries churn from the capital bound for Paget, Warwick, and Somerset parishes. Ringside seats for this show are the benches beneath the trees of Albuoy's Point, a pleasant waterside park. Nearby is the **Royal Bermuda Yacht Club,** built in the 1930s. The idea for the yacht club was conceived in 1844 beneath the Calabash Tree at Walsingham (☞ Tom Moore's Tavern *in* The Parishes, *below*), and Prince Albert approved the club's use of the word "Royal" in 1845. Today royalty, international yachting celebrities, and the local elite hobnob at this posh center, which sponsors the Newport–Bermuda Ocean Yacht Race and the Gold Cup International Match Race Tournament. Barr's Bay Park, to the west of Albuoy's Point, also affords a good view of the yacht club and the harbor. Just beyond Bermudiana Road on Pitts Bay Road (a continuation of Front Street), steps and a ramp lead from the street to the park, with its vast expanse of green grass, its vistas, and its benches for taking it all in.

❷ **Bank of Bermuda.** Pigs were the only inhabitants Sir George Somers and his crew encountered when their ship, the *Sea Venture,* foundered on Bermuda's shores in 1609. Bermuda's earliest coin, called "hog money," commemorated those first residents. The coin is appropriately stamped on one side with a wild hog ringed with the words "Somer Ilands," and on the other with a replica of Sir George's ruined ship. If you're interested in coins, go up to the mezzanine of the Bank of Bermuda, where British and Spanish coins, many of them ancient, are displayed in glass cases. The collection includes some pieces of hog money, which the Bermuda Company issued in 1616. ⊠ *6 Front St.,* ☎ *441/ 295–4000.* ⌸ *Free.* ☉ *Nov.–Mar., Mon. 9:30–4, Tues.–Thurs. 8:30– 4, Fri. 8:30–4:30; Apr.–Oct., Fri. 8:30–7 only.* ⌇

☺ ⑭ **Bermuda Underwater Exploration Institute.** Opened in 1997, the enormous BUEI is designed to acquaint visitors with the vast deep and its various residents. Smack on the harbor, the two-story building has an exhibit hall—the Ocean Discovery Centre—with more than 40 displays, an auditorium for films and lectures, gift shops, boardrooms, and a restaurant. Bermuda sits 12,000 ft above the ocean floor on an extinct volcano, and the showpiece of the exhibit hall is a simulated capsule dive to the bottom, introduced by a videotaped Peter Benchley. The

TOURING BY MOPED

THERE ARE NO RENTAL CAR FIRMS in Bermuda, which will come as no surprise to the informed. Still, the anxiety that some visitors feel when they arrive at the airport and hear that they cannot rent an automobile can be striking in its intensity.

Residents of Bermuda are allowed to own vehicles (one per family, thank you!), but Bermuda's small size, its narrow roads, and its concern for the environment has led to a governmental ban on rental cars. Once the nervous visitor has calmed down and understands the many options for transportation around the island (ferry, bicycle, taxi, bus, and scooter), a truly automobile-free vacation begins.

Because of the ban on rental cars, the streets in Hamilton, and on the rest of the island, are not congested. It may appear busy during the brief morning and afternoon rush, but compared to that in U.S. or European cities, Bermuda "traffic" is gentle and quiet. Courteous hand signals, slow speeds, and spectacular scenery turn an ordinary outing into a sublime experience.

There are various routes that can be enjoyed by moped drivers, and it depends on one's taste in adventure, along with cooperating weather, to determine which route to follow. Some visitors prefer a trip to Dockyard because there are ferry services from that location that will return moped and passenger to home base in Hamilton, or to any of the smaller ferry terminals going back toward the south shore. Taking the ferry back avoids having to drive back over the same road.

Driving to St. George's Parish has its advantages too, as at Flatts Village the road splits, with the North Shore Road continuing east along the Atlantic while Harrington Sound Road dips south and east along the Sound and passes Tucker's Town, a delightful stopover. Harrington Sound Road meets the North Shore Road again at Bailey's Bay, just before the causeway to the airport and St. George village.

Whichever route you take, do remember that the most interesting sights in Bermuda are often along the little side roads, the ones with lyrical names like Point Finger Road, My Lords Bay Road, Tamarind Vale Road, and the Khyber Pass. On these smaller roads you will see lovely residences, historic markers, and even a few small farms.

A few things to remember, however. Bermudians, in the English fashion, drive on the left-hand side of the road. And even though visitors don't need drivers' licenses to rent mopeds (although they must be over 16 years of age), they are required to follow all the rules of the road. Another warning—dress appropriately. It is not uncommon for new drivers to take a spill, usually when they are going quite slowly, perhaps while navigating a country lane or even the driveway of their hotel. So Bermuda shorts aren't the thing because even a little fall could result in a nasty loss of leg skin. Wear long pants, at least until you feel really secure on your two-wheeler. And with those cool nights, and sometimes chilly drizzles, its also smart to pack a sweater or windbreaker for the long ride back from the parishes. And, finally, remember to wear the helmet that comes with the bike. It's the law in Bermuda. (☞ Moped & Scooter Rental in Smart Travel Tips A to Z for more information on rentals.)

expedition is actually an elevator trip to the lower floor, where displays include a scale model of a ship that sank off Bermuda hundreds of years ago, a cargo inventory, and artifacts from sunken vessels. A big screen shows jellyfish cruising the waters, there are huge murals of sea creatures, and an aural display lets you hear the sounds sea animals make as they communicate with each other. There's also a place to test your preparatory scuba skills. In addition, the institute has a precious-metals exhibit and a display featuring the restored rigging of some 18th-century ships. ✉ *E. Broadway*, ☎ *441/292–7219*, 𝔽𝔸𝕏 *441/236–6141.* 🎫 *$9.75.* ☉ *Daily 9–5.* ✍

⑪ Cabinet Building. Bermuda's Senate—the upper house of Parliament—sits in the dignified two-story Cabinet Building, surrounded by trees and gardens. Amid great ceremony, the formal opening of Parliament takes place in the Senate Chamber, traditionally on the first Friday of November. His Excellency the Governor, dressed in a plumed hat and full regalia, arrives on the grounds in a landau drawn by magnificent black horses and accompanied by a police escort. A senior police officer, carrying the Black Rod made by the Crown jewelers, then asks the Speaker of the House, elected representatives, and members of the Senate Chamber to convene. The governor makes his Throne Speech from a tiny cedar throne, dating from the 1600s, which is carved with the words "Cap Josias Forstore Govornour of the Sumer Islands Anodo 1642" (Josias Foster was governor in 1642). The portraits above the dais are of King George III and Queen Charlotte. The chamber is open to visitors, but you should come on a Wednesday if you want to watch the Senate in action. Call first to inquire about the schedule. Take some time to admire the ☞ **Cenotaph** out front. ✉ *Front St.*, ☎ *441/292–5501.* 🎫 *Free.* ☉ *Weekdays 9–5.*

★ ⑨ Cathedral of the Most Holy Trinity. One of the island's most impressive structures, this is the seat of the Anglican Church of Bermuda. The cathedral is the second church to have been built on this site. Twelve years after its completion in 1872, Trinity Church was burned to the ground by an arsonist. Work began on the present church the following year, and it was consecrated in 1911. Designed in Early English style with Gothic-revival flourishes, the church is constructed of Bermuda limestone and materials imported from Scotland, Nova Scotia, France, Ireland, and Indiana. The tower rises to 143 ft, and the clerestory in the nave is supported by piers of polished Scottish granite. The four smaller columns in each aisle were added after a hurricane shook the cathedral—and its architect—during construction. The altar in the Lady Chapel is of Italian marble, and above it is a copy of Andrea del Sarto's *Madonna and Child.*

The Warrior Chapel, dedicated in 1977, honors those who have served in the armed forces of the Crown. The Great Warrior Window is a memorial to 85 Bermudian men who died in World War I. The flags represent military units of Bermuda and England. The choir stalls and bishop's throne were carved from English oak, and the pulpit is a replica of the one in St. Giles Cathedral, Edinburgh. On a wall near the lectern, the Canterbury Cross, set in stone taken from the walls of Canterbury Cathedral, is a copy of one made in Kent in the 8th century. The stained-glass windows are lovely. Note especially the Angel Window on the east wall of the north transept, which was made by local artist Vivienne Gilmore Gardner. After exploring the interior, climb the 150-odd steps to the tower, at the top of which you'll have spectacular views of Hamilton. ✉ *Church St.*, ☎ *441/292–4033.* 🎫 *Tower $3.* ☉ *Church daily and for Sun. services; tower weekdays 10–3.*

NEED A
BREAK?
Executives, secretaries, shoppers, and store owners flock to **The Spot** (⊠
6 Burnaby St., ☎ 441/292–6293) for breakfasts, plate lunches, burgers, sandwiches, and coffee. In business for more than 50 years, this
nook serves full meals and daily specials for less than $10, and sand-
wiches for about $5. It's one of the best values on the island. The Spot is
open Monday to Saturday 6:30 AM to 7 PM.

⑫ Cenotaph. This memorial to Bermuda's war dead stands in front of the
Cabinet Building. On Remembrance Day (November 11), the Governor and other dignitaries lay wreaths at its base. The Cenotaph is a
smaller version of the famous monument in Whitehall, London. The
cornerstone was laid in 1920 by the Prince of Wales, who, as King Edward VIII, abdicated to wed Mrs. Wallis Simpson. The Cenotaph lies
between Parliament and Court streets. Although Court Street is safe
in daylight, it's best not to wander around here at night. Bermuda does
have some problems with drugs, and what traffic there is centers on
Court and Victoria streets after dark.

★ **❻ City Hall.** Set back from the street behind a lawn, fountains, and a lily
pond is a large white structure topped by a weather vane shaped like
the *Sea Venture.* This relatively new building (1960) houses Hamilton's
City Hall, whose massive cedar doors open into a large lobby with great
chandeliers, high ceilings, and a portrait gallery. The large portrait of
Queen Elizabeth II was painted by Curtis Hooper and unveiled in 1987
by the duke of Gloucester. Oil paintings of Hamilton's former mayors
hang here as well. Behind tall cedar doors on the right are the Coin
and Note Display of the Bermuda Monetary Authority, the extensive
Benbow Collection of 20th-century stamps, and occasional displays
of historic Bermudiana. The City Hall Theatre often hosts concerts,
plays, and dance performances. A handsome cedar staircase leads to
the second-floor galleries.

Upstairs, the East Exhibition Room houses the **Bermuda National
Gallery,** the island's only climate-controlled gallery. Opened in 1992,
the gallery displays European paintings from the early 16th to 19th
centuries, including works by Thomas Gainsborough, Sir Joshua
Reynolds, and George Romney. There are also 20th-century lithographs,
oils, sculptures, and acrylics, and an extensive collection of Bermudian
artists and works by painters who visited the island from the late 19th
century to the 1950s.

In the West Wing of City Hall, changing exhibits are displayed in the
Bermuda Society of Arts Gallery. The juried annual Spring, Summer,
Autumn, and Winter Members' Shows attract talented local artists, who
display high-quality works painted and drawn with watercolors, oils,
pastels, acrylics, and charcoals; collage and sculpture are also included
occasionally. The Photographic Show in January features underwater
and shoreside shots. Solo shows by local and visiting artists are also
held in the Society's small gallery throughout the year. ⊠ *Church St.,*
☎ *441/292–1234 City Hall; 441/295–9428 Bermuda National Gallery
(East Wing); 441/292–3824 Bermuda Society of Arts Gallery (West
Wing).* ▣ *City Hall free, Bermuda National Gallery $3, Bermuda So-
ciety of Arts Gallery free (donations accepted).* ☉ *City Hall weekdays
9–5; Bermuda National Gallery and Bermuda Society of Arts Gallery
Mon.–Sat. 10–4.*

NEED A
BREAK?
Paradiso Cafe (⊠ 7 Reid St., at the entrance to Washington Mall, ☎
441/295–3263) and the **Windsor Garden** (⊠ Windsor Pl. Mall, across
Queen St. and north of the library, ☎ 441/295–4085) are great
places to relax over light lunch fare or diet-busting pastries.

★ ⓭ **Fort Hamilton.** On the eastern outskirts of Hamilton is this imposing old fortress, complete with a moat, 18-ton guns, and underground passageways that were cut through solid rock by Royal Engineers in the 1860s. The restored fort is one of several built by order of the duke of Wellington. Outdated even before its completion, the fort never fired a shot in aggression. Today you can enjoy splendid views of the capital and the harbor from here. Accompanied by drummers and dancers, the kilted Bermuda Isles Pipe Band performs a stirring skirling ceremony on the green every Monday at noon from November through March. One-way streets make getting here a little circuitous. From downtown Hamilton head east on Victoria Street, turn left on King Street and then turn left onto Happy Valley Road. ⊠ *Happy Valley Rd., Pembroke,* ☎ *no phone.* 🎫 *Free.* ⊙ *Daily 9:30–5.*

➊ **Front Street.** Hamilton's main drag runs alongside the harbor. Front Street bustles with small cars, mopeds, bicycles, buses, pedestrians, and the occasional horse-drawn carriage, and is lined with colorful little buildings, many with balconies and arcades that house shops and boutiques. This is Bermuda's main shopping area, and shoppers will probably want to spend plenty of time—and money—here (☞ Chapter 8). The Visitors Service Bureau, with its friendly staff and abundance of free brochures, is in Front Street's Ferry Terminal Building.

★ ➎ **Museum of the Bermuda Historical Society/Bermuda Public Library.** Mark Twain admired the giant rubber tree that stands on Queen Street in the front yard of this Georgian house, once home to Hamilton's first postmaster, William Bennet Perot, and his family. Although charmed by the tree, which had been imported from Demerara (now Guyana) in the mid-19th century, Twain lamented that it didn't bear fruit in the form of hot-water bottles and rubber overshoes.

The house now contains the Bermuda Public Library and Museum of the Bermuda Historical Society. The library, which was founded in 1839, moved to its present quarters in August 1916. One early librarian was an eccentric gentleman with the Dickensian name of Florentius Frith, who rode in from the country on horseback and struck terror into the heart of anyone who interrupted his chess games to check out a book. The reference section has virtually every book ever written about Bermuda, as well as a microfilm collection of Bermudian newspapers dating back to 1784. The rare-book collection contains a 1624 edition of John Smith's *Generall Historie of Virginia, New England and the Somers Isles.* In the museum's entrance hall are portraits of Sir George Somers and his wife, painted about 1605. Portraits of Postmaster Perot and his wife hang there, too. Notice Admiral Sir George Somers's lodestone (circa 1600), used for magnetizing compass needles, and a Bermuda map from 1622 that shows the division of the island into 25-acre shares by the original Bermuda Company. The museum also contains an eclectic collection of old English coins and Confederate money, Bermuda silver, Asian porcelains, and pictures of horse-and-buggy Bermuda juxtaposed with modern-day scenes. There are several cedar pieces, including two Queen Anne chairs from about 1740, a handsome grandfather clock, a glass chandelier, handmade palmetto hats, and a recently restored sedan chair from around 1770. Ask to see the letter George Washington wrote in 1775 "to the inhabitants of Bermuda," requesting gunpowder. ⊠ *13 Queen St.,* ☎ *441/295–2905 library; 441/295–2487 museum.* 🎫 *Free (donations accepted).* ⊙ *Library weekdays 9–6, Sat. 9–5; museum Mon.–Sat. 9:30–3:30. Tours by appointment.*

There is a popular branch of the **Ice Queen** (✉ Reid and Queen Sts., ☎ 441/292–6497), Paget's late-night burger joint, right in Hamilton. The restaurant, which is open late, has ample seating and a lineup of burgers, ice cream, and such.

4 Perot Post Office. Bermuda's first postage stamps (1848) originated in this two-story white building, which dates from around 1840 and still serves as the island's main post office. Bermuda's first postmaster was William Bennet Perot, appointed in 1818. Perot would meet arriving steamers, collect the mail, stash it in his beaver hat, and then stroll around Hamilton to deliver it. To post a letter, residents came and paid Perot, who hand-stamped each one. Obviously, the postmaster had to be at his station to do so, but this annoyed Perot, as he preferred pottering around in the garden. Local historians credit Perot's friend, the pharmacist J. B. Heyl, with the idea for Bermuda's first book of stamps. Heyl suggested that Perot make a whole sheet of postmarks, write "Wm B. Perot" on each postmark, and sell the sheet for a shilling. People could then tear off a postmark, paste it on a letter, and mail it—without having to extricate Perot from the shrubbery. The extremely rare Perot stamps, some of which are now in the Queen's Royal Stamp Collection, are coveted by collectors. At press time the record price for an 1848 Perot stamp was £225,000 ($350,000). ✉ *Queen St.,* ☎ *441/ 295–5151.* ☜ *Free.* ☉ *Weekdays 9–5.*

The garden where Perot liked to pass his time is now **Par-la-Ville Park,** a pleasant spot that occupies a large portion of Queen Street. The Queen Street entrance (there's another on Par-la-Ville Road) is next to the post office. Paths wind through the luxuriant gardens, and the park benches are ideal for picnicking or enjoying a short rest. You may have trouble finding a place to sit at noontime, as this is a favorite lunch spot for Hamilton office workers.

8 St. Theresa's Church. St. Theresa's is a Spanish Mission–style church that serves as the seat of the island's six Roman Catholic Churches. It houses the gold and silver chalice that Pope Paul VI presented to Bermuda's diocese during a 1968 visit. Mass was first celebrated in here in 1932. The church is two blocks north of Victoria Park. ✉ *Cedar Ave. and Elliot St.,* ☎ *441/292–0607.* ☉ *Daily 7:30–7.*

10 Sessions House. Bermuda's Parliament, the world's third oldest, met for the first time in 1620 in St. Peter's Church, in St. George's. It later moved to the State House, where deliberations were held for almost 200 years until the capital was moved to Hamilton. The eye-catching Italianate edifice called Sessions House now houses the House of Assembly (the lower house of Parliament) and the Supreme Court. The original two-story structure was built in 1819. The Florentine towers and colonnade, decorated with red terra-cotta, were added in 1887 to commemorate Queen Victoria's Golden Jubilee. The Victoria Jubilee Clock Tower made its striking debut at midnight on December 31, 1893.

In its present location, the House of Assembly meets on the second floor, where business is conducted in a style befitting such an august body. The sergeant-at-arms precedes the Speaker of the House into the chamber, bearing a silver-gilt mace. (Introduced in 1921, the mace is fashioned after a James I mace in the Tower of London.) The Speaker, in wig and flowing black robe, solemnly calls the meeting to order with a cedar gavel made from the old Belfry Tree, which has been growing in St. Peter's churchyard since before 1620. The proceedings are no less ceremonious and colorful in the Supreme Court, on the lower floor, where judges in red robes and full wigs hear the arguments of barristers in black robes and wigs. You're welcome to watch the proceedings in the Assembly and the Supreme Court, but you'll want to call to find out when sessions are scheduled. ⊠ *Parliament St. between Reid and Church Sts.,* ☎ *441/292–7408.* 🎫 *Free.* ⊘ *Weekdays 9–12:30 and 2–5.*

❼ Victoria Park. Nestled amid gardens and shaded by trees, a Victorian bandstand is the focal point of the 4-acre Victoria Park and sometimes hosts concerts in summer. The park was built in 1887 in honor of Queen Victoria's Golden Jubilee and opened with great fanfare in 1890. It's perfectly safe when filled with people, but it isn't a good place to wander alone. Some fairly seedy-looking characters hang out here. ⊠ *Behind City Hall on Victoria St.*

The Town of St. George

The settlement of Bermuda began on St. George's end of the island nearly 400 years ago, when the *Sea Venture* was wrecked off the coast. Much of the fun of St. George's is exploring the alleys and walled lanes that wind through the town. You can easily tour the town on foot.

A Good Walk

Start your tour in **King's Square** ⑮, stopping first in the Visitors Bureau to pick up maps and brochures. Stroll out onto **Ordnance Island** ⑯ to see the statue of Sir George Somers and a replica of the *Deliverance II.* The **White Horse Tavern** ⑰ is a pleasant place for lunch or general refreshment. Just up the street is the **Bermuda National Trust Museum at the Globe Hotel** ⑱, which houses fascinating historical exhibits pertinent to American history. Across the square is **Town Hall** ⑲, with King Street running alongside it. As you walk up King Street, notice the fine Bermudian architecture of **Bridge House** ⑳. Walk up King Street to Princess Street, and on your left is **Reeve Court** ㉑, a Bermuda National Trust property. Across from it, at the top of King Street, is the **Old State House** ㉒, the oldest stone house in Bermuda.

Walk along Princess Street and cross Duke of York Street to **Somers Garden** ㉓ to see the putative burial site of the heart of Sir George Somers. After walking through the garden, ascend the steps to Blockade Alley, where you'll see on a hill ahead the **Unfinished Church** ㉔. To your left are Duke of Kent Street, Featherbed Alley, and the **St. George's Historical Society Museum** ㉕. Around the corner is the **Featherbed Alley Printery** ㉖. Cross Clarence Street to Church Street and then turn right on Broad Alley to reach the **Old Rectory** ㉗. Straight ahead (as straight as you can go among these twisted alleys), is Printer's Alley, where Joseph Stockdale published Bermuda's first newspaper on January 17, 1784. The short street connecting Printer's Alley with Old Maid's Lane is **Nea's Alley** ㉘, which looks like something out of a tale retold by the Brothers Grimm.

Return to Church Street and enter the yard of **St. Peter's Church** ㉙, an ancient Anglican church (the main entrance is on Duke of York Street). From the church, continue down Duke of York Street to Barber's Alley, but before turning left to reach **Tucker House** ㉚ notice, on the right, **Petticoat Lane** ㉛. After visiting Tucker House, cross Water Street to Somers Wharf, where you'll find the **Carriage Museum** ㉜, although it may be closed for renovations.

TIMING

Despite its small size, St. George's encompasses much of historical interest, and you should plan to spend a full day poking around the houses and museums.

Between March and November, the government sponsors several free events, including walking tours. The island is usually fairly uncrowded

36

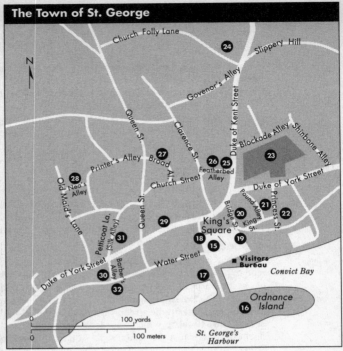

The Town of St. George

during the low season, so this is a good time to see the town crier and the mayor of St. George's, both of whom are around. Note, however, that St. George's can be very crowded between late spring and early fall, when cruise ships dock here (as they do in Hamilton), and shoppers flood the streets near and around King's Square.

Sights to See

★ ⑱ **Bermuda National Trust Museum at the Globe Hotel.** Governor Samuel Day built the house that is now the Bermuda National Trust Museum in 1700. The building served as the Globe Hotel for 150 years, and then housed the Confederate Museum until 1995. Visitors are shown a video, *Bermuda, Centre of the Atlantic,* and an exhibit entitled "Rogues and Runners: Bermuda and the American Civil War." Based on photos and documents from public and private collections, the exhibit tells the colorful story of St. George's career as a port for Confederate blockade runners. A diorama of the town's waterfront, a model of the blockade-runner *Fergus,* and a Victorian seal press that reproduces the Great Seal of the Confederacy are also on display.

The story behind one of the museum's former displays is worth recounting. Major Norman Walker, who came to Bermuda as a Confederate agent, used the building as his office during the U.S. Civil War. Having suffered a depression after the capital moved to Hamilton in 1815, St. George's sided with the South for economic reasons, and the town became a hotbed of blockade-running. The first woman to run the blockade was Georgiana Walker, Major Walker's pregnant wife, who risked capture by the North to join her husband in Bermuda. She was determined that their baby would be born on Confederate soil, underneath the Stars and Bars. So the four-poster bed in the birthing room was draped with the Confederate flag, and it's said that Confederate soil was spread beneath the bed. ⊠ *Duke of York St.,* ☎ *441/*

297–1423. ☜ $4; $5 combination ticket includes admission to Tucker House and Verdmont, in Smith's Parish. ☉ Tues.–Sat. 10–4.

㉟ Bridge House. Named for a bridge that once crossed a small tidal creek nearby, this house was built sometime prior to 1700. It's a fine example of Bermudian architecture, and has served as the home of several of Bermuda's governors. Now owned by the Bermuda National Trust, it has been restored and is privately leased as several small apartments, an art studio, and a shop.

㉜ Carriage Museum. With the arrival of cars on Bermuda in 1946, horse-drawn carriages were put out to pasture, so to speak. Although this museum is presently closed to the public, it is expected to open again in late 2000. Displays here offer a fascinating look at some of the island's old carriages. The surrey with a fringe on top, along with isinglass curtains that roll down, was a favorite. Among other previous displays, which are expected to be shown again, are a dignified brougham, a six-passenger enclosed Opera Bus, and a small two-wheeler for children, called the Little Red Dog Cart. The museum is at Somers Wharf, part of a multimillion-dollar waterfront restoration. St. George's passenger-ship terminal is nearby. ☒ *Water St.*

㉖ Featherbed Alley Printery. As quaint as its name, the Featherbed Alley Printery is in a little cottage that houses a working printing press of the sort invented by Johannes Gutenberg in the 1450s. ☒ *Featherbed Alley,* ☎ *441/297–0423.* ☜ *$4 (includes admission to St. George's Historical Society Museum).* ☉ *Apr.–Nov., weekdays 10–4.*

⑮ King's Square. Now the hub and heartbeat of St. George's, King's Square is actually comparatively new. For 200 years after the town was settled the square was a marshy part of the harbor. It was filled in only in the 1800s.

Prominently displayed in King's Square are cedar replicas of the stocks and pillory originally used to punish criminals. The grisly gizmos now serve as props for tourist photos and for special activities staged here on Wednesday during low season. If you decide to take the walking tour (☞ Sightseeing *in* Smart Travel Tips A to Z), you'll be greeted in the square by the mayor of St. George's. The town crier, whose resounding voice is almost enough to wake the dead, is on hand in full colonial costume. After the official welcome, he bellows a few pronouncements and places any perceived malefactors in the stocks. The main event, however, is when a woman in colonial garb is branded a "gossip" and dunked in the harbor. You can stop at the Visitors Service Bureau here for maps, brochures, and advice.

㉘ Nea's Alley. The 19th-century Irish poet Tom Moore lived on this street, then known as Cumberland Lane, during his four-month tenure as registrar of the admiralty court. Moore, who was endowed with considerable charm, had an impact on the island that endures to this day. He was invited to stay in the home of Admiral Mitchell, the neighbor of Mr. William Tucker and his wife, Hester, who is the "Nea" to whom Moore pours out his heart in several poems. Moore is thought to have first seen Hester here in Cumberland Lane, which he describes in one of his odes as "the lime-covered alley that leads to thy home." However discreet Nea and Moore may have been about their affair, his odes to her were on the steamy side—much to the dismay of her husband. Although it was rather like locking the barn door after the horse has bolted, Tucker eventually refused to allow his former friend into his house. Some Bermudians speculate that Nea was very much in love with Tom, but that he considered her merely a pleasant diversion. He returned to Ireland after his assignment, and Nea died in 1817 at the age of 31. Bermudians are much enamored of the short-lived romance between Hester and Moore, and travelers are likely to hear a good deal about it.

㉗ Old Rectory. Built around 1690 by a local pirate, George Dew, this house takes its name from a later owner, Alexander Richardson. Called the "Little Bishop," he was rector of St. Peter's from 1755 to 1805, excepting a six-year stint on St. Eustatius. Richardson's diary is filled with anecdotes about 18th-century St. George's. Traditional architectural features, such as cedar beams, chimneys, and a welcoming-arms staircase are handsome. A garden is open to the public as well. The house is now owned by the Bermuda National Trust. ⊠ *Broad Alley,* ☎ *441/297–0879.* ☜ *Free (donations accepted).* ☉ *Nov.–Mar., Wed. noon–5.*

㉒ Old State House. A curious ritual takes place every April in King's Square. One peppercorn, regally placed upon a velvet pillow, is presented to the mayor of St. George's amid much pomp and circumstance. The peppercorn is the annual rent paid to the town by the Masonic Lodge St. George No. 200 of the Grand Lodge of Scotland, which has occupied the Old State House ever since the capital moved from St. George's to Hamilton in 1815. The oldest house in Bermuda, it was built in 1620 in what Governor Nathaniel Butler believed was the Italian style. The limestone building used a mixture of turtle oil and lime as mortar, and set the style for future Bermudian buildings. Upon completion, it became home to the Parliament, which had been meeting in St. Peter's Church, and also hosted dances and social gatherings. The Old State House is closed on public holidays. ⊠ *Princess St.,* ☎ *441/292–2480; 441/297–1206 (Wed. only).* ☜ *Free.* ☉ *Wed. 10–4.*

★ ☾ **⑯ Ordnance Island.** *Land Ho!*—a splendid Desmond Fountain statue of Sir George Somers—dominates Ordnance Island. The dunking stool is a replica of the one used to dunk gossips, nagging wives, and suspected witches. Demonstrations are sometimes given, although volunteers report that getting dunked is no fun, even in fun.

Also on the island is the ***Deliverance II,*** a replica of one of the ships built by the survivors of the 1609 shipwreck. (Somers and his crew built two ships, the *Deliverance* and the *Patience,* to carry them to Jamestown, Virginia, after the incident.) Below deck, life-size mannequins in period costume depict the realities of ocean travel during the 17th century. It wasn't the *QE2.* ⊠ *Ordnance Island,* ☎ *441/297–2750.* ☜ *$3.* ☉ *Mar.–Nov., daily 9–5.* ☜

㉛ Petticoat Lane. Also called Silk Alley, this little street received its name in 1834 after the emancipation of Bermudian slaves. Legend has it that two freed slaves who had always wanted petticoats like those worn by their mistresses strolled down the lane on Emancipation Sunday with much rustling of petticoat skirts.

㉑ Reeve Court. The Bermuda National Trust purchased this three-story house on Princess Street to ensure protection from development around the State House. Although the building is not open to the public, you can wander through the colonial garden to admire plantings of fruits and herbs and a formal parterre. ⊠ *Princess St.*

㉕ St. George's Historical Society Museum. Furnished to resemble its former incarnation as a private home, this typical Bermudian building from the early 1700s houses artifacts and documents pertaining to the island's earliest days. One of Bermuda's oldest pieces is a table believed to have been used as the High Court bench in the State House. The house is also filled with documents—including a doctor's bill from

1790—old letters, and displays of pewter, china, and rare books. There's even a whale-blubber cutter.

The U.S. Civil War relics include a torpedo raft. Built of heavy timber with projecting arms to hold torpedoes, the raft was part of a Union plan to blow up the submarine barricade in Charleston harbor. After breaking loose from its towing ship during a gale, the raft drifted for six years before washing ashore in Dolly's Bay on St. David's Island. When the captain of the towing ship later visited Bermuda, he recognized the raft and explained its purpose to the puzzled Bermudians.

On the south wall of the house is an iron grate said to have come from the cell where Bermuda's first Methodist missionary, the Reverend John Stephenson, was confined for preaching to slaves. Stephenson persisted in preaching from his cell to a crowd that collected outside. The cottage gardens behind the building are beautiful, and there is no fee to view them. ⊠ *Featherbed Alley,* ☎ *441/297–0423.* ▨ *$4 (includes admission to Featherbed Alley Printery).* ☉ *Apr.–Dec., weekdays 10–4; Jan.–Mar., weekdays 11–3.*

★ ㉙ **St. Peter's Church.** The tombstones here, in Bermuda's oldest churchyard, tell some interesting tales, indeed. This is the resting place of governors, doctors, simple folk, and pirates alike. East of the church is the grave of Hester, or "Nea," marked "Mr. William Tucker's Family Vault." One of the best-known monuments stands over the grave of Richard Sutherland Dale, who died in 1815 at age 20. An American Navy midshipman, Dale was mortally wounded during a sea battle with the British in the War of 1812. The monument was erected by his parents as a tribute to the St. Georgians, whose "tender sympathy prompted the kindest attentions to their son while living and honoured him when dead." In an enclosure to the west of the church is the slaves' graveyard. The ancient cedar tree, which antedates 1620, is the old Belfry Tree, from whose wood the gavel that begins each session of the House of Assembly is still made.

Because parts of St. Peter's Church date back to its construction in 1620, it holds the distinction of being the oldest continuously operating Anglican church in the Western Hemisphere. It was not the first church to stand on this site, however. It replaced a 1612 structure of posts and palmetto leaves that was destroyed in a storm. The present church was extended in 1713, and the galleries on either side were added in 1833. The oldest part of the church is the area around the 17th-century tripletier pulpit. The dark-red cedar altar is the oldest piece of woodwork in the colony, carved under the supervision of Richard Moore, a shipwright and Bermuda's first governor. The baptismal font, brought to the island by the early settlers, is about 500 years old, and the late-18th-century bishop's throne is believed to have been salvaged from a wreck. Among the treasures displayed in the vestry are a 1697 William of Orange communion set and a Charles I chalice, sent from England by the Bermuda Company in 1625. Commemorative plaques hang on the walls, and some of the names are wonderful. One large memorial is to Governor Allured Popple. If you enter through the back door, be sure to look at the front of the church when you leave. ⊠ *Duke of York St.,* ☎ *441/297–8359.* ▨ *Free (donations accepted).* ☉ *Daily 10–4:30.*

NEED A BREAK?   Sitting almost cheek-by-jowl with St. Peter's Church, **Temptations Cafe & Bakery** (⊠ 31 Duke of York St., ☎ 441/297–1368) is a popular spot for heavenly pastries and sandwiches; it's open Monday to Saturday 8:30 AM to 5 PM. **Reid's Restaurant** (⊠ 109 Mullet Bay Rd., ☎ 441/ 297–1039) has both counter service and a tiny outdoor terrace for good, hearty breakfasts; casual lunch and dinner food (chowder, hamburgers, hotdogs, meat pies) are also served. It's open Monday to Saturday 7 AM to 9 PM, Sunday until 6 PM.

㉓ Somers Garden. After sailing to Jamestown and back in 1610, Sir George Somers fell ill and died. According to local lore, Somers told his nephew Matthew Somers that he wanted his heart buried in Bermuda, where it belonged. Matthew, who never seemed to pay much attention to his uncle's wishes, sailed for England soon afterward, sneaking Somers's body aboard in a cedar chest to avoid alarming the superstitious seamen. (Somers's body is buried near his birthplace in Dorset.) When the tomb where Somers's heart was supposedly interred was opened many years later, only a few bones, a pebble, and some bottle fragments were found, so no one knows whether Matthew Somers ever carried out his uncle's wishes. Nonetheless, ceremonies were held at the empty grave upon the 1920 visit of the prince of Wales, during which the prince christened this pleasant, tree-shrouded park Somers Garden. ⊠ *Bordered by Shinbone Alley, Blockade Alley, and Duke of Kent and Duke of York Sts.,* ☏ *no phone.* 🎫 *Free.* ☉ *Daily 9–4.*

⑲ Town Hall. St. George's administrative offices are housed in this two-story building that was constructed in 1808. The hall is paneled and furnished with cedar, and there's a delightful collection of photographs of former mayors. Many years ago Town Hall was the scene of a memorable con. A gentleman calling himself Professor Trott appeared in town and announced a spectacular production of *Ali Baba and the Forty Thieves.* A great crowd collected at Town Hall for the play, and thievery was duly performed: having lured residents away from their homes, the wily "professor" made off with an iron safe. A worthwhile slide presentation, "About St. George's," is shown in the theater on the second floor. ⊠ *King's Sq.,* ☏ *441/297–1425; 441/297–1532 for information on "About St. George's."* 🎫 *Free.* ☉ *Town Hall Mon.–Sat. 10–4; "About St. George's" Nov.–Mar., weekdays 10:05, 11:05, and 3:15 (call for hrs Dec.–Apr.).*

㉚ Tucker House. Antiques aficionados will find much of interest in this historic house, one of the showplaces of the Bermuda National Trust. Built of native limestone in 1711, the house sat close to the waterside (the area is now built up). Henry Tucker, president of the Governor's Council, lived here with his family from 1775 to 1807. His grandson donated most of the furnishings, which date from the mid-18th and early 19th centuries. Much of it is cedar, but there are some handsome mahogany pieces as well. The mahogany dining table was crafted in Bermuda from a tree grown in Cuba, and the English mahogany breakfront holds a collection of Tucker family silver.

A short flight of stairs leads down to the kitchen, originally a separate building, and a doorway leads to the enclosed kitchen garden. Through the small courtyard is an archaeological exhibit that uses artifacts recovered through excavations of the site to explore the connections between the St. George's and Williamsburg branches of this interesting family. A bookstore, appropriately called The Book Cellar, now occupies the cellar.

The Tucker name has been important in Bermuda since the birth of the colony, and a number of interesting family portraits hang in the house. Henry Tucker's father and brother were both involved in the famed "Gunpowder Plot" of 1775. The Continental Congress had imposed a ban on exports to all British colonies not taking part in the revolt against England, but Bermuda depended upon the American colonies for grain, so a delegation of Bermudians traveled to Philadelphia offering salt in exchange for the resumption of grain shipments.

Congress rejected the salt, but agreed to lift the ban if Bermuda sent gunpowder instead. A group of Bermudians, including the two Tuckers, then sneaked into the island's arsenal, stole the gunpowder, and shipped it to Boston. The ban was soon lifted.

The house sits at the corner of Barber's Alley, named for Joseph Hayne Rainey, a former slave from South Carolina whose father had bought him his freedom. Rainey and his French wife fled to Bermuda at the outbreak of the U.S. Civil War. Renting one of the outbuildings on the Tucker property, Rainey set up shop as a barber, while his wife developed a large clientele for her dressmaking business. After the U.S. Civil War the couple returned to South Carolina, where Rainey went into politics. His career advanced quickly, and in 1870 he became the first black man to be elected to the U.S. House of Representatives. ⊠ *Water St.,* ☎ *441/297–0545.* ▭ *$4; $5 combination ticket includes admission to Bermuda National Trust Museum and Verdmont Museum, in Smith's Parish.* ☉ *Mon.–Sat. 10–4.*

NEED A BREAK?

As midday approaches, you might want a latte or espresso and a snack or a pastry from **Caffe Latte** (8 York St., ☎ 441/297–8196). There's a second branch in Hamilton. Everything here is moderately priced, and they are open from 8 AM to between noon and 4 PM depending on the day of the week.

㉔ Unfinished Church. Considering how much attention and affection is lavished on St. Peter's these days, it's hard to believe that residents in the 19th century wanted to replace the old church with a new one. Work began on this church in 1874, but construction was halted when a schism developed within the church. Money for construction was later diverted to rebuild Hamilton's Trinity Church after it burned down. Work on the new church in St. George's was abandoned by the turn of the century. In 1992 the Bermuda National Trust obtained a 50-year lease on the church and is repairing and stabilizing the structure. Access is subject to completion of the work. ⊠ *Up Kent St. from King's Sq. (where Kent St. becomes Government Hill Rd. at intersection of Church Folly La.).*

⑰ White Horse Tavern. For much of the 19th century this popular waterside restaurant was the Davenport home. After his arrival in St. George's in about 1815, John Davenport opened a small dry-goods store on the square. He was able to wangle a profitable contract to supply beef to the garrison, and gold and silver began to pour in. There were no banks in Bermuda, but Davenport wasn't the trusting sort anyway. He stashed the money in a keg and kept it beneath his bed. When the keg was full, he took it down to the cellar and put another one under his bed. By the time he was an old man, Davenport was spending hours each day gloating over the kegs that filled his cellar. After his death, it was discovered that the old miser had amassed a £75,000 fortune in gold and silver. ⊠ *8 King's Sq.,* ☎ *441/297–1838.* ☉ *Mon.–Sat. 10 AM–1 AM, Sun. noon–1 AM.*

The West End

In contrast to Hamilton and St. George's, the West End is a rather bucolic part of Bermuda. With the notable exception of Dockyard, many of the attractions here are natural rather than man-made: nature reserves, wooded areas, and beautiful harbors and bays. In the waters off Daniel's Head, the Sea Gardens are regularly visited by glass-bottom boats from Hamilton. With its bow jutting out of the water, the coral-wrapped wreck of HMS *Vixen* is a major attraction. The ship was deliberately sunk by the British to block the channel and protect

THE BERMUDA TRIANGLE

"IF SATAN NEEDED PEOPLE to fight he wouldn't just kill people in the bermuda triangle he would kill them all over . . ."

"The ships and people were taken, they went to hell; had to fight the war in the holy land, war is still pending in the holy land!!! satan needed an army to fight against god, god uses unorthodox forces to fight back (hail, fire, etc.) . . ."

"I think the bermuda triangle is just a big hoax."

"Some people actually lost loved ones so watch the jokes . . ."

These are actual postings on some of the dozens of World Wide Web sites devoted to the infamous Bermuda Triangle. Nothing much has occurred in the triangle—also called Devil's Triangle, Limbo of the Lost, the Twilight Zone, and Hoodoo Sea—since the 1960s, but these comments are from the present day. Someone named Bubba, The Salty Dog, maintains a Web page largely devoted to debunking Triangle myths.

Strangely enough, "The U.S. Board of Geographic Names does not recognize the Bermuda Triangle as an official name and does not maintain an official file on the area." But the Naval Historical Center addresses the subject on its "Frequently Asked Questions" Web site, and the U.S. Navy and U.S. Coast Guard have a "Bermuda Triangle Fact Sheet" on their sites.

The area in question covers some 500,000 square mi of the Atlantic Ocean. Its apexes are most commonly defined as Bermuda; the southernmost tip of Florida; and San Juan, Puerto Rico. (Some place a boundary closer to Chesapeake Bay than to Miami.) It seems to have been christened in February 1964, when Vincent Gaddis wrote an article titled "The Deadly Bermuda Triangle" for *Argosy* magazine.

Weird incidents have been documented here ever since Columbus noted in his logbook a haywire compass, strange lights, and a burst of flame falling into the sea. In the past 500 years at least 50 ships and 20 aircraft have vanished in the Triangle, most without a trace—no wreckage, no bodies, no nothing. Many disappeared in reportedly calm waters, without having sent a distress signal. Among the legends is that of the *Mary Celeste*, a 103-ft brigantine found floating and abandoned in 1872—with warm food on the stove, according to some accounts. But the real mystery of the *Mary Celeste* is that she turns up in Triangle tales at all. The ship was actually found off the coast of Portugal.

One of the most famous Triangle cases is that of Flight 19. At 2:10 on the afternoon of December 5, 1945, five TBM Avenger Torpedo Bombers took off from Fort Lauderdale, Florida, on a routine two-hour training mission. Their last radio contact was at 4 PM. They were never seen or heard from again. The official Navy report said the planes disappeared "as if they had flown to Mars."

Perhaps not surprisingly, theories of alien abduction abound in Triangle lore. According to one beaut, famous persons wishing to evaporate (and thus foil the paparazzi) pay the president of the United States $100,000 in cash. This buys them a top-secret trip to the Bermuda Triangle, where they abandon a ship (which will conveniently be found empty), and eventually disappear into a witness-protection program. Needless to say, Elvis Presley signed up, and is, somewhere, alive and well—just a hundred grand poorer.

On a simpler note, one Web surfer posts, "Bermuda is such a beautiful island it's no wonder so many people disappear."

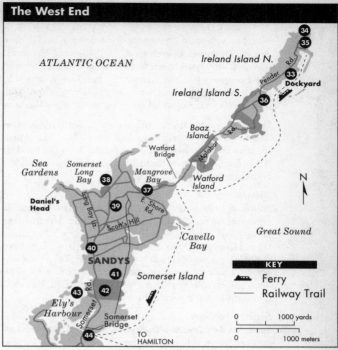

Dockyard from attack by torpedo boats. The West End is part of Sandys Parish, named after Sir Edwin Sandys, an investor in the Bermuda Company. Local lore contends that Sir George Somers took a keen interest in this region, and in the early days it was known as "Somers's seate"—hence the name of Somerset Village. Somerset is now a sleepy little hamlet with banks, several restaurants, a few shops, and not much else. The West End's big attraction is the Royal Naval Dockyard, a bastion of the British Royal Navy for nearly 150 years.

A Good Tour

The Somerset ferry from Hamilton stops at Somerset Bridge, Cavello Bay, Watford Bridge, and Dockyard. Disembark from the ferry at the Dockyard landing to begin your walk through the **Royal Naval Dockyard** ⑳ on Ireland Island, a sprawling complex with several notable attractions. Start at the former fortress that houses the **Maritime Museum** ㉞. The museum's collections are in several large stone buildings spread over 6 acres. Across the street from the museum is the Old Cooperage, a barrel-maker's shop dating from 1831. The reconstructed building houses the Neptune Cinema, which shows first-run films, as well as the Craft Market. To see some fine examples of Bermudian art, stop at the nearby **Bermuda Arts Centre at Dockyard** ㉟.

From here, you can travel by bicycle. Bike down the main road out of Dockyard along Ireland Island South. Turn left on Craddock Road and cycle down to see **Lagoon Park** ㊱ and the little inlet called the Crawl.

Cross over Boaz and Watford islands to Somerset Island. The largest of all these islets, Somerset Island is fringed on both sides with beautiful secluded coves, inlets, and bays. **Somerset Village** ㊲ nestles sleepily beside pretty Mangrove Bay. A short distance farther along Cambridge Road is pretty **Long Bay Park and Nature Reserve** ㊳. Continue along Cambridge Road (which becomes Somerset Road) until you see the arched gateway leading to **Springfield and the Gilbert Nature Reserve** ㊴.

Nearby, high atop a promontory against a backdrop of the sea, you can see **St. James Church** ㊵. A short distance beyond the church, opposite Willowbank guest house, is the entrance to the idyllic **Heydon Trust property** ㊶. Just around the bend on your left is **Fort Scaur** ㊷, which affords sweeping views of the Great Sound, and at the bottom of the hilly, twisting road lies spectacular **Ely's Harbour** ㊸.

Linking Somerset Island with the rest of Bermuda is **Somerset Bridge** ㊹, said to have the world's smallest draw. Near the bridge is the Somerset ferry landing, where you can catch a ferry back to Hamilton. Across the bridge, Somerset Road becomes Middle Road, which leads into Southampton Parish.

TIMING

Allow at least a day for exploring this area. If you take the ferry to Somerset, look closely at the ferry schedule. The trip can take anywhere from a half hour to more than an hour, depending on which ferry you take. However, there are worse ways to while away an hour than churning across Bermuda's Great Sound. Take your bicycle or moped aboard the ferry, too, because after you stroll around Dockyard you'll need wheels to see other parts of the West End. Bus service is available if you don't have your own transport.

Sights to See

㉟ **Bermuda Arts Centre at Dockyard.** Since it was opened by Princess Margaret in 1984, this spot has been a showcase for local artists and artisans and an excellent place to see Bermudians' work (☞ Specialty Stores *in* Chapter 8). Exhibits, which change often, include watercolors, oils, and photography. Beautifully crafted silver jewelry, hand-dyed scarves, and quilts are sold throughout the year. The selection of note cards and posters emphasizes Bermudian motifs. ✉ *Dockyard,* ☎ *441/234–2809.* ☞ *Free (donations accepted).* ☉ *Daily 10–5.*

㊸ **Ely's Harbour.** This small sheltered harbor (pronounced *ee*-lees), with pleasure boats dotting its brilliant turquoise waters, was once a hangout for smugglers. ✉ *Off Middle Rd. west of Somerset Bridge.*

㊷ **Fort Scaur.** Perched on the highest hill in Somerset, the fort was begun in 1868 and completed in the 1870s. British troops were garrisoned here until World War I, and during World War II, American forces from Battery D, 52nd Coast Artillery Battalion, were stationed here. Little remains to be seen of that now, although the 22 acres of gardens are quite pretty, and the view of the Great Sound is fantastic. Almost worth the long climb is the Early Bermuda Weather Stone, the "perfect weather indicator." The plaque reads: "A wet stone means . . . it is raining; a shadow under the stone . . . means the sun is shining; if the stone is swinging, it means there is a strong wind blowing; if the stone jumps up and down it means there is an earthquake; if ever it is white on top . . . believe it or not . . . it is snowing." ✉ *Somerset Rd., Ely's Harbour.* ☞ *Free.* ☉ *Apr.–Oct., daily 9–4:30; Nov.–Mar., daily 9–4.*

㊶ **Heydon Trust property.** A reminder of what the island was like in its early days, this quiet, peaceful property has been maintained as undeveloped open space. On its 43 acres are citrus orchards, banana groves, flower and vegetable gardens, and bird sanctuaries. Pathways dotted with park benches wend through the preserve, affording some wonderful views of the Great Sound. If you persevere along the main path, you'll reach the tiny, rustic **Heydon Chapel,** which dates from before 1620. A rugged cross is planted in the hillside, and a welcome mat lies at the door. Inside are a few wooden pews, cedar beams, and an ancient oven and hearth in a small room behind the altar. Services, which include Gregorian chant, are still held in the chapel at 3 PM Monday–Saturday. ⊠ *Somerset Rd.,* ☎ *441/234–1831.* ⌖ *Free.* ☉ *Daily dawn–dusk.*

36 **Lagoon Park.** Hidden in the mangroves are a lovely lagoon, footpaths, wild birds, and places to picnic. The Crawl, next to the park, is a picturesque inlet with fishing boats bobbing in the water and lobster pots on the dock. The park is always open, and there's no charge for entry. ⊠ *Lagoon Rd. off Malabar Rd.*

38 **Long Bay Park and Nature Reserve.** This park has a great beach, shallow water, and picnic areas. The Bermuda Audubon Society owns the adjacent nature reserve and its pond, which attracts migrating birds in the spring and fall. Peaceful as the area is now, it was the scene of one of Bermuda's most sensational murders. Skeeters' Corner, at the end of Daniel's Head Road, was the site of a cottage once owned by a couple of the same name. One night in 1878, Edward Skeeters strangled his wife and dumped her in the water. His long, rambling confession revealed that he was irked because she talked too much.

34 **Maritime Museum.** Opened by Queen Elizabeth II in 1975, the sprawling 6-acre Maritime Museum is housed in Bermuda's largest fort, which was built to defend the Royal Naval Dockyard. You enter the museum over a moat. The exhibits are in six old magazines and munitions warehouses arranged around the parade grounds and the Keep Pond area. Several of the rather tired displays pertain to the *Sea Venture* and the early history of the island. Artifacts and relics from some of the approximately 300 ships wrecked on the island's reefs are shown, and the Age of Discovery exhibit traces some of their voyages. Sailors will appreciate the Bermuda dinghies, 14-ft sailboats that can carry as much as 1,000 ft of canvas, on display in the Boat Loft. You can also explore the restored ramparts to take in commanding views of the Great Sound and North Shore. A renovation is expected to be completed at the end of 2000. The 19th-century Commissioner's House, set high on a bluff, is the world's oldest cast-iron–frame residence. Home to Dockyard commissioners from 1827 to 1837, and later a barracks, the house was formally commissioned as a ship—the HMS *Malabar*—in 1919.

Across the street, the **Neptune Cinema** shows first-run films and the **Craft Market** displays the works of local craftspeople and commercial artists. Jaded tourists who think of crafts as tacky souvenirs are in for a pleasant surprise. There are some delightful items on sale here, including wood carvings and miniature cedar furniture (☞ *Specialty Stores* in Chapter 8). ⊠ *Dockyard,* ☎ *441/234–1418 Maritime Museum; 441/234–1333 Craft Market.* ⌖ *Maritime museum $7.50, craft market free.* ☉ *Both daily 10–5.*

NEED A BREAK? While you stroll through the displays of handicrafts at the Dockyard, you might want to stop off at the **Frog & Onion Pub** (☎ 441/234–2900), which specializes in "creative pub fare" at moderate prices. This dark and expansive hideaway is ideally situated across from the Maritime Museum and right next to the craft market in the Cooperage Building, and dining is indoors or alfresco. Sweet lamb-and-curry pie, fish-and-chips, and bangers and mash, along with plenty of good ales, should fortify hearty explorers. It's open 11 AM to 10 PM for food, and the pub remains open until 1 AM.

33 **Royal Naval Dockyard.** After the American Revolution, Britain found itself with neither an anchorage nor a major ship-repair yard in the western Atlantic. Around 1809, when Napoléon started to make threatening noises in Europe and British ships became increasingly vulnerable to pirate attack, Britain began construction of a major stronghold in Bermuda. The work was done by slaves and English convicts toiling under appalling conditions. Thousands of workers died before the project was completed. The shipyard functioned as such for nearly 150 years. It was closed in 1951, and the Royal Navy left Bermuda in 1995 after a 200-year presence.

With the opening of the ☞ **Maritime Museum** in 1975, the decision was made to transform the entire naval port into a tourist site. Every year brings new Dockyard attractions, and Bermudians are justifiably proud of the project. The area includes a shopping arcade and a visitor center in the handsome, century-old Clocktower Building (now called the Clocktower Centre), a cruise-ship terminal, a snorkel park, restaurants, a marina with deepwater berths, and water-sports facilities. The former shipyard has literally blossomed, having undergone extensive landscaping to replace its vast stretches of concrete with shrubs, trees, and grassy lawns. Hold on to your hat when you're strolling in the area. It's often very windy, particularly along the water.

You can reach the Dockyard in 40 minutes from Hamilton on an express bus that leaves the capital every 15 minutes. Walking tours meet regularly from November through March (☞ Sightseeing *in* Smart Travel Tips A to Z), and from April through October you can make arrangements in advance through the Royal Naval Dockyard's public-relations department (☎ 441/234–1709, FAX 441/234–3411). There's also a Visitors Service Bureau (The Cooperage Bldg., ☎ 441/234–3824) here that's open year-round, Monday through Friday 9:30 to 4, Sunday 11 to 3.

NEED A
BREAK?

Amid the shops in the Clocktower Centre is **Nannini's Häagen-Dazs** (☎ 441/234–2474), that staple of the sweet-tooth trade. Choose one of the 16 flavors of ice cream or nonfat soft yogurt, or enjoy a cup of freshly brewed espresso, cappuccino, or hot chocolate at a table outside. Look also for Nannini cakes and Perugina chocolates from Italy, and have a chat with owner Fosco Nannini, who weaves his share of interesting yarns. The shop is open daily 9:30 to 5.

40 **St. James Church.** The entrance to this church is marked on the main road by handsome wooden gates, designed by a Royal Engineer in 1872. A long pathway curls past glistening white tombs in the churchyard. The first church on this site, made of wood, was destroyed by a hurricane in 1780. The present structure, one of the loveliest churches on the island, was consecrated in 1789. The tall, slender spire is a faithful replica of the 1880 spire that was hit by lightning in 1937 and sent crashing down into the church's center aisle. ⊠ *Main Rd., Somerset,* ☎ *441/234–2025.* ▧ *Free.* ☉ *Daily dawn–dusk.*

44 **Somerset Bridge.** Reputed to have the smallest draw in the world, this bridge on Somerset Road opens a mere 18 inches, just wide enough to accommodate a sailboat mast.

37 **Somerset Village.** A quiet retreat, this village is quite different from St. George's, Hamilton, and Dockyard. Only one road runs through it, and its few shops are mostly branches of Hamilton stores, along with two banks. In low season, tour guides concentrate on the area's history as well as its natural beauty and unusual medicinal plants. Somerset Island itself is heavily populated, laced with roads and pathways through quiet residential areas.

③⑨ **Springfield and the Gilbert Nature Reserve.** Set in five heavily wooded acres, Springfield—a branch of the Bermuda Library, and owned by the National Trust—is an old plantation home dating from around 1700. Restoration began in 1997 on the main house and outbuildings—the kitchen, slave quarters, and buttery—which are built around an open courtyard. Unfortunately, the house is closed to the public while under renovation.

The Gilbert Nature Reserve, named after the family that owned the property from 1700 to 1973, was acquired by the Bermuda National Trust in conjunction with the Bermuda Audubon Society. It has a number of walking trails. ⊠ *Main Rd., Somerset,* ☎ *441/236–6483.* ⊠ *Free.* ☉ *Daily.*

The Parishes

Bermuda's other points of interest—and there are many—are scattered throughout the island's parishes. This final section covers the length and breadth of the colony, commenting only on the major sights. Half the fun of exploring Bermuda, though, is wandering down forgotten lanes or discovering some little-known beach or cove. A moped or bicycle is ideal for this kind of travel, even though most of the island is served by buses and ferries. It would be foolish, if not impossible, to try to see all the sights here in one day. The tour below, which leaves from Hamilton, can easily be broken into two halves. The first, exploring parishes on the eastern part of the island; the second, traveling through the western ones. Keep in mind that you'll probably end up touring the parishes piecemeal—a couple of sights here, a church there, and plenty of time at the beach in between.

A Good Tour
EASTERN PARISHES

Follow Cedar Avenue north out of Hamilton to **St. John's Church** ㊺, the parish church of Pembroke. Marsh Folly Road, which runs between the church and Bernard Park, will take you to the limestone passageway called **Black Watch Pass** ㊻. The road got its name from Black Watch Well, at the intersection of Black Watch Pass and North Shore Road. The residence of Bermuda's governor, imposing **Government House** ㊼, sits atop Langton Hill, which overlooks North Shore Road, Black Watch Well, and the sea. North Shore Road merges with Spanish Point Road near **Spanish Point** ㊽, at the tip of the peninsula, where a park affords pleasant vistas. En route to Spanish Point you'll pass **Admiralty House Park** ㊾, a pretty spot with several caves and sheltered coves. Head back along North Shore Road to Devonshire Parish. Ideal for cycling and quiet picnics, Devonshire is a serene part of the island, with much to offer in the way of natural beauty. Locals come to **Devonshire Dock** ㊿ to buy fresh fish (something to bear in mind if you're staying in a housekeeping apartment). A short distance farther along North Shore Road is **Palmetto House** ⑤①, an 18th-century cruciform house.

If you continue along North Shore Road, you'll reach **Flatts Village** ⑤②, home of the estimable **Aquarium, Museum, and Zoo** ⑤③, and the small but interesting **Railway Museum and Curiosity Shop** ⑤④. Continuing east, North Shore Road climbs Crawl Hill, a high point offering spectacular views over the island and sea. "Crawl" derives from the Afrikaans word *kraal,* meaning animal enclosure. On Bermuda the word was applied to several ponds containing turtles and fish. This part of Hamilton Parish was also a shipbuilding site in the colony's early days.

Turn right on Trinity Church Road to see the early 17th-century **Holy Trinity Church** ⑤⑤. Just off Trinity Church Road is Mt. Wyndham, the

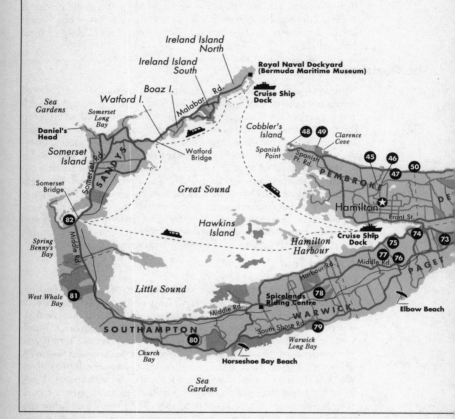

ATLANTIC OCEAN

Ireland Island North

Ireland Island South

Boaz I.

Watford I.

Malabar Rd.

Royal Naval Dockyard
(Bermuda Maritime Museum)

Cruise Ship Dock

Sea Gardens

Somerset Long Bay

Daniel's Head

Cobbler's Island

Spanish Point

48 49

Clarence Cove

Spanish Pt. Rd.

Somerset Island

SANDYS

Somerset Rd.

Watford Bridge

PEMBROKE

45 46

47 50

DE

Somerset Bridge

Great Sound

Hamilton

Front St.

82

Middle Rd.

Spring Benny's Bay

Hawkins Island

Hamilton Harbour

Cruise Ship Dock

75 74

73

PAGET

77 76

Middle Rd.

Harbour Rd.

West Whale Bay

81

Little Sound

Elbow Beach

Spicelands Riding Centre

78

WARWICK

SOUTHAMPTON

Middle Rd.

South Shore Rd.

79

Warwick Long Bay

80

Church Bay

Horseshoe Bay Beach

Sea Gardens

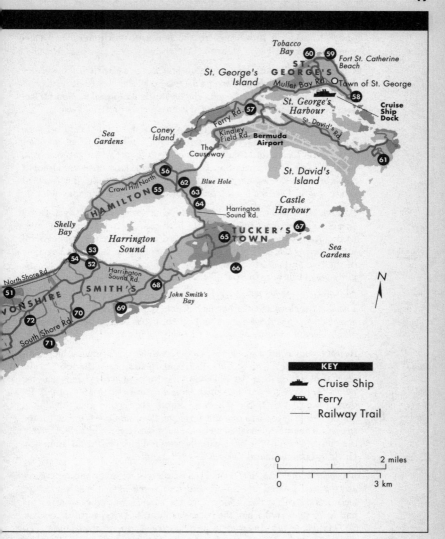

KEY

Cruise Ship

Ferry

Railway Trail

peak from which Admiral Sir Alexander Cochrane surveyed the British fleet prior to its attack on Washington, D.C., in 1814. Follow North Shore Road as it dips south to the **Bermuda Perfumery and Gardens** (56). Blue Hole Hill leads to the causeway over Castle Harbour.

Once across the causeway you're in St. George's Parish. Take Kindley Field Road around the airport, turn left onto Mullet Bay Road, and cross Swing Bridge over Ferry Reach. The **Bermuda Biological Station for Research** (57) will interest you if you're keen on environmental issues.

There is magnificent scenery along the stretch of road that runs between Mullet Bay and the sea. A little farther east, Mullet Bay Road becomes Wellington Road, and finally Duke of York Street when you reach St. George's (☞ The Town of St. George, *above*). East of town, Duke of York Street becomes Barrack Hill Road. From the road, the views of the town, St. David's Island, and Castle Harbour are spectacular.

Barrack Hill Road turns into Cut Road, which leads all the way to **Gates Fort** (58), a reconstruction of an early 17th-century fort. The main camp of the *Sea Venture* survivors is believed to have been in this general area. Leaving Gates Fort via Barry Road, you'll pass Buildings Bay. One of the two ships that carried Sir George Somers and his crew to Virginia was built here in 1610, hence the bay's name.

Continue up Barry Road to the very impressive **Fort St. Catherine** (59). The fort overlooks St. Catherine's Beach, where the survivors from the *Sea Venture* scrambled ashore on July 28, 1609. Nearby **Tobacco Bay** (60) also played a prominent role in the island's history.

Retrace your route through St. George's to Swing Bridge, which connects St. George's with St. David's Island. In addition to Bermuda's airport, about 2 square mi of St. David's has for many years been occupied by a U.S. naval air station, which closed operations in 1995. In 1940, during World War II, Sir Winston Churchill agreed to give the United States a 99-year lease to operate a base on Bermuda in exchange for destroyers. The entire area taken up by the air station is now called St. David's, but construction of the base actually required linking three islands—St. David's, Longbird, and Cooper's—with landfills.

Apart from the base, St. David's is a rustic spot whose inhabitants have always led isolated lives. It is said that some have never visited St. George's, let alone the other end of the island. A number of residents had to be relocated when the base was built, but they refused to leave St. David's, so the government purchased a section of the island called "Texas" and built cottages there for the displaced islanders. The area is just off the naval base. You can see Texas Road at the tip of the island near the lighthouse. When **St. David's Lighthouse** (61) is open, you can take in fantastic views from inside.

Head back across the causeway and turn left on Wilkinson Avenue. A network of caves, caverns, and subterranean lakes runs beneath the hills on this part of the island. Two of them are on the property of the nearby Grotto Bay Beach Hotel & Tennis Club (☞Resort Hotels *in* Chapter 5). South of the hotel are the **Crystal Caves** (62), the most impressive of the caves that are open to the public.

Harrington Sound Road runs along the strip of land between the Sound and Castle Harbour. At Walsingham Lane, you'll see a white sign for the restaurant called **Tom Moore's Tavern** (63). Harrington Sound Road leads southward to the amber-color **Leamington Caves** (64) (the caves were closed at press time but may reopen in 2001).

Farther south on Harrington Sound Road is **Tucker's Town** ⑥⑤, where you'll find the exclusive Mid Ocean Club and a community of well-heeled Bermudians. Below the clubhouse on the south shore are the **Natural Arches** ⑥⑥, one of the island's oldest and most photographed attractions. A chain of islands dots the channel into the harbor between St. David's and Tucker's Town Bay. In the colony's early days these islands were fortified to protect Castle Harbour from possible enemy attack. Soon after his arrival in 1612, Governor Moore built his first and best fort on **Castle Island** ⑥⑦.

Back on Harrington Sound Road, the **Devil's Hole Aquarium** ⑥⑧ is touted as Bermuda's first tourist attraction, dating from the mid-19th century. Take steep Knapton Hill Road, which leads westward to South Shore Road and **Spittal Pond** ⑥⑨, a lovely nature park. West of Spittal Pond on South Shore Road is the turnoff to Collector's Hill, which is a very steep climb indeed. The hill is named for Gilbert Salton, a 19th-century customs collector who lived in a house near the top. The house has long since disappeared. At the very top of Collector's Hill is **Verdmont** ⑦⓪, Bermuda's finest historic house. Return to South Shore Road and follow it west to the 18-acre **Palm Grove** ⑦①, whose gardens are a singular delight of Devonshire Parish.

WESTERN PARISHES

The western group of parishes begins with Paget, south of Hamilton town. Brighton Hill Road, just west of Palm Grove, runs north to Middle Road and the **Old Devonshire Church** ⑦②, the parish's biggest attraction. Turn left off Middle Road onto Tee Street, and then right onto Berry Hill Road. One mile farther on the left is the turnoff to Point Finger Road and the **Botanical Gardens** ⑦③, a landscaped park laced with roads and paths. A few minutes away by moped are the offices of the **Bermuda National Trust** ⑦④, a prestigious preservation organization. From the Trust offices, go west on Harbour Road, and near the Lower Ferry Landing is **Clermont** ⑦⑤, a historic house (not open to the public).

If you're on foot, turn left on Valley Road to reach the late–18th-century **St. Paul's Church** ⑦⑥. If you're riding a moped, take Chapel Road and turn east on Middle Road to Valley Road, or walk the bike up the narrow one-way stretch of hill past the SPCA headquarters on the left. St. Paul's sits on the edge of **Paget Marsh** ⑦⑦, notable for its natural splendors. From St. Paul's, head west into Warwick Parish along Middle Road. Just after the intersection with Ord Road (opposite the now-closed Belmont Hotel, Golf & Country Club), look to your left to see **Christ Church** ⑦⑧. Turn left off Middle Road onto Camp Hill Road, which winds down to the south-shore beaches. Along the way is Warwick Camp, built in the 1870s to guard against any enemy landing on the beaches. The camp was used as a training ground and rifle range during World War I. Pearl White, of *The Perils of Pauline* fame, came to Bermuda to shoot a movie in 1920, bringing an entourage that included lions, monkeys, and a host of other exotic fauna. Scenes for the film were shot on Warwick Bay, below the rifle range. Most Bermudians had never seen either a lion or a movie star, and great crowds gathered to watch the filming.

Some of the island's prettiest beaches are off South Shore Road. Two of them are at Warwick, as is peaceful, green **Astwood Park** ⑦⑨. Two miles west along South Shore Road is the turnoff for Lighthouse Road, which takes you to **Gibbs Hill Lighthouse** ⑧⓪ and unsurpassed views of the island.

If you're still feeling adventurous, head west, turn left off Middle Road onto Whale Bay Road (just before the Port Royal Golf & Country Club), and go down the hill to **Whale Bay Fort** ⑧. Continuing west, a small road near Somerset Bridge has the odd name of **Overplus Lane** ㉒, which harks back to the 17th century. Across Somerset Bridge is the West End (☞ The West End, *above*). If you're traveling by bike or by moped, you can catch a ferry from Somerset Bridge back to Hamilton. Otherwise, take your pick of Middle, Harbour, or South Shore Road to find your way back to the capital.

TIMING

The parishes, outside of Hamilton and St. George's (Somerset is a rural community), are considered by Bermudians to be "out in the country." These parts of the island *are* less congested than the towns, but the area to the east of the capital—especially the traffic circle where Crow Lane intersects with the Lane and Trimingham Road—is very busy during morning and afternoon rush hours. Those unaccustomed to riding on mopeds and driving on the left should take particular care at the traffic circles, especially during rush hours.

Sights to See

㊾ **Admiralty House Park.** This pretty spot was the estate of John Dunscombe in the early 19th century. Dunscombe, who later became lieutenant governor of Newfoundland, sold the property in 1816 to the British military, which decided to build a house for the commanding British admiral of the naval base at Dockyard. The house was reconstructed several times through the years, notably in the 1850s by an eccentric admiral with a weakness for subterranean tunnels. He had several caves and galleries cut into the cliffs above the sea. The house was closed when the Royal Navy withdrew in 1951 and was later demolished. All that remains of the complex is the ballroom. Within the park, Clarence Cove offers a sheltered beach and pleasant swimming. ⊠ *Off North Shore Rd. at intersection with Spanish Point Rd., Pembroke Parish.*

㊼ ㊾ **Aquarium, Museum, and Zoo.** The aquarium has always been a pleasant diversion, but thanks to an ambitious expansion project it has become awesome indeed. The state-of-the-art North Rock Exhibit, in the main gallery, is a 145,000-gallon tank that displays Bermuda's famed living coral reefs. A crystal-clear acrylic wall that curves overhead gives you the impression of actually being underwater with all manner of sea creatures.

In addition to colorful marine life, among the zoo's displays are a beehive, octopuses, and a touch pool in the Local Tails Exhibit, and a reptile walkway that gives you a close-up look at alligators and Galápagos tortoises. For children, there is a Discovery Room, with activities pertaining to Bermuda. And the natural history museum has a geology display with explanations of Bermuda's volcanic origins, information on the humpback whales that migrate past the island, and a deep-sea exhibit that documents the half-mile dive of marine biologist Dr. William Beebe in the early 1930s. A walk-through Australasian Exhibit contains wildlife indigenous to Australia, New Guinea, Borneo, and Malaysia. ⊠ *Flatts Village, Smith's Parish,* ☎ *441/293–2727.* ☜ *$10.* ☉ *Daily 9–5 (last admission at 4:30), guided tours 1:10.* ☜

㊲ **Astwood Park.** A 3-mi chain of sandy beaches, coves, and inlets begins at Warwick Long Bay and extends to Horseshoe Bay in the east (☞ Beaches *in* Chapter 7). East of Warwick Bay, Astwood Park is a lovely public park with picnic tables and two beaches. The larger of the two beaches—the one to the left as you face the park—is ideal for snorkeling. ⊠ *Off South Shore Rd., Warwick and Southampton Parishes.*

NEED A
BREAK? **Bailey's Ice Cream Parlour & Food D'Lites** (✉ Blue Hole Hill, ☎ 441/
293–8605) has 40 varieties of freshly made natural ice cream, as well
as shakes, sodas, yogurts, and sorbets. For something a bit stronger,
cross the road for a rum swizzle and a "swizzleburger" at the **Swizzle
Inn** (✉ Blue Hole Hill, Hamilton Parish, ☎ 441/293–1845).

🖐 ➎ **Bermuda Biological Station for Research.** In 1903—long before environmental issues were in fashion—scientists began researching marine
life here. Facilities include ships for ocean research, 13 laboratories, a
250-seat lecture hall, and a 20,000-volume library. Research programs
at the station focus on such issues as global change and the health of
Bermuda's reefs, and have focused extensively on acid rain. Guided tours
of the grounds and laboratory are conducted Wednesday at 10 AM only,
beginning in the main building. ✉ *17 Biological La., Ferry Reach, St.
George's Parish,* ☎ *441/297–1880.* 🎟 *Free (donations accepted).*

OFF THE
BEATEN PATH **BERMUDA GOLF ACADEMY –** As you're tooling west along Middle Road
about 1 mi past the South Road intersection, watch for Granaway
Heights Road on the left across from a pond. Slow down and prepare
for a left turn onto Industrial Park Road for the Academy. You'll want to
come here for the 320-yard driving range, practice greens, 40 practice
bays, and, of course, lessons, videotaping, and club repair and rental.
But there is also a small restaurant that serves light meals and shows the
Golf Channel continuously, and a playground for kids. ✉ *Industrial Park
Rd., Southampton Parish,* ☎ *441/238–8800.* ☉ *Daily 9 AM–10 PM.*

➐ **Bermuda National Trust.** The nonprofit organization that oversees the
restoration and preservation of many of the island's gardens, open spaces,
and historic buildings has its offices in Waterville, a rambling 18th-
century house built by the Trimingham family. The drawing and dining rooms are open to the public during business hours. Waterville also
houses the Trustworthy gift shop, which sells handmade crafts, nov-
elties, and Trust logo items. The Trust is a solid source of information
about the island. ✉ *29 The Lane, Paget Parish,* ☎ *441/236–6483.* 🎟
Free (donations accepted). ☉ *Bermuda National Trust weekdays 9–5,
gift shop Mon.–Sat. 10–4.*

➎ **Bermuda Perfumery and Gardens.** In 1929 the Lili Perfume Factory
began extracting natural fragrances from the island's flowers, and the
enterprise eventually blossomed into the present perfumery and tourist
attraction. You can take a guided tour of the factory, which is in a 200-
year-old cottage with cedar beams, but the biggest draw is the aromatic
nature trail that you can walk on your own. A complimentary map
helps you sniff your way around the oleanders, frangipani, jasmine,
orchids, and passionflowers that are the raw material for the factory.
The adjoining Calabash Gift Shop carries a large selection of soaps and
toiletries. ✉ *212 North Shore Rd., Hamilton Parish,* ☎ *441/293–0627
or 800/527–8213.* 🎟 *Free.* ☉ *Apr.–Oct., Mon.–Sat. 9:15–5, Sun. 10–
4; Nov.–Mar., Mon.–Sat. 9:15–4:30.*

NEED A
BREAK? **Shelly Bay Pizza** (✉ Shelly Bay Plaza, St. George's Parish, ☎ 441/
293–8465) is a wonderful little pizzeria that has been serving great
slices for the past 15 years. They also have submarine sandwiches,
chicken, fish dinners, and home-baked pies. It's a five-minute walk to the
beach, where you can sit on the seawall and watch the windsurfers skim
by as you eat lunch. They're open Monday to Saturday 7 AM–10 PM,
Sunday 1 PM to 10 PM.

46 **Black Watch Pass.** The Public Works Department excavated about 2.5 million cubic ft of solid limestone during construction of the awesome passageway that leads from Hamilton to North Shore Road. This pass took its name from the **Black Watch Well.** During a severe drought in 1849 the governor ordered a well dug on government ground to alleviate the suffering of the local poor. Excavated by a detachment of the famed Black Watch regiment, the well is marked by a commemorative plaque and shaded by a tiered concrete slab. The site is not particularly inspiring, however, and only the most dedicated well-wishers will want to make the pilgrimage. ⊠ *Black Watch Pass and North Shore Rd., Pembroke Parish.*

73 **Botanical Gardens.** A fragrant haven for the island's exotic subtropical plants, flowers, and trees—and for whoever enjoys them—the park has within its 36 acres a miniature forest, aviary, a hibiscus garden with more than 150 species, and a Garden for the Blind filled with the scents of sweet geranium, lemon, lavender, and spices. Seventy-five-minute walking tours of the gardens leave the visitor center at 10:30 on Tuesday, Wednesday, and Friday (Tuesday and Friday only from November through March). To arrange tours at other times, talk to the curator of the gardens or make a donation to the Botanical Society. The center has information and gift and tea shops. Bermuda's Agriculture Department also has offices on the grounds.

The pretty white house within the Gardens is **Camden** (☎ 441/236–5732, ☾ Tues. and Fri. noon–2), the official residence of Bermuda's premier. The large, two-story house is more typical of West Indian estate architecture than traditional Bermudian building. The house is open for tours except when official functions are scheduled. ⊠ *Point Finger Rd., Paget Parish,* ☎ *441/236–4201.* ☞ *Free.* ☾ *Botanic garden daily dawn–dusk.*

67 **Castle Island.** According to an oft-told tale, two Spanish ships appeared outside the channel in 1613 and attempted to attack the colony. Two shots were fired from the fort: one fell into the water, and the other hit one of the ship's hulls. The Spaniards fled, unaware that the fortress had expended two-thirds of its stock of ammunition. The colonists had less than a barrel of gunpowder and only one cannonball left. ⊠ *Smith's Parish.*

78 **Christ Church.** This one-story, gray stone church with four soaring towers was built in 1719. It is reputedly the oldest Presbyterian house of worship in any British colony or dominion. It's open for Sunday services only. ⊠ *Middle Rd., Warwick Parish.*

75 **Clermont.** Bermuda's first tennis court was on the grounds of this imposing house, once the residence of Sir Brownlow Gray, chief justice of Bermuda (and also noted for its fine woodwork). Miss Mary Outerbridge learned to play here during a visit from New York in 1874. Upon her return to the United States, she asked the Staten Island Cricket Club to build a court, and armed with her racket and a book of rules, she introduced tennis to America. The house is not open to the public. ⊠ *On Harbour Rd. (to left as you head west) between Lovers and Highwood Las., Paget Parish.*

62 **Crystal Caves.** In 1907 while playing ball, two boys made a startling discovery. When the ball disappeared down a hole, the boys burrowed after it and found themselves in a vast cavern 120 ft underground, surrounded by fantastic stalagmite and stalactite formations. You approach along a wet, sloping walkway and a wooden pontoon bridge across the underground lake. After explaining the formation of stalactites and stalagmites, a tour guide uses a lighting system to make silhou-

THE BERMUDA RAILWAY

THE HISTORY OF THE Bermuda Railway is as fascinating as it is brief. Along with horse-drawn carriages, boats, and bicycles, Old Rattle and Shake was the primary means of transportation on the island from 1931 to 1948. The Bermuda Public Works Department bandied about proposals for a railroad as early as 1899. Over the objections of livery stable owners, the Bermuda Parliament finally granted permission in 1922 for a narrow-gauge line to run from Somerset to St. George's.

The laying of the tracks was a formidable undertaking, requiring the construction of long tunnels and swing bridges. By the time it was finished the railway had cost investors $1 million. Mile for mile, it was the most expensive railroad ever built, and the construction, which proceeded at a somnolent 2½ mi per year, was the slowest ever recorded. Finally, on October 31, 1931, the little train got its roaring start with festive opening ceremonies at Somerset Bridge.

First-class passengers sat in wicker chairs; second-class cars were outfitted with benches. One American visitor spoke in glowing terms of her first train ride in Bermuda, waxing lyrical about rolling cedar-covered hills, green velvet lawns, and banks of pink oleanders. Certainly, it was a vast improvement over the 19th-century horse buses that lumbered from Somerset to St. George's, carrying freight as well as passengers. Not everyone was happy, though. One writer groused that

the train was "an iron serpent in the Garden of Eden."

Old Rattle and Shake began going downhill during World War II. Military personnel put the train to hard use, and it proved impossible to obtain the necessary maintenance equipment. At the end of the war the government acquired the distressed railway for $115,000. Automobiles came to Bermuda in 1946, and train service ended in 1948, when the government sold the railway in its entirety to British Guiana (now Guyana).

Today's secluded, 18-mi Bermuda Railway Trail runs the length of the island along the route of the old Bermuda Railway. Restricted to pedestrians, horseback riders, and cyclists, the trail is a delightful way to see the island, away from the traffic and noise of main roads. The Bermuda Department of Tourism's "The Bermuda Railway Trail Guide," available at all Visitors Service Bureaus, includes seven walking tours, ranging from about two to four hours, and an outline of what you can expect to see along the way. (For more information about sights along the way, see "Off Bermuda's Beaten Track" in Chapter 9.) Note that many of the trails are isolated, and none is heavily trafficked. Although Bermuda has no major crime problem, unpleasant incidents can occur. Women travelers especially should avoid setting out on remote trails alone. Apart from reasons of safety, the Railway Trail is more enjoyable shared with a companion.

ettes. People who suffer from claustrophobia will probably want to skip the caves, as space can be quite tight. And the caves are not open to children under 11 years of age. ✉ *8 Crystal Caves Rd., off Wilkinson Ave., Hamilton Parish,* ☎ *441/293–0640,* ℻ *441/293–1656.* ☎ *$7.50.* ◷ *Apr.–Oct., daily 9:30–4:30; Nov.–Mar., call for hrs.*

🖐 ⑱ **Devil's Hole Aquarium.** In 1830 a Mr. Trott built a wall around his fish pond—evidently to prevent people from fishing in it—and was besieged with questions about what he was hiding. In 1843, yielding to the curiosity of the Bermudians, Mr. Trott permitted people to view his fish pond—for a fee. The deep pool contains about 400 sea creatures, including giant grouper, sharks, and huge turtles. You can play at fishing, using baited—but hookless—lines. ✉ *92 Harrington Sound Rd., Smith's Parish,* ☎ *441/293–2072,* ℻ *441/292–6707.* ☎ *$5.* ◷ *Daily 10–4:30.*

NEED A
BREAK?

For a relaxing, inexpensive lunch of Bermuda fish, or homemade codfish cakes, visit **The Village Cafe** (✉ 29 Mangrove Bay Rd., Sandys Parish, ☎ 441/234–3167), a little place with charm and friendly service. You can order takeout or eat on one of the outdoor patios. Full lunch costs $7 to $12. The café is open daily until 5 PM.

⑩ **Devonshire Dock.** Local fishermen return here each afternoon to unload their catch. It's a great place to buy fresh fish for dinner, something to keep in mind if your accommodations have cooking facilities. ✉ *North Shore Rd., Devonshire, near the border with Pembroke.*

⑫ **Flatts Village.** One of the earliest settlements on the island, Flatts occasionally hosted the House of Assembly, although much of the village's activity involved flouting the law rather than making it. Hoping to avoid customs officers, Bermudians returning from the West Indies would sometimes sail into the village in the dead of night to unload their contraband cargoes. ✉ *Smith's Parish.*

★ ⑲ **Fort St. Catherine.** Apart from Dockyard, this restored fortress is the most impressive on the island. It has enough cannons, tunnels, and ramparts to satisfy the most avid military historian. One of a host of fortifications constructed in St. George's, the original fort was begun around 1613. It was remodeled and enlarged at least five times, and work continued on it until late in the 19th century. As you travel through the tunnels, you'll come across some startlingly lifelike figures tucked into niches. Several dioramas depict the island's development, and an audiovisual presentation describes the building and significance of the fort. There is also a small but elaborate display of replicas of the Crown Jewels of England. ✉ *15 Coot Pond Rd., St. George's Parish,* ☎ *441/297–1920.* ☎ *$5.* ◷ *Daily 10–4:30.*

⑱ **Gates Fort.** St. George's has always had the greatest concentration of fortifications on Bermuda. Gates Fort is a reconstruction of a small militia fort dating from the 1620s. Don't expect turrets, towers, and tunnels, however. There is little to see here apart from the sea. The fort and Gates Bay, which it overlooks, were named for Sir Thomas Gates, the first of the survivors of the *Sea Venture* to reach dry land. Upon doing so, he is said to have shouted, "This is Gates, his bay!" Public speaking was obviously not Gates's forte, even though he was by profession a politician—he later became governor of Virginia. ✉ *Cut Rd., St. George's Parish,* ☎ *no phone.* ☎ *Free.* ◷ *Daily 10–4.*

★ ⑳ **Gibbs Hill Lighthouse.** The second cast-iron lighthouse ever built soars above Southampton Parish. Designed in London and opened in 1846, the tower stands 117 ft high and 362 ft above the sea. The light was originally produced by a concentrated burner of four large, circular wicks. Today the beam from the 1,000-watt bulb can be seen by ships 40 mi out to sea and by planes 120 mi away at 10,000 ft. You can climb to the top, although it's not a trip for anyone who suffers from vertigo. The haul up the 185 spiral stairs is a long one, but you can stop to catch your breath at platforms along the way, where photographs and drawings of the lighthouse divert your attention. At the top you can stroll the balcony for a spectacular view of Bermuda, but the wind may snatch your hat, and the tower is known to sway in high winds. ✉ *Lighthouse Rd., Southampton Parish*, ☎ *441/238–0524.* 🎫 *$2.50.* ☉ *Daily 9–4:30.*

NEED A BREAK?   A charming place to relax over breakfast, lunch, or tea and take in the island vistas is the **Lighthouse Tea Room** (☞The Parishes *in* Chapter 4) located in the lighthouse keeper's cottage.

47 **Government House.** Bermuda's governor's residence, which overlooks North Shore Road, Black Watch Well, and the sea, is not open to the public. The 45 acres of land were purchased when the capital was transferred from St. George's to Hamilton in 1815. A simple two-story house served as the governor's home until the present, rather austere mansion was completed in 1892. Various royals and other distinguished visitors planted the trees and shrubs on the pretty, landscaped lawns. Among the guests who have been entertained here are Sir Winston Churchill, President Kennedy, and, more recently, Queen Elizabeth II and Prince Philip, Prince Charles, Margaret Thatcher, and President George Bush. The mansion was also the scene of the 1973 assassination of Governor Richard Sharples and his aide, Captain Hugh Sayers. ✉ *Pembroke Parish.*

55 **Holy Trinity Church.** Built in 1623 as one long room with a thatched roof, Holy Trinity is said to be the oldest Anglican church on Bermuda. The church has been much embellished during the past 370-some years, but the original building remains at its core. The small graveyard is encircled by palms, royal poinciana, and cherry trees. ✉ *Church Bay, Harrington Sound, Hamilton Parish*, ☎ *441/293–1710.* ☉ *Open for services only.*

64 **Leamington Caves.** Although closed at press time, Leamington Caves may open under new management in 2001. An amber-tint Statue of Liberty is among the fanciful formations of stalagmites and stalactites here, though by and large these caves are smaller and less impressive than Crystal Caves. Aboveground, a restaurant, formerly the Plantation, had served some of the island's best food and may also reopen in 2001. ✉ *Harrington Sound Rd., Hamilton Parish*, ☎ *441/293–1188 for information.*

66 **Natural Arches.** Carved over the centuries by the wind and ocean, these two limestone arches rise 35 ft above the beach. Look for the signs pointing to Castle Harbour Beach and the Natural Arches near the end of South Shore Road. ✉ *Smith's Parish.*

72 **Old Devonshire Church.** A church has stood on this site since 1612, although the original was replaced in 1716. That replacement church was almost wholly destroyed in an explosion on Easter Sunday in 1970, and the present church is a faithful reconstruction. A small, simple building of limestone and cedar, it looks much like an early Bermuda cottage. The three-tier pulpit, the pews, and the communion table are believed to be from the original church. Some pieces of church silver date back to 1590 and are said to be the oldest on the island. ✉ *Middle Rd., Devonshire Parish*, ☎ *441/236–3671.* 🎫 *Free.* ☉ *Daily 9–5:30.*

⑧ Overplus Lane. The name of this lane harks back to the 17th century, when Richard Norwood divided the island into shares and tribes. He allotted 25 acres to each share, and 50 shares to each tribe. When the survey was completed, 200 acres (too small to form a tribe) remained unallotted and were listed as "overplus." Governor Tucker directed the surveyor to keep an eye peeled for an attractive chunk of territory that could be designated as the surplus land. Norwood recommended a piece of real estate in the western part of the island, whereupon the governor claimed it and built a fine house on it. Upon hearing of the governor's action, the Bermuda Company lodged a complaint, forcing Tucker to return to London to sort everything out. The surplus land was eventually divided into seven parts, with Tucker retaining the section on which his house sat. The remainder was given to the Church. ✉ *Sandys Parish.*

⑦ Paget Marsh. Protected by the Bermuda National Trust, this lovely marsh contains cedars and palmettos, endangered plants, and a mangrove swamp. ✉ *Middle Rd., Paget Parish,* ☎ *441/236–6483.*

★ ⑦ Palm Grove. On the grounds of this private estate, there is a pond within which is a relief map of Bermuda. Each parish is divided by carefully manicured grass sections. Desmond Fountain statues stand around the edge, peering into the pond's depths. ✉ *South Shore Rd. across from Brighton Hill, Smith's Parish,* ☎ *no phone.* 🎟 *Free.* ☉ *Mon.–Thurs. 9–5.*

㉛ Palmetto House. In the 18th century, when this cruciform house was built, cross-shape houses were thought to ward off evil spirits. Three rooms, furnished in period antiques, can be seen on a house tour. The house is now owned by the Bermuda National Trust and is open to the public on a limited basis. In **Palmetto Park** you can pick up one of the North Shore stretches of the Railway Trail. ✉ *North Shore Rd., Devonshire Parish,* ☎ *441/236–6483.* 🎟 *Free.* ☉ *Thurs. only 10–5.*

㊽ Railway Museum and Curiosity Shop. The old Aquarium Station of the island's erstwhile narrow-gauge railroad houses a tiny museum cluttered with photos, signs, wicker chairs from the first-class compartment, and other memorabilia. "Old Rattle and Shake," as the railway was known, is so fondly remembered by Bermudians that you'll wonder why the line was shut down. The museum recently installed rarely seen footage of the railway in operation. ✉ *37 North Shore Rd., Hamilton Parish,* ☎ *441/293–1774.* 🎟 *Free (donations accepted).* ☉ *Weekdays 10–4 and some Sats.; ring bell and curator will let you in if she's home.*

㉛ St. David's Lighthouse. Built in 1879 of Bermuda stone, and occupying the highest point on Bermuda's eastern end, the lighthouse rises 208 ft above the sea. Although only about half the height of Gibbs Hill Lighthouse in Southampton Parish, it nevertheless has spectacular views. From the balcony you can see St. David's and St. George's, Castle Harbour, and the reef-fringed south shore. The lighthouse is not always open. Check with the Park Rangers Office (☎ 441/236–5902) for hours. ✉ *St. George's Parish.*

NEED A BREAK? | Right on the water near St. David's Lighthouse, the **Black Horse Tavern** (✉ Clarkes Hill, ☎ 441/297–1991) is a casual spot that's popular with locals. Seafood is the specialty. The fish sandwiches are delicious, and shark hash and curried conch stew are also offered. There are outdoor picnic tables as well as indoor seating. It's closed Monday. (*See* Chapter 4 for more details.)

㊺ St. John's Church. The first church on this site was built in 1621. The present church was consecrated in 1826 as the parish church of Pembroke. During a funeral in 1875, the churchyard was the scene of a verbal duel between the Anglican rector and a Wesleyan minister. The Anglican church insisted that all burial services in parish churchyards be conducted by the rector, but the Wesleyans challenged the church in the case of a deceased woman named Esther Levy. Claiming he'd been asked by her friends to perform the funeral service, a Wesleyan minister appeared in the churchyard despite the efforts of the Anglican rector to stop him. Simultaneous services were held over poor Mrs. Levy's body, with the minister and the adamant Anglican trying to outshout each other. The rector subsequently filed charges of trespassing against the Wesleyan, and the celebrated case went before the Supreme Court. The jury found for the rector, and fined the minister one shilling. ⊠ *St. John's Rd., Pembroke Parish,* ☎ *441/292–0299.* ⊡ *Free.* ⊙ *Daily 8–5:30.*

76 **St. Paul's Church.** Around the turn of the century, the "Paget Ghost" began to be heard in and around St. Paul's. Nothing could be seen, but the mysterious sound of tinkling bells was plainly audible, coming from several directions. The ghost became quite famous, and a veritable posse—armed with firearms and clubs—gathered to find it. Vendors even set up refreshment stands. Finally, a visiting American scientist proclaimed that the tinkling sound came from a rare bird, the fililo. According to the scientist, the fililo was a natural ventriloquist, which explained why the sound jumped around. No one ever saw the bird, however, and no one saw the ghost either. It disappeared as mysteriously as it had come. The present church was built in 1796 to replace an earlier church on this site. ⊠ *Middle Rd., Paget Parish,* ☎ *441/236–5880.* ⊡ *Free.* ⊙ *Weekdays 8–4:30, Sat. by appointment, Sun. 7:30–1.*

48 **Spanish Point.** Survivors of the wrecked *Sea Venture* thought they found evidence here of an earlier visit by the Spanish, and historians now believe that Captain Diego Ramirez landed here in 1603. There is a small park for picnicking, a sheltered bay for swimming, public facilities, and a lovely view of Somerset across the sound. Here you can also see the remains of a 19th-century floating dock from Dockyard, which looks a bit like a dinosaur's skeleton. Unfortunately, some rather seedy characters hang out here, so don't come alone. In summer lots of people camp here, and the noise level can be far from peaceful. Cobbler's Island, across Cobbler's Cut from Spanish Point, has a grisly history. Executed slaves were put on display here as a warning to others of the consequences of disobedience. ⊠ *Pembroke Parish.*

★ **69** **Spittal Pond.** A showcase of the Bermuda National Trust, this nature park has 60 acres for carefree roaming, although you're requested to keep to the walkways. More than 25 species of waterfowl winter here between November and May. On a high bluff overlooking the ocean, Spanish Rock stands out as an oddity. Early settlers found a rock crudely carved with the date 1543 and other markings that were unclear. It is now believed that a Portuguese ship was wrecked on the island in 1543, and that her sailors built a new ship on which they departed. The carvings are thought to be the initials RP (for *Rex Portugaline,* King of Portugal), and the cross to be a badge of the Portuguese Order of Christ. The rock was removed to prevent further damage by erosion, and the site is marked by a bronze casting of the original carving. A plaster-of-paris cast of the Spanish Rock is also on display at the Bermuda Historical Society Museum, in Hamilton. ⊠ *South Shore Rd., Smith's Parish,* ☎ *no phone.* ⊡ *Free.* ⊙ *Daily dawn–dusk.*

60 **Tobacco Bay.** In 1775 gunpowder bound for Boston was secretly loaded on this bay (☞ Tucker House *in* The Town of St. George, *above*). Nowadays there are changing facilities and a refreshment stand on its fine beach. Nearby St. Catherine's Beach is a pleasant place for a swim and a quiet contemplation of the events of July 28, 1609. ✉ *St. George's Parish.*

63 **Tom Moore's Tavern.** Now a popular restaurant (☞ The Parishes *in* Chapter 4), the house was originally the home of Samuel Trott, who built it in the 17th century and named it Walsingham. When Tom Moore, the Irish poet, arrived in Bermuda in 1804, the house was occupied by a descendant of the original owner (also named Samuel Trott) and his family. The Trotts befriended the poet, who became a frequent visitor to the house. In "Epistle V," Moore immortalized the Trott estate's calabash tree, under which he liked to write his verses. In 1844, the idea for the Royal Bermuda Yacht Club (☞ Albuoy's Point *in* Hamilton, *above*) was conceived under the very same tree. ✉ *Walsingham La. and Harrington Sound Rd., Hamilton Parish,* ☎ *441/293–8020.*

65 **Tucker's Town.** In 1616 Governor Daniel Tucker, for whom the town was named, wanted to abandon St. George's in favor of a new settlement here on the shores of Castle Harbour. A few streets were laid out and some cottages built, but the plan was eventually shelved. For 300 years Tucker's Town remained a small fishing and farming community; cotton was grown for a while, and a few whaling boats operated from here. Dramatic change overtook the community soon after World War I, however. Seeking to raise the island's appeal in order to attract passengers on its luxury liners to Bermuda, a steamship company called Furness, Withy & Co. purchased a large area of Tucker's Town for a new country club. The result was the exclusive Mid Ocean Club, with its fine golf course. The Castle Harbour Resort, now run by Marriott, adjoins the club. Members of the club started building residences nearby, and the Tucker's Town boom began. Today, only members of the club can buy a house in the area, and private residences have been known to sell for more than $3 million. ✉ *Smith's Parish.*

★ **70** **Verdmont.** It may have been prominent shipowner John Dickinson who built this house around 1710. At the end of the American War of Independence, Verdmont was the home of John Green, an American Loyalist who fled to Bermuda from Philadelphia. Green married the stepdaughter of Dickinson's granddaughter Elizabeth, and he was appointed judge of the Court of Vice Admiralty. Green was also a portrait artist, and his family portraits remain on the walls. The house resembles a small English manor house and has an unusual double roof and four large chimneys: each of the eight rooms has its own fireplace. Elegant cornice moldings and paneled shutters grace the two large reception rooms downstairs, originally the drawing room and formal dining room. The sash windows reflect a style fashionable in English manors.

Although it contains none of the original furnishings, Verdmont is a treasure house of Bermudiana. Some of the furniture is imported from England—there is an exquisite early 19th-century piano—but most of it is fine 18th-century cedar, crafted by Bermudian cabinetmakers. In particular, notice the desk in the drawing room, the lid and sides of which are made of single planks. Also displayed in the house is a china coffee service, said to have been a gift from Napoléon to President Madison. The president never received it. The ship bearing it across the Atlantic was seized by a Bermudian privateer and brought to Bermuda. Look carefully, too, at the handmade cedar staircase; the newel posts on each landing have removable caps to accommodate candles in the evening. Upstairs is a nursery with antique toys and a cedar cradle. The last occupant of Verdmont was an eccentric woman who lived here for 75 years without installing electricity or any other modern trappings. After her death, her family sold the house to the Bermuda Historic Monuments Trust—the forerunner of the Bermuda National Trust, which opened it as a museum in 1956. ⊠ *Collector's Hill, Smith's Parish,* ☎ *441/236–7369.* 🎟 *$3; $5 combination ticket with Bermuda National Trust Museum and Tucker House in St. George's.* ⊙ *Tues.–Sat. 10–4.*

NEED A BREAK? The simple and popular **Speciality Inn** (⊠ South Shore Rd., foot of Collector's Hill, ☎ 441/236–3133) serves pasta, pizza, sandwiches, soups, shakes, ice cream, and good breakfasts. It's open Monday to Saturday from 6 AM to 10 PM.

⑧₁ Whale Bay Fort. Overgrown with grass, flowers, and subtropical plants, this small, 19th-century battery offers little in the way of a history lesson, but it does overlook a secluded pink-sand beach, gin-clear water, and craggy cliffs. The beach is accessible only on foot, but it's a splendid place for a swim. Bear in mind that you have to climb back up the hill to your moped or bike. *In Southampton Parish, turn off Middle Rd. to Whale Bay Rd.; the road ends and the fort is at the bottom of a steep hill in Sandys Parish.*

4   DINING

Bermuda's culinary lineup has expanded
and, on the whole, improved during the
past decade. A steady stream of
internationally acclaimed chefs have come
to the island, and the once-dominant Italian
cuisine has given way to Japanese sushi
bars and menus that combine Asian
ingredients in island specialties. But the
island's cuisine begins and ends with
Bermudian ingredients—and therein lies its
culinary identity.

Updated by
Judith Wadson

W ITH ABOUT 150 RESTAURANTS from which to choose—nearly seven per square mile—you'll have little trouble getting your fill in Bermuda. An international medley of cuisines is served these days. Italian, Indian, Caribbean, Chinese, English, French, Japanese, and Mexican restaurants are within walking distance of one another in Hamilton. Much harder to swallow than the average spoonful of fish chowder, though, are the prices. Bermuda has never sought a reputation for affordability, and restaurateurs are no exception. A few greasy spoons serve up standard North American fare at a decent price, but by and large you should prepare for a bit of sticker shock.

What you won't find on Bermuda are McDonald's, Burger King, or any of their ilk. Apart from a lone Kentucky Fried Chicken outlet, which sneaked in several years ago, the fast-food chains have been barred by Bermuda's government. After the island's last premier, Sir John Swan, saw his plans for independence rejected in a referendum, he resigned and promptly applied for permission to open a McDonald's outlet but was opposed by Parliament in 1996. After taking the case through several appeals, the highest court—the London-based Privy Council—declared that no new fast-food franchises would be permitted on the island. Most residents breathed a sigh of relief on hearing the news in 1999.

Although Bermudian cuisine is seemingly elusive, many restaurants are highlighting local dishes amid their international offerings. Cassava pie—formerly reserved for Christmas dinner—can be found along with mussel pie. Fish chowder is found at high-end establishments and diners alike, accompanied by the traditional splash of sherry peppers and black rum. Local fish is usually offered. Try it panfried and topped with a lemon-banana sauce. And Bermuda spiny lobster, seasonally available from September through March, is succulent, particularly when dipped in drawn butter with lemon. Other local highlights can usually be found at The Black Horse Tavern, an out-of-the-way place on the water in St. David's, where the menu is dictated by what the fishermen catch. Shark hash and mussel pie are usually available. The traditional Sunday codfish breakfast is best at Freeport Gardens, in the Royal Naval Dockyard. A huge plate of boiled or steamed salt cod, boiled potatoes and onions, and sliced local bananas topped with a creamy egg or tomato sauce with avocado slices will stave off hunger for the better part of the day.

Dining in Bermuda is typically expensive. Don't be surprised if dinner for two at one of the very top places—the Newport Room or Fourways Inn, for example—puts a $200–$300 dent in your pocket. And a 15% service charge is almost always added to the bill "for your convenience." Between the Newport Room and the Kentucky Fried Chicken, however, are myriad dining opportunities and some truly innovative menus. Many hotels offer a choice of meal plans as well, which can provide significant savings (☞ Chapter 5). Ask about these when booking your room.

As with most rituals in Bermuda, dining tends to be rather formal. For men, jackets are rarely out of place and are required in most upscale restaurants. Credit cards are generally accepted, though some smaller taverns and lunch spots take only cash and traveler's checks. Note that late breakfasts and lunches and early dinners can be hard to come by, because most restaurants close between meals.

CATEGORY	COST*
$$$$	over $50
$$$	$35–$50
$$	$20–$35
$	under $20

*per person, excluding drinks and service (a 15% service charge is some-times added)

HAMILTON & ENVIRONS

Asian

$$–$$$ ✕ **House of India.** The north side of Hamilton, across from a home-
★   less shelter, isn't exactly the best location, but the food here is well worth
a taxi ride. The authentically made dishes are bursting with flavor and
feature offerings from across the subcontinent. Start with vegetable
samosas (small deep-fried turnovers). Any entrée you choose—meat,
fish, or vegetarian—will be memorable. All the breads are freshly
made in the tandoor, and the *pappadams* (lentil-flour tortillas) are light
and full of flavor. A weekday brunch ($11) is worth every cent. The
lassi (sweetened yogurt) drinks, particularly the mango, are excellent
and refreshing. ✉ *57 North St.,* ☎ *441/295–6460. MC, V.*

$–$$$ ✕ **Chopsticks.** This restaurant features a mix of Szechuan, Hunan, and
Cantonese favorites, as well as Thai and Filipino food. The best Chi-
nese selections include jumbo shrimp with vegetables in black-bean sauce,
hoisin (sweet and spicy) chicken, and lemon chicken. Thai and Filipino
chefs lend a taste of their home countries with such favorites as *pla
pae sa* (boneless fish fillet steamed on a bed of cabbage and celery with
ginger, sweet pepper, scallions, red chilies, and cilantro), and beef
panang (cooked in coconut sauce, curry paste, and lime leaves). All dishes
are made to order, special diets can be accommodated, and MSG can
be omitted. Specially priced dinner menus are available for $15.50 or
$21.95 from November through March. Takeout is available. ✉ *Reid
St. E,* ☎ *441/292–0791. AE, MC, V.*

$$ ✕ **The Bombay.** The culinary scene of any British colony would be in-
complete without a curry house, and this Indian restaurant captures
the flavor of the subcontinent without becoming a caricature. All the
traditional favorites are prepared remarkably well here. Order the
peeaz pakora (onion fritters) and mulligatawny soup as starters. Then
opt for the *jhinga vindaloo* (shrimp in hot curry), mutton *saagwala*
(braised lamb in creamy spinach), or anything from the clay tandoor
oven. Nan, *paratha,* and pappadam are terrific breads and snacks to
accompany the meal. Ask about the discounted dinner menus, or stop
by on a weekday for the buffet lunch. Takeout is available. ✉ *Reid
St.,* ☎ *441/292–0048 or 441/292–8865. AE, MC, V.*

Bermudian

$$ ✕ **The Pickled Onion.** Set in an old whiskey warehouse with exposed
cedar beams, this restaurant serves a variety of familiar dishes with a
Bermudian twist. The walls are painted in Bermuda's trademark pas-
tels, though bright tablecloths, wrought-iron furniture, and a wonderful
harbor view make the patio the most popular dining area. Try the stir-
fried rockfish with vegetables and cashews in hoisin-oyster sauce, or the
Pickled Onion pizza (with the works). For dessert try the fried bananas
with black-rum banana salsa or chocolate pâté with raspberry sauce. Live
musicians (pop, jazz, and blues) entertain evenings from April through
November. ✉ *53 Front St.,* ☎ *441/295–2263. AE, MC, V.*

$–$$ ✕ **Monty's.** Try this pleasant, tropically themed spot when you're in
the mood for Bermudian, English, or Caribbean cuisine. Fluffy omelets,
pancakes, and French toast are on the breakfast menu. For lunch the

$ ✕ **Jamaican Grill.** Try this casual, family-run restaurant for well-seasoned Jamaican cooking. Colorful murals surround patrons with island scenes such as the multitiered Dunns River Falls. You can order at the take-out counter downstairs or dine upstairs. Either way, treat yourself to coconut or *escovich* (salt-cured) fish, red beans and rice, brown stew chicken, akee and salt fish, beef patties, curried goat, and of course, peppery jerk chicken or fish. No alcohol is served, but the refreshing pineapple-ginger, carrot, mango, and other natural juices hit the spot. ✉ *32 Court St.,* ☎ *441/296–6577. MC, V. Closed Sun.*

French

$$$ ✕ **La Coquille.** Some diners sail right up to the dock for the delicious Provençal food at this restaurant overlooking Hamilton Harbour. The decor, fish and shells painted on the walls, highlights the house specialty—seafood. Sitting either outside or in an enclosed veranda, sample the tiger prawns with carrot mousse, panfried local fish, or chicken stuffed with sun-dried tomatoes. Complement your meal with a selection from the extensive wine list. *40 Crow La. (Bermuda Underwater Exploration Institute),* ☎ *441/292–6122. AE, MC, V.*

$$$ ✕ **Waterloo House.** This restaurant and small Relais & Château hotel
★ in a former private house on Hamilton Harbour serves Bermudian and Continental cuisine. You can dine either on the waterside patio (in summer) or in the elegant dining room, where deep-raspberry walls, rich chintzes, and elegant sconces set the mood. The restaurant usually offers a daily special or two, but don't overlook the menu items, especially the well-seasoned Bermuda fish chowder and the tender lamb. Service is outstanding. ✉ *Pitts Bay Rd.,* ☎ *441/295–4480. Jacket and tie. AE, MC, V.*

$$–$$$ ✕ **Le Figaro Bistro & Bar.** Oversized posters adorn the walls of this at-
★ tractive French bistro. An archway separates the two dining areas, which are decorated in warm tones and often filled with locals, from bank tellers to businesspeople. Among the most popular dinner selections are the peppered tuna with garlic mashed potatoes, the cassoulet, and steaks. ✉ *63 Reid St.,* ☎ *441/296–4991. Reservations essential. AE, MC, V.*

$–$$ ✕ **Monte Carlo.** Some of Bermuda's best meals are served in this cheer-
★ ful Mediterranean restaurant behind Hamilton's City Hall. The ceiling is adorned with beams of old Bermuda cedar. The room is decorated with copies of impressionist works painted on the walls and china and copper pans hanging by the fireplace. For lunch, the fresh tuna marinated in Provençal oil and herbs and served with caper sauce is outstanding, as are the sautéed scallops served with spinach and a light orange sauce. For dinner, try the Bouillabaisse Marseillaise—fish and shellfish in a delicious broth. A special lighter menu (with lighter prices) includes a variety of crepes. The dessert trolley brings white-chocolate crème brûlée and homemade pastries. ✉ *Victoria St.,* ☎ *441/ 295–5453. AE, MC, V.*

International

$$$ ✕ **Fresco's Wine Bar & Restaurant.** Fresco's is known for its homemade pasta dishes prepared tableside, its award-winning pork tenderloin stuffed with papaya and star fruit, and its nightly wine tastings. At lunchtime head outdoors to eat in the courtyard, which is accented with a fountain, palms, and flowers. Inside there's a wine cellar–like room with a vaulted ceiling. The upstairs wine bar serves some excellent vintages by the glass, along with late-night snacks and desserts. You're in luck if you see something you like on the walls. These works by local artists are for sale. ✉ *Chancery La. off Front St.,* ☎ *441/295–5058. Reservations essential weekends. AE, MC, V.*

$$–$$$ ✕ **The Red Carpet.** This tiny restaurant is very popular at lunch, es-
★ pecially among local politicians and businesspeople, who savor the traditional yet creatively prepared international fare. The clever use of
mirrors creates an illusion of space, while plentiful brass gives the place
a stylish look. Among the culinary highlights are the grilled lamb
chops with rosemary, the rockfish with fried banana and almonds, and
the seafood platter. ⊠ *Armoury Bldg., Reid St.,* ☎ *441/292–6195. AE,
MC, V. Closed Sun.*

$$–$$$ ✕ **Ristorante Primavera and Omakase Sushi Bar.** Understated ele-
★ gance reigns at this pleasing Mediterranean dining room in the west
end of Hamilton. You'll sit under a cleverly designed ceiling of grape
vines and lattice to enjoy the extensive menu. Spectacular starters are
carpaccio primavera (thin slices of beef tenderloin with Parmesan
cheese and olive oil on arugula) and scampi and scallops *innamorati*
(sautéed in cognac, paprika, and shallots). The well-seasoned *zuppa di
pesce* (fish soup) is a wonderful combination of scallops, clams, salmon,
rockfish, and mushrooms. You can also choose from a variety of consistently good pastas. *Triangolo di paste* is a combination of three different
pastas with three different sauces. Upstairs is a popular new sushi eatery,
Omakase, with terrific seafood delicacies. Try Jurassic Maki—a core of
salmon skin and soft-shell crab with flying fish roe, seaweed, and rice topped
with smoked eel. It's definitely enough for two. Another great taste (and
name) is the Pink Cadillac—spicy tuna, snapper, salmon, nori seaweed,
and rice dusted with pink bonita flakes. ⊠ *Pitts Bay Rd.,* ☎ *441/295–
2167. AE, MC, V. No lunch weekends.*

$$ ✕ **Harbourfront.** Few eateries on Front Street have as much variety as
★ this busy place, where sushi is served alongside Continental and
Mediterranean specialties. Sit on the porch or behind the large glass
doors and watch the action along Front Street and the harbor as you
peruse the extensive menu. This is the place to come at lunchtime for
a good burger or salad. For dinner start with grilled calamari or carpac-
cio followed by lobster, rack of lamb, or any of the excellent pastas.
The small sushi bar is usually filled with locals, but you can order at
a table as well. ⊠ *Front St.,* ☎ *441/295–4207. AE, MC, V.*

$ ✕ **The Beach.** Across Front Street from the cruise-ship dock, this laid-
back dining spot brings Hamilton some tropical flair. Colorful picnic
tables, surfboards, and murals of the sand and sea evoke the shore.
Dining is both indoors and out, with soups, salads, sandwiches, pasta,
burgers, and chicken dishes on the casual menu. Among the frozen drinks,
the Dark and Stormy (black rum and ginger beer) is a winner. ⊠ *103
Front St.,* ☎ *441/292–0219. AE, MC, V.*

$ ✕ **Paradiso Cafe.** When you're ready for a break from shopping, a high
stool in this coffee bar is a good people-watching perch. Assorted
Euro-coffees and herbal teas, served hot or iced, are on the light menu,
along with salads, soups, pasta, quiche, and gourmet sandwiches. ⊠
7 Reid St., Washington Mall, ☎ *441/295–3263. AE, MC, V. Closed
Sun. No dinner.*

Italian

$$–$$$ ✕ **Harley's Bistro.** Popular with Hamilton businesspeople, this pool-
side eatery overlooking Hamilton Harbour serves up Asian and Ital-
ian fare either indoors or alfresco. Pizzas with standard toppings and
the usual lineup of pasta dishes are offered alongside Asian-inspired
choices like wok-charred rockfish with curried sticky rice and peanut
sauce. ⊠ *76 Pitts Bay Rd., at the Fairmont Hamilton Princess,* ☎ *441/
295–3000. AE, DC, MC, V.*

$$–$$$ ✕ **Little Venice.** Bermudians head for this trattoria when they want more
from Italian cooking than pizza. Little Venice can be expensive, but
it's worth it, and the service is expert. Try an abundant plate of an-

tipasto, or chicken-and-apple sausage over mixed vegetables with mustard sauce. Salads are first-rate, particularly the Caesar salad and the spinach salad topped with Gorgonzola croutons. All of the pastas are commendable, especially the linguine with mussels. Good choices for main courses include veal with mushrooms and asparagus in red wine, and the duck with peaches in a honey–Grand Marnier sauce. The tiramisu is delicious. ⊠ *Bermudiana Rd.,* ☎ *441/295–3503. Reservations essential. AE, MC, V.*

$$–$$$ ✕ **Portofino.** This popular Italian restaurant is often busy and noisy. If pizza's your game, you'll appreciate the wide array of toppings available (phone 15 minutes ahead if you want a pie to go). The sirloin steak *pizzaiola* (with olives, anchovies, capers, and tomato sauce) is also good, as is calamari fried in a delicate batter. For a bit of undersea adventure, consider octopus cooked in red sauce with olives and capers and served over risotto. Homemade pasta and other risotto specials are excellent. ⊠ *Bermudiana Rd.,* ☎ *441/292–2375 or 441/295–6090. AE, MC, V. No lunch weekends.*

$$ ✕ **La Trattoria.** Tucked in a Hamilton alley, this no-nonsense trattoria has red-check tablecloths and a familiar mom-and-pop feel. Recommended entrées are cheese ravioli in a tomato cream sauce and fillet of fish sautéed in white wine with oregano, garlic, and olives. The pizzas have creative toppings, such as arugula and prosciutto. ⊠ *Washington La.,* ☎ *441/295–1877. AE, MC, V.*

$$ ✕ **Tuscany.** The balcony of this owner-run spot overlooks Front Street and has a view of Hamilton Harbour. Inside, a mural of the Tuscan countryside dominates one wall. The pizzas are good, especially the *4 Stagioni* (four seasons), with tomato, mozzarella, artichoke hearts, and asparagus. The linguine with seafood and the veal with mushrooms are also delicious. ⊠ *Front St.,* ☎ *441/292–4507. AE, MC, V.*

$ ★ ✕ **Pasta Basta.** This restaurant and Pasta Pasta (☞ Italian *in* Town of St. George, *below*) share virtually the same menu and decor. Both are Bermudian favorites, with brightly painted interiors, colorful tables and chairs, and a lively (if slightly institutional) atmosphere. The food is tasty and well prepared, and the ever-changing menu of simple Northern Italian cuisine offers good value. The St. George's location serves pizza. At either branch, try penne with chicken-and-pepper sauce, classic or vegetable lasagna, *orecchiette* pasta with pesto and potato, Caesar salad, or any of the daily specials. Liquor is not served at either restaurant, and smoking is not allowed. ⊠ *1 Elliot St. W, Hamilton,* ☎ *441/295–9785;* ⊠ *York St., St. George's,* ☎ *441/297–2927. Reservations not accepted. No credit cards.*

Mexican

$ ✕ **Rosa's Cantina.** Bermuda's only Tex-Mex eatery has a festive atmosphere and a predictable decor of sombreros, serapes, and south-of-the-border bric-a-brac. Despite its monopoly on the island's Mexican cuisine, the food here is consistently good. Popular favorites include Nachos Unbelievable (melted cheese, refried beans, beef, onions, tomatoes, peppers, jalapeños, and guacamole), fajitas, and burritos. Any item can be made as mild or as spicy as you like. Along with Mexican fare, the menu includes hearty Texas-style steaks, chicken, and seafood. Rosa's has a loyal local following and is always filled with a crowd of Bermudians and vacationers; on balmy evenings it's fun to sit on the balcony overlooking Front Street. ⊠ *121 Front St.,* ☎ *441/295–1912. AE, MC, V.*

Seafood

$$–$$$$ ✕ **Lobster Pot.** Bermudians swear by this place, which dishes out some of the best versions of island standards in Bermuda, including local lobster (from September through March), Maine lobster, and a host of other local shellfish and fish. Try the yellowtail or rockfish with bananas and almonds, or the delicious Lobster Pot snails in their buttery secret sauce. The maritime decor includes shining brass instruments and sun-bleached rope. ✉ *Bermudiana Rd.,* ☎ *441/292–6898. AE, MC, V. Closed Sun.*

$$–$$$ ✕ **Fisherman's Reef.** Above the Hog Penny Pub, this upscale restaurant draws a local crowd for seafood and steak lunches and dinners. The fish chowder is excellent, as is the St. David's conch chowder. Of the wide selection of seafood entrées, the best are Bermuda lobster (in season); wahoo Mangrove Bay (seasoned and broiled with slices of Bermuda onion and banana); and the Cajun-style, baked, or panfried catch of the day. ✉ *Burnaby Hill off Front St.,* ☎ *441/292–1609. AE, DC, MC, V. No lunch weekends.*

$$–$$$ ✕ **Port O' Call.** For lunch or dinner, this delightfully intimate restaurant is one of Hamilton's most popular eateries. Many choose to begin with escargots. Fresh local fish—such as wahoo, tuna, grouper, and snapper—is cooked perfectly, and the sauces are pure silk. The early bird specials, served between 6 and 7 Monday through Thursday, cost around $23 for soup or salad and entrée. ✉ *87 Front St.,* ☎ *441/295–5373. AE, MC, V. Closed Sun. No lunch Sat.*

THE TOWN OF ST. GEORGE

British

$$ ✕ **Carriage House.** Hearty British and international food is the daily bread at this attractive slice of the Somers Wharf restoration. Try to secure a table outside on the patio or inside by a window so you can watch the action on the harbor. Dinner can be pricey, but many items are reasonable. This is the place to tuck into roast prime rib of beef, cut to order tableside. But don't overlook the fresh Bermuda fish when it's on the menu. On Sunday the Carriage House lays out a generous buffet brunch that includes champagne. Afternoon tea with all the trimmings is served every day except Sunday. ✉ *Somers Wharf,* ☎ *441/297–1270. AE, DC, MC, V.*

$$ ✕ **Wharf Tavern.** This English-style watering hole enjoys a steady flow of patrons from breakfast until 3 AM every night, except Sunday, when it closes at 6. Vacationers—especially families and yachties—sit on the porch or on the wharf and take in the activity on St. George's Harbour. The menu's mainstays are a varied selection of sandwiches and burgers of typical pub quality, chicken or shrimp and chips, and panfried wahoo or tuna. Service can be slow. ✉ *Somers Wharf,* ☎ *441/297–1515. MC, V.*

International

$$–$$$ ✕ **San Giorgio.** The choice of inside dining room or waterside terrace on St. George's Harbour make this restaurant one of the most romantic settings on the island. Owners Nick and Ginny Brown are dedicated to serving a variety of good food. Daily Italian or Asian-inspired specials and fresh local fish and island produce draw a faithful following. For lunch the Italian creations—pizza, gnocchi, and other pasta dishes—are consistently good. Or try the salad of grilled shrimp with shaved fennel, arugula, and orange in a Thai-inspired dressing. Dinner antipasti are for the most part traditional, but the spring rolls of chicken, shrimp, and sundried tomato with a chipotle plum sauce are decidedly eclectic. Delicious entrées include penne Gorgonzola with spinach and pine nuts, and ravioli stuffed with morel mushrooms, leeks, peas, and cheese in a cream sauce. ✉ *36 Water St.,* ☎ *441/297–1307. MC, V.*

Italian

$ ✕ **Pasta Pasta.** This restaurant shares its menu and decor with Pasta
★ Basta (☞ Italian *in* Hamilton & Environs, *above*). ✉ *Duke of York St.,* ☎ *441/297–2927. Reservations not accepted. No credit cards.*

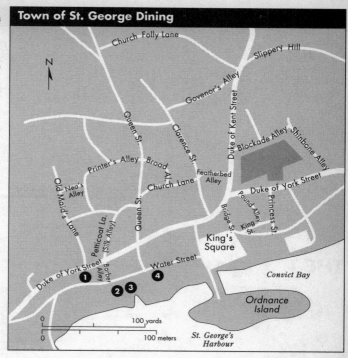

Town of St. George Dining

THE PARISHES

The West End

British

$$–$$$ ✕ **Somerset Country Squire.** Overlooking Mangrove Bay in the West End, this typically English tavern is all dark wood and good cheer, with a great deal of malt and hops in between. Much of the food isn't good enough to warrant a special trip across the island, but some of it is. The Bermuda fish chowder, the panfried mahimahi, and the steak-and-kidney pie are all delicious. ✉ *Mangrove Bay, Somerset,* ☎ *441/234–0105. AE, MC, V.*

International

$$$–$$$$ ✕ **Seahorse Grill.** Set on the Elbow Beach Hotel property five minutes from Hamilton, this chic establishment, decorated in a minimalist manner, is the perfect place for an expense-account meal. The varied and frequently changing menu showcases locally grown produce, much of it pesticide-free. This is the type of place that describes the ingredients in minute detail, naming their exact geographic origins, so be prepared for some involved reading. The service can be slow, so be prepared to linger between courses. Start with cedar-smoked magret duck with cherry compote or the foie gras. The black rum barbecued tuna is outstanding, as is the rack of lamb. A satisfying end is the sticky ginger cake with passion-fruit sauce or the homemade banana ice cream. Lunch offerings of a two- or three-course meal cost $25 or $33, respectively, which gives diners a chance to sample the fare at much lower prices. ✉ *Elbow Beach Hotel, Paget,* ☎ *441/236–3535. AE, MC, V.*

72

Dining in the Parishes

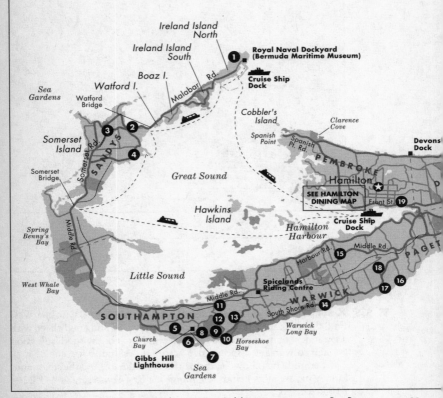

Black Horse Tavern 26	Freeport Gardens . . . 4	Lighthouse Tea Room 7	Paw-Paws 14
The Bouquet Garni 22	Frog & Onion Pub 1	Lillian's 6	Rib Room 9
Cafe Lido 16	Green Lantern . . . 19	Longtail Cafe 6	Seahorse Grill 16
Coconuts 5	Henry VIII 8	Newport Room 12	Somerset Country Squire 2
Dennis's Hideaway 25	Horizons 18	North Rock Brewing Company 21	Specialty Inn 20
Fourways Inn 15	Il Palio 3	Norwood Room . . . 17	Swizzle Inn 24
			Tio Pepe 13

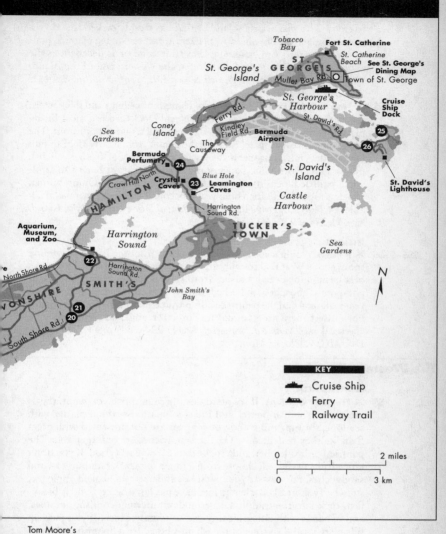

Tobacco
Bay

St. George's
Island

ST.
GEORGE'S

Fort St. Catherine

St. Catherine
Beach

See St. George's
Dining Map

Mullet Bay Rd.   Town of St. George

St. George's
Harbour

Cruise
Ship
Dock

St. David's Rd.

Ferry Rd.

Coney
Island

Sea
Gardens

Kindley
Field Rd.

The
Causeway

Bermuda
Airport

Bermuda
Perfumery

24

25

26

St. David's
Island

St. David's
Lighthouse

Crawl Hill North

Crystal
Caves

23

Blue Hole

Leamington
Caves

Harrington
Sound Rd.

HAMILTON

Castle
Harbour

TUCKER'S
TOWN

Aquarium,
Museum,
and Zoo

Harrington
Sound

Sea
Gardens

22

Harrington
Sound Rd.

North Shore Rd.

SMITH'S

John Smith's
Bay

VONSHIRE

21

20

South Shore Rd.

N

KEY

Cruise Ship

Ferry

Railway Trail

0   2 miles
0   3 km

Tom Moore's
Tavern **23**

Waterlot Inn **11**

Whaler Inn **10**

Wickets
Brasserie **12**

$$ ✕ **Longtail Cafe.** Adjacent to the lobby of the Sonesta Beach Resort, this newly redesigned and renamed dining spot is a great casual place to enjoy tasty pizzas or a salad bar that has freshly picked island vegetables and terrific dressings. Appetizers are served on big platters, family-style. Desserts can be as simple as fruit salad or as decadent as the chocolate cake. It's a good addition at the western end of the island. ⊠ *Sonesta Beach Resort, South Shore Rd., Southampton,* ☎ *441/238-8122. AE, MC, V.*

$–$$ ✕ **Frog & Onion Pub.** With its vaulted limestone ceilings and thick walls, the former warehouse of the Royal Naval Dockyard is a most fitting place for this nautically decorated eatery and its large poolroom. The food caters to every taste, running the gamut from hearty English pub fare to delicious European dishes to a selection of fresh local fish plates. Pub favorites are bangers and mash, the Argus Bank fish sandwich, panfried local rockfish or tuna, and the Frog & Onion burger, which is topped with fried onions and bacon. A children's menu is available. ⊠ *The Cooperage Bldg., Royal Naval Dockyard, Ireland Island,* ☎ *441/234-2900. MC, V.*

Italian

$$$–$$$$ ✕ **Il Palio.** A ship's spiral staircase ascends from the bar to the dining
★ room at this West End restaurant, where you'll find some of the island's best pasta and specialty dishes from several Italian regions. Spinach-and-potato gnocchi with herbed tomato or meat sauce is a winner. The veal scallopini and the panfried wahoo with balsamic jus are other treats. For dessert there are assorted Italian ice creams and an Italian-style cheesecake. ⊠ *Main Rd., Somerset,* ☎ *441/234–1049 or 441/234–2323. DC, MC, V. Closed Mon.*

The Western Parishes

Bermudian

$$ ✕ **Freeport Gardens.** If it's good, locally caught fish you want, this is the place. The fish platter and the combination seafood platter with scallops, shrimp, and wahoo or snapper are not presented with great flair, but they're delicious. The fish sandwiches are unforgettable. The panfried or broiled Bermuda rockfish is particularly good. If you don't fancy fruits of the sea, choose from a range of pizzas, hamburgers, and sandwiches. For dessert you might be offered freshly baked apple pie, strawberry shortcake, or lemon meringue pie. For a hearty Sunday breakfast, tuck into the traditional Bermudian offering: codfish, potatoes, and bananas with either creamy egg or tomato sauce. If you pass up this tasty local dish (one of the island's best), try a Spanish omelet or waffles with bacon. ⊠ *Pender Rd., Dockyard, Sandys,* ☎ *441/234–1692. AE, MC, V.*

British

$$–$$$$ ✕ **Henry VIII.** As popular with locals as it is with tourists from nearby Southampton resorts, the lively Henry VIII effects an Old English look that stops just short of "wench" waitresses and Tudor styling. The mix of English and Bermudian favorites on the menu includes such classics as mussel pie. The fish chowder is wonderful, as are the very British steak-and-kidney pies. The rack of lamb is always cooked to perfection. Save room for sticky toffee pudding—it's tops. Strolling minstrels serenade during dinner most nights. Afterward, join the local crowd in the bar to hear visiting comedians or island acts, including calypso singers. ⊠ *South Shore Rd., Southampton,* ☎ *441/238–1977. AE, MC, V.*

$ ✕ **Lighthouse Tea Room.** At the base of the famous Gibbs Hill Lighthouse in Southampton, a selection of delicious teas, properly brewed, and such English favorites as scones with clotted cream make this a charming spot to rest after the big climb. Homemade soups, quiche, smoked trout, and pork pie with chutney satisfy larger appetites. Breakfast (sausage, eggs, and crumpets, anyone?) is also served. ⊠ *Lighthouse Hill, Southampton,* ☎ *441/238–8679. AE, MC, V. No dinner.*

Caribbean

$$$$ ✕ **Coconuts.** Nestled between high cliff rocks and a pristine beach on
★ the southern coast at the Reefs resort (☞ Small Hotels *in* Chapter 5), this outdoor restaurant is one of the best places to nab that table overlooking the ocean. The view is made even more dramatic at night by floodlights. An annually changing menu includes freshly grown produce prepared with Caribbean flavor. A fixed price of about $50 (excluding 15% gratuity) includes four courses. A simpler lunch menu includes daily specials, burgers, sandwiches, and good salads. ⊠ *South Shore Rd., Southampton,* ☎ *441/238–0222. Reservations essential. AE, MC, V. Closed Nov.–Apr.*

French

$$$–$$$$ ✕ **Newport Room.** With its nautical decor—glistening teak and mod-
★ els of victorious America's Cup yachts—this fine restaurant in the Fairmont Southampton Princess has had a special place in the hearts of the island's elite for years. The dining room focuses on French cuisine with American and Bermudian touches. Each dish is beautifully presented, and the service is exceptional. Salads are a step away from the traditional, with such offerings as a five-leaf salad with citrus, sautéed corn, crab cakes, and champagne grapes. The seafood entrées are especially noteworthy, and, for dessert, the Grand Marnier soufflé and crêpes suzettes (for two) are great choices. The Newport Room closes some winter months, so call ahead for information. ⊠ *Fairmont Southampton Princess, South Shore Rd., Southampton,* ☎ *441/239–6964. Jacket required. AE, DC, MC, V. Closed some winter months. No lunch.*

International

$$$$ ✕ **Horizons.** The dining room at Horizons cottage colony in Paget is one of Bermuda's most elegant, and reservations are difficult to secure on short notice. Occupying what once was a private home, this Relais & Châteaux property has an impeccably trained staff who will do their best to make this an unforgettable dining experience. The menu, which changes daily and features local ingredients, has such offerings as mesclun greens with a loquat vinaigrette, a vegetable terrine with basil oil and tomato coulis, and roasted snapper set on sun-dried tomato polenta. ⊠ *South Shore Rd., Paget,* ☎ *441/236–0048. Reservations essential. Jacket and tie. No credit cards.*

$$$$ ✕ **Norwood Room.** Don't be put off by the fact that this restaurant in the Stonington Beach Hotel is run by students of the Hospitality and Culinary Institute of Bermuda: under the supervision of their mentors, they offer superb food and service. The oversize training kitchen uses local ingredients and European culinary techniques to create a range of bright, fresh tastes. The cold fruit soup (piña colada, strawberry, or watermelon), warm duck confit with sherry vinaigrette dressing, mahimahi on spinach and roasted garlic, and grilled beef tenderloin with red bell pepper pesto are especially good. Enjoy a preprandial cocktail at the sunken bar overlooking the swimming pool. ⊠ *South Shore Rd., Paget,* ☎ *441/236–5416. Jacket and tie. AE, MC, V.*

$$$–$$$$ ✕ **Fourways Inn.** This restaurant has risen to preeminence as much for its lovely 18th-century surroundings as for anything coming out of the kitchen. After a recent refurbishment, the airy interior evokes a wealthy plantation home, with plenty of fine china, crystal, and silver. Order rockfish in a crabmeat crust with crayfish sauce or beef tenderloin with chanterelle mushrooms and candied parsnips. The fish chowder is superb as a starter, as is the Caesar salad. But leave enough room for a Dark and Stormy (black rum and ginger) soufflé for dessert. Try a Fourways Special cocktail, made with the juice of Bermuda loquats and other fruits, and a dash of bitters. ⊠ *1 Middle Rd., Paget,* ☎ *441/236–6517. Jacket required. AE, MC, V.*

$$–$$$$ ✕ **Waterlot Inn.** This Bermudian treasure resides in a graceful, two-
★ story manor house that dates from 1670. Service is impeccable, and the dining-room staff has just enough island exuberance to take the edge off European-style training. The savory fish chowder prevails as one of Bermuda's best, and the panfried Bermuda fish and the rack of lamb are both superb. ⊠ *Middle Rd., Southampton,* ☎ *441/238–0510. Jacket required. AE, DC, MC, V. Closed Jan.–mid-Mar. No lunch.*

$$$ ✕ **Lillian's.** This restaurant in the Sonesta Beach Resort is the premier
★ place for Northern Italian cuisine on the island, and its new sushi bar is also of the same high caliber. On the Italian side, the Gorgonzola whip with roasted snails is unforgettable, and the osso bucco is superbly tender. The freshly made pasta is always a sure bet, and the sauces are done to perfection. The newly created sushi bar, in a quiet corner of the spacious restaurant, is tiny, and reservations to sit here are essential. But the fresh and innovative sushi may also be enjoyed at tables, even alongside a plate of pasta. ⊠ *Sonesta Beach Resort, South Shore Rd., Southampton,* ☎ *441/238–8122. AE, MC, V.*

$$ ✕ **Paw-Paws.** This bistro can seat you on a patio overlooking busy South Shore Road or in a cozy dining room with colorful murals of Italian garden scenes. The varied menu features Bermudian, European, and North American dishes, but the chef may attempt a bit too much variety, as dishes are uneven in quality. Best bets are Bermuda fish chowder, ravioli *d'homard et saumon* (homemade lobster ravioli with strips of smoked salmon), and grilled jumbo shrimp stuffed with crabmeat. During Sunday lunch you can order the traditional Bermudian dish of codfish and potatoes with bananas. ⊠ *South Shore Rd., Warwick,* ☎ *441/236–7459. MC, V.*

$ ✕ **Wickets Brasserie.** Prints of the game of cricket decorate Wickets, whose international fare will suit just about any palate. Bermuda fish chowder is a classic starter. Follow it up with a salad, burger, sandwich, pizza, pasta, or chicken. Top off the meal with key lime pie or a piece of Oreo chocolate cheesecake. Note that the restaurant closes for a few weeks in the winter for repairs. ⊠ *Fairmont Southampton Princess Hotel, South Shore Rd., Southampton,* ☎ *441/238–8000. Reservations essential. AE, DC, MC, V. Closed a few wks in winter.*

Italian

$$$ ✕ **Cafe Lido.** On the beachfront terrace at the Elbow Beach Hotel, with
★ waves breaking just below, Cafe Lido is one of the island's most romantic settings. Signature dishes at this award-winning contemporary Italian-Mediterranean restaurant include the seafood casserole and pastas, most of which are freshly made on the premises. The ever-changing dessert menu might include crème brûlée or Italian gelato. ⊠ *Elbow Beach Hotel, off Shore Rd., Paget,* ☎ *441/236–9884. Reservations essential. AE, MC, V.*

$$ ✕ **Tio Pepe.** You needn't spend much money for a satisfying meal at this Italian restaurant with a Mexican name. The easygoing atmosphere makes it an ideal stop for bathers returning from a day at Horseshoe Bay Beach. Try the spicy eggplant baked in tomato sauce and topped with cheese to start, and follow it up with lobster ravioli or seafood linguine. The grilled local tuna and wahoo are sensational. ⊠ *South Shore Rd., Southampton,* ☎ *441/238–1897 or 441/238–0572. Reservations essential. AE, MC, V.*

Seafood

$$$–$$$$ ✕ **Whaler Inn.** Perched above the rocks and surf at the Southampton Princess, this seafood house has one of the most dramatic settings on the island. The fresh seafood comes mainly from local fishermen, making the food pleasing and plentiful. Desserts, such as the brownie sundae, are stupendous. ⊠ *Fairmont Southampton Princess Hotel, South Shore Rd., Southampton,* ☎ *441/238–0076. AE, DC, MC, V. Closed 1 month in winter. No lunch Nov.–Mar.*

Steak

$$–$$$ ✕ **Rib Room.** This is the best place on the island for char-grilled steaks
★ and chops and barbecued ribs. The conservative country club–style dining room overlooks the Fairmont Southampton Princess Golf Course, and the service is superior. The house specialty, prime rib, is perfection in the genre and served in its juices with traditional Yorkshire pudding. The lamb chops are also superlative, as is the rotisserie-cooked half chicken. Salads are served buffet style, and the Bermuda fish chowder is a sensation. ⊠ *Fairmont Southampton Princess Hotel, South Shore Rd., Southampton,* ☎ *441/238–8000. AE, MC, V. No lunch.*

The Eastern Parishes

Bermudian

$$ ✕ **Dennis's Hideaway.** Eccentric Dennis Lamb hunches over his pots
★ discussing everything from plumbing and the government to the fate of man. These days, however, his son, Sea Egg, does most of the cooking. Dennis's Hideaway is little more than a ramshackle pink structure with a scattering of homemade picnic tables—it's decidedly grubby—but it serves what may be Bermuda's best local food. Order the "fish dinner with the works"—$30-plus for a feast of shark hash on toast, conch fritters, mussel stew, conch stew, fish chowder, fried fish, conch steak, shark steak, shrimp, and scallops. Owner Dennis Lamb may even throw in some bread-and-butter pudding for good measure. Only the most determined diners can partake, as hours are erratic and the place is way off the beaten path. ⊠ *Cashew City Rd., St. David's,* ☎ *441/297–0044. Reservations essential. No credit cards.*

$–$$ ✕ **Black Horse Tavern.** Islanders fill the casual dining room hung with
★ mounted fish from local waters and the outside picnic tables to savor the chef's culinary magic. Curried conch stew with rice is a favorite, as are the straightforward renderings of amberjack, rockfish, shark, tuna, wahoo, and Bermuda lobster, in season. For lunch the fish sandwich is a perfect order. This is a great place for island originals. ⊠ *St. David's Island,* ☎ *441/297–1991. AE, MC, V. Closed Mon.*

International

$$$ ✕ **Tom Moore's Tavern.** Set in a house that dates from 1652, this restaurant in Bailey's Bay enjoys its colorful past. Irish poet Tom Moore visited friends here frequently in 1804 and wrote odes under the nearby calabash tree. Today fireplaces, casement windows, and shipbuilders' cedar joinery capture a sense of history that in no way interferes with the fresh, light, and innovative cuisine. Broiled scampi, Bermuda lobster (in season), and sautéed-then-broiled Bermuda fish with pine nuts stand out. The soufflés are always excellent, as is the chef's pastry. Both change daily. Dine in one of five cozy rooms or, by special arrangement, groups may dine alfresco on a terrace that overlooks Walsingham Bay. ⊠ *Bailey's Bay, Hamilton Parish,* ☎ *441/293–8020. Jacket required. AE, MC, V. Closed Jan.–mid-Feb. No lunch.*

$$ ✕ **North Rock Brewing Company.** The copper and mahogany tones of the handcrafted beers and ales are reflected in the warm decor of this bar and restaurant. Pub seating surrounds the glass-enclosed brewery where David Littlejohn, who runs North Rock with his wife, Heather, tinkers with the gleaming copper kettles. Sit in the dining room or outside on the breezy patio for fish-and-chips, codfish cakes, or pork tenderloin. ⊠ *10 South Rd., Smith's,* ☎ *441/236–6633. AE, MC, V.*

$–$$ ✕ **The Bouquet Garni.** This new eatery on the premises of the former Halfway House Restaurant & Bar opens for morning coffee at 10. The menu changes daily, but lunch offerings usually include burgers, fish sandwiches, and salads. Dinner specials include fresh local fish when available and beef and chicken dishes. Vegetarians will enjoy good salads or quiches. ⊠ *North Shore Rd., Flatts Village,* ☎ *441/295–5212. MC, V. No dinner Sun.*

$–$$ ✕ **Swizzle Inn.** People come here as much to drink as to eat. Just west of the airport near the Bermuda Perfume Factory, this inn created one of Bermuda's most hallowed (and lethal) drinks—the rum swizzle. Grab a spot in the shadowy bar—plastered with business cards from all over the world—to sip one of these delightful concoctions, or sit on the porch or upstairs balcony and watch the mopeds whiz by. If you get hungry, try a "swizzleburger" (a hamburger dressed up with bacon and cheese), shepherd's pie, liver and onions, or a delicious Bermuda fish sandwich. The nightly special might include tasty *pad thai* (stir-fried rice noodles) or fresh fish cooked to your preference. ⊠ *Blue Hole Hill, Bailey's Bay,* ☎ *441/293–1854. AE, MC, V.*

Italian

$ ✕ **Speciality Inn.** A favorite with locals, this south-shore restaurant is cheerful and clean, with low prices that seem to match the sparse decor. The food is Bermudian with an Italian accent. You might find fish chowder or red-bean soup on the menu, along with chicken cacciatore, pizza (vegetarian or pepperoni), and panfried fish with almonds. ⊠ *Collectors Hill, Smith's,* ☎ *441/236–3133. MC, V.*

5 LODGING

If all the accommodations available on
Bermuda were reviewed here, this book
would barely qualify as carry-on luggage.
Those that we cover include a huge array of
full-service resort hotels, cottage colonies,
small inns, guest houses, and housekeeping
apartments.

Updated by
Vivienne
Sheath

THE MOST FAMOUS BERMUDIAN LODGING is probably the beachfront cottage colony—freestanding cottages clustered around a main building that houses a restaurant, a lounge, and an activities desk. Many island properties, especially these cottage colonies, are sprawling affairs set in extensive grounds and connected by walkways and steps. At some of the smaller guest houses and housekeeping apartments, you must carry your own luggage on the long walk to your room. If you have a disability or would rather not climb hills, you may be happier at a conventional hotel with elevators and corridors.

Like everything else in Bermuda, lodging is expensive. Rates at Bermuda's luxury resorts are comparable to those at posh hotels in New York, London, and Paris. These prices would be easier to swallow if you received first-class service in return, but in fact such features as 24-hour room service and same-day laundry service are rare.

You can shave about 40% off your hotel bill by visiting Bermuda in low or shoulder seasons. The trick is trying to pin down the dates. Low season runs roughly from November through March. However, each property sets its own schedule, which may even change from year to year. Some hotels begin high-season rates on April 1, others April 15, and a few kick in as late as May 1. Your best bet is to call and ask about low- and shoulder-season rates.

Because temperatures rarely dip below 60°F in the winter, low-season weather is ideal for tennis, golf, and shopping, although the water is a bit chilly for swimming. Low-season packages are attractively priced, and a host of government-sponsored special events (many of them free) are staged for visitors. Some hotels and smaller properties close each January and/or February to prepare for the high season.

The greatest concentration of lodgings is along the south shore, in Paget, Warwick, and Southampton parishes, which have the best beaches. If shopping is your bag, however, you might prefer a hotel near the main shopping area—Front Street in Hamilton—or one of the many Hamilton Harbour properties, which are a 5- to 10-minute ferry ride from the capital. The West End is a bit remote, but it's ideal for boaters, fishermen, and those who just want to get away from it all. The ferry travels regularly across the Great Sound to Hamilton. The East End has its share of nautical activities, but its major attraction is the charming historic town of St. George's. In truth, Bermuda is so small that it's possible to see and do everything you want without much travel.

Whether or not they're officially classified as cottage colonies, a large number of guest accommodations are in cottages—most of them pink with white trim and gleaming, white tiered roofs. There are some sprawling resorts, but no high-rises and no neon signs. An enormous property like The Fairmont Southampton Princess is hard to miss, but many hotels and guest houses are identifiable only by small, inconspicuous signs or plaques. Bermuda is noted for its lovely gardens and manicured lawns, and the grounds of almost every hotel and cottage are filled with subtropical trees, flowers, and shrubs.

Typical Bermudian architecture is a limestone house, usually painted a pastel color, with a white tiered roof and most likely a white stone chimney. Many houses have exterior stairs that make a welcoming gesture—banisters curving outward at the base like open arms. Tray ceilings (shaped like inverted trays) are quite common in Bermuda, as are "knee-high fireplaces," which come up roughly knee-high.

Return visitors to the island will appreciate the annual improvements that most properties make. The Hotels Refurbishment (Temporary) Customs Duty Relief Bill of 1991 substantially reduced the duty on goods imported to Bermuda, and hotels and guest house owners have taken advantage of this to further upgrade their facilities.

A 7.25% government occupancy tax is tacked onto all hotel bills, and a service charge is levied. Some hotels calculate a service charge as 10% of the bill, whereas others charge a per diem amount. All guests must make a two-night deposit two to three weeks before their arrival. Those properties that don't accept credit cards for deposits—and many do not—accept personal checks. Virtually every hotel on the island offers at least one vacation package—frequently some kind of honeymoon special—and many of these are extraordinarily good deals. It's worth learning about the various policies and programs at the properties that interest you before booking.

Bermuda was not traditionally a family destination, but that has changed. Most hotels, guest houses, and cottage colonies welcome families with children, and most have day-care and children's-activity programs. Some hotels—including the Elbow Beach Hotel, the Grotto Bay Beach Resort, The Fairmont Southampton Princess, Willowbank, and most smaller properties—have supervised programs for children, some of which are part of attractive packages. Many hotels can also arrange for baby-sitters.

Most lodgings have a choice of meal plans, and their room rates vary according to the meal plan you choose. Under a Full American Plan (FAP), breakfast, lunch, and dinner are included in the hotel rate. A modified American Plan (MAP) covers breakfast and dinner. A Bermuda Plan (BP) includes only a full breakfast, while a breakfast-only Continental Plan (CP) means pastries, juice, and coffee. Unless otherwise noted, the rates quoted below are based on the European Plan (EP), which includes no meals at all.

Many hotels also have a variety of "dine-around" plans that allow you to eat at other restaurants on the island as part of the meal plan. The Fairmont Hamilton Princess and The Fairmont Southampton Princess offer a Royal Dine-Around program year-round, which allows you to eat at any of the several Princess restaurants. Horizons and Waterloo House have similar dine-around arrangements, as do the five properties in the Bermuda Collection (Ariel Sands, Cambridge Beaches, the Reefs, Stonington Beach, and the Pompano). Hotel and cottage colony dinners are usually formal. Men are asked to wear jackets and ties, and casual but neat dress is suggested for women. Many hotels will pack you a picnic lunch if you want to get out and about.

Bermuda's Small Properties Ltd. is a group of small hotels and guest houses that share a toll-free information/reservations line and a fax number. The properties include Angel's Grotto, Greenbank, Marley Beach Cottages, and Grape Bay Cottages. To reserve at any of these properties, call 800/637–4116 or fax 441/236–1662.

Cottage colonies and hotels host entertainment at least one night a week in high season, offering everything from jazz to classical music. Barbecues and dinner dances are also popular. Afternoon tea is served daily, in keeping with British tradition, and a rum-swizzle party is usually held on Monday night. Guest houses and housekeeping apartments do not have regularly scheduled entertainment, but informal gatherings are not uncommon.

Hotel Facilities Chart

	Access for Disabled	On The Beach	Swimming Pool	Restaurant	Cable T.V.	Fitness Facilities	Golf Nearby	Tennis Courts	Conference Fac.	Accept Children	Children's Prog.	Access To Spa	On-Site Water-Sports	Accept Credit Cards	Air-Conditioned	Entertainment	Boat Dock/Marina
Angel's Grotto	•				•		•			•				•	•		
Ariel Sands	•	•	•	•	•	•	•	•	•		•	•	•	•	•	•	
Astwood Cove			•		•		•			•				•	•		
Aunt Nea's Inn at Hillcrest						•				•				•	•		
Barnsdale Guest Apartments			•		•		•			•				•	•		
Cambridge Beaches		•	•	•		•	•	•	•	•		•	•	•	•		•
Edgehill Manor			•		•		•			•					•		
Elbow Beach Hotel	•	•	•	•	•	•	•	•	•	•	•	•	•	•	•	•	
Fourways Inn			•	•	•		•		•	•				•	•		
Grape Bay Cottages		•								•				•	•		
Greenbank Cottages							•			•			•	•			
Grotto Bay Beach Hotel	•		•	•		•	•	•	•	•	•		•	•	•	•	•
Harmony Club			•	•	•		•	•						•	•	•	
Horizons & Cottages			•	•			•	•		•				•	•	•	
Little Pomander Guest House	•				•					•				•	•		•
Loughlands Guest House			•				•	•		•				•	•		
Marley Beach Cottages		•	•		•		•			•			•	•	•		
Marriott's Castle Harbour	•	•	•	•	•	•	•	•	•	•				•	•	•	•
Newstead			•	•			•	•		•		•		•	•	•	•
Oxford House					•					•				•	•		
Palmetto Hotel & Cottages			•	•			•		•	•			•	•	•	•	•
Paraquet Guest Apartments			•	•	•		•			•					•		
Pink Beach Club & Cottages		•	•	•			•	•	•	•			•	•	•	•	
Pompano Beach Club		•	•	•		•	•	•	•	•			•	•	•	•	•
The Princess, Hamilton	•		•	•	•	•	•	•	•	•		•	•	•	•	•	•
The Reefs	•	•	•	•		•	•	•	•	•			•	•	•	•	

	Access for Disabled	On The Beach	Swimming Pool	Restaurant	Cable T.V.	Fitness Facilities	Golf Nearby	Tennis Courts	Conference Fac.	Accept Children	Children's Prog.	Access To Spa	On-Site Water-Sports	Accept Credit Cards	Air-Conditioned	Entertainment	Boat Dock/Marina
Rosedon			•							•					•		
Royal Heights Guest House			•				•			•				•	•		
Royal Palms Hotel			•	•	•					•				•	•		
St. George's Club	•	•	•	•	•		•	•	•	•			•	•	•	•	
Salt Kettle House							•			•					•		•
Sky Top Cottages							•			•					•		
Sonesta Beach Hotel & Spa	•	•	•	•	•	•	•	•	•	•	•	•	•	•	•	•	
Soundview Cottage			•				•			•					•		
Southampton Princess	•		•	•	•	•	•	•	•	•	•	•	•	•	•	•	•
Stonington Beach Hotel		•	•	•	•		•	•	•					•	•	•	
Surf Side Beach Club		•	•	•	•	•	•		•	•				•	•	•	
Waterloo House			•	•					•	•				•	•	•	
Whale Bay Inn		•			•		•			•					•		
White Sands & Cottage			•	•	•					•				•	•		
Willowbank		•	•	•			•	•	•	•	•						

Most large hotels have their own water-sports facilities where you can rent Windsurfers, Sunfish, paddleboats, and other equipment. Even the smallest property, however, can arrange sailing, snorkeling, scuba, and deep-sea fishing excursions, as well as sightseeing. The Coral Beach & Tennis Club and the Mid Ocean Club are posh private clubs, and require an introduction by a member for access to their excellent beach, tennis, and golf facilities. However, many hotels have arrangements with one or the other to allow guests certain privileges.

Unless otherwise noted, rooms in all lodgings below are equipped with private bathrooms.

CATEGORY	COST*
$$$$	over $250
$$$	$150–$250
$$	$100–$150
$	under $100

*Except where otherwise noted, all prices are for a standard double room for two (EP) during high season, excluding 7.25% tax and 10% service charge (or equivalent).

⬤ *following the text of a review is your signal that the property has a Web site, where you will find details and, usually, images; for a link, visit www.fodors.com/urls.*

Resort Hotels

$$$$ 🏨 **Elbow Beach Hotel.** You would never guess from its pristine appearance that this is Bermuda's oldest seaside resort. It opened in 1908. Guests approach the huge pillars of the entrance via a long driveway, and once inside, the marble floors and wood paneled lobby tell you this is definitely a luxury resort. The rooms, suites, and junior suites are spread among the main building, outlying multiunit lanais, and duplex cottages. All have a balcony, patio, ocean view, Internet access, and 24-hour room service. The majority offer comfortably sized lounges and bedrooms with marble bathrooms. The jewel of the resort is the two-floor Penthouse where guests (at a price) can enjoy filled bookshelves, a small kitchen, butler/maid quarters across the hall, master and junior bedrooms, two balconies (one with a whirlpool) with perfect ocean views, marble bathrooms, steam room, and traditional mahogany furniture throughout. The outstanding beach features cabanas and a grill with bar. The resort's beachside Cafe Lido offers one of the island's very best inside and outside dining venues. Excellent business facilities include a boardroom. ✉ *Box HM 455, Hamilton HM BX,* ☎ *441/236–3535; 800/223–7434 in U.S. and Canada;* 🖷 *441/236–8043. 169 rooms, 75 suites. 3 restaurants, 4 bars, air-conditioning, in-room safes, minibars, room service, pool, beauty salon, hot tub, putting green, 5 tennis courts, croquet, exercise room, beach, motorbikes, shops, children's program (ages 5–13), concierge, business services. AE, DC, MC, V. EP.*

$$$$ 🏨 **The Fairmont Hamilton Princess.** This big pink landmark opened in
★   1884 and is credited with launching Bermuda's tourist industry. It's named in honor of Princess Louise, Queen Victoria's daughter, who visited the island in 1883. The atmosphere is slightly formal, and the staff provides swift, courteous service. The walls at the entrance to the Tiara Room restaurant are covered with pictures of the politicians and royals who have stopped by through the years. Ideally located on Hamilton Harbour, the hotel caters to businesspeople (voice mail and Internet access available), convention groups, and others who want to be near downtown Hamilton. Plush upholstery, bedspreads, and drapes are used throughout, and most rooms have balconies. A ferry makes

regular runs across the harbor to the Fairmont Southampton Princess (☞ *below*), which has a golf course and other sports facilities (at extra cost). The Hamilton Princess has no beach, but you may use the one at the Southampton Princess. The dine-around plan between the two Princess hotels offers a choice of nine restaurants—from casual to formal. ☒ *Box HM 837, Hamilton HM CS,* ☎ *441/295–3000; 800/ 441–1414 (worldwide);* ℻ *441/295–1914. 413 rooms, 60 suites. 3 restaurants, 2 bars, air-conditioning, in-room data ports, in-room safes, minibars, 2 pools (1 saltwater), beauty salon, spa, putting green, tennis court, exercise room, motorbikes, shops, laundry service, concierge, business services. AE, DC, MC, V. BP, EP, MAP.* 🕭

$$$$ 🏨 **The Fairmont Southampton Princess.** This modern, six-story hotel
★ dominating a hilltop near Gibbs Hill Lighthouse is the island's most complete full-service resort. It's not the place for a quiet retreat, but its extensive activities, the island's top children's program, and several of its best restaurants make it very appealing. The 300-year-old Waterlot Inn (☞ The Parishes *in* Chapter 4) occupies a dockside spot on the north side, and the Whaler Inn beach club is perched above the surf on the south-shore side. A jitney churns over hill and dale to connect them all. All standard rooms are decorated in soft coral hues and light woods and have marble bathrooms. Avoid rooms on the first three floors of the west and north wings as they overlook rooftops. The oceanfront deluxe rooms are the nicest. Two beautiful penthouses and two magnificent wood-paneled duplex suites with enormous windows overlooking the ocean are also available. Perks on the 54-room Gold Floor include Continental breakfast, all-day drinks, afternoon tea, and a private lounge. Use of the health club, sauna, par-3 golf course, and tennis courts all cost extra. A first-class spa is planned for winter 2001. The excellent Dolphin Quest program, in a 3-acre, open-to-the-sea lagoon, allows you to interact with friendly bottlenose dolphins for $95. Admission is by lottery. ☒ *Box HM 1379, Hamilton HM FX,* ☎ *441/238–8000; 800/441–1414 (worldwide);* ℻ *441/238–8968. 594 rooms, 24 suites. 5 restaurants, 4 bars, air-conditioning, minibars, no-smoking rooms, indoor and outdoor pools, beauty salon, spa, 18-hole golf course, 11 tennis courts, croquet, health club, beach, motorbikes, shops, nightclub, theater, children's programs (ages 4–17), concierge. AE, DC, MC, V. MAP.* 🕭

$$$$ 🏨 **Sonesta Beach Resort.** Set on a low promontory fringed by coral reefs, this six-story modern building has a stunning ocean view and direct access to three superb natural beaches. The hotel caters to guests who want an action-packed vacation. An activities director coordinates bingo games, theme parties, movies, water sports, an excellent children's program, teen activities, and other diversions. South Side Scuba Watersports has a rental outlet here and dive and snorkel boats leave the resort daily from April through November and on request the rest of the year. A shuttle takes you to the hotel's beach at Cross Bay, but beach lovers should insist on a Bay Wing Beachfront Junior Suite that opens onto a private sandy beach. All rooms on the 25-acre property have balconies, but island-view rooms in the main building have just that— land views only. The Sonesta also has one of Bermuda's best health and beauty spas, and special spa packages are available. A shuttle bus transports guests between the hotel and South Road, where buses to Hamilton are available. ☒ *Box HM 1070, Hamilton HM EX,* ☎ *441/ 238–8122; 800/766–3782 in U.S.;* ℻ *441/238–8463. 365 rooms, 34 suites. 3 restaurants, 2 bars, air-conditioning, in-room safes, minibars, 2 pools (1 indoor), hot tub, massage, spa, steam room, 6 tennis courts, exercise room, beach, motorbikes, shops, children's programs (ages 3– 12), playground, concierge. AE, DC, MC, V. EP (BP and MAP on request).* 🕭

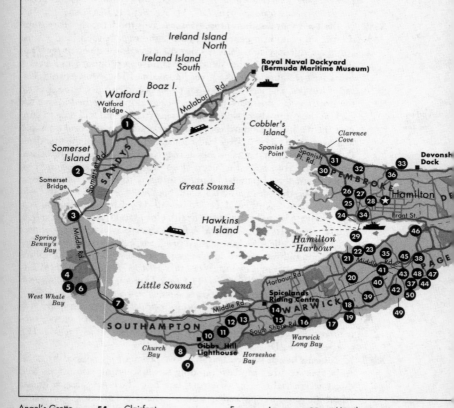

ATLANTIC OCEAN

Ireland Island
North

Ireland Island
South

Boaz I.

Watford I.

Watford
Bridge

Royal Naval Dockyard
(Bermuda Maritime Museum)

Malabar Rd.

Cobbler's
Island

Clarence
Cove

Somerset
Island

Spanish
Point

Spanish
Pt. Rd.

Devonsh
Dock

SANDYS

Somerset
Bridge

Somerset Rd.

Great Sound

PEMBROKE

Hamilton

Front St.

Spring
Benny's
Bay

Middle Rd.

Hawkins
Island

Hamilton
Harbour

West Whale
Bay

Little Sound

Harbour Rd.

Spicelands
Riding Centre

WARWICK

PAGET

Middle Rd.

Middle Rd.

SOUTHAMPTON

South Shore Rd.

Warwick
Long Bay

Church
Bay

Gibbs Hill
Lighthouse

Horseshoe
Bay

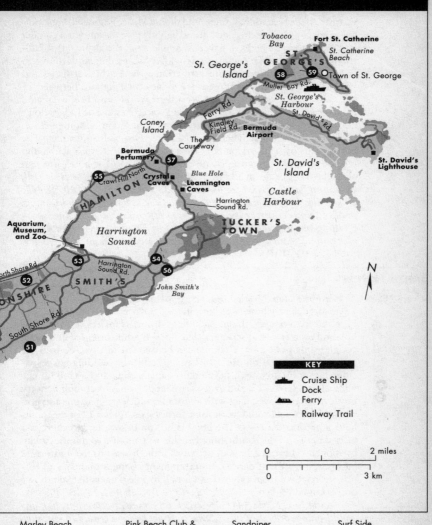

Tobacco Bay

Fort St. Catherine

St. Catherine Beach

St. George's Island

ST. GEORGE'S

58 59 Town of St. George

Muller Bay Rd.

St. George's Harbour

St. David's Rd.

Coney Island

Ferry Rd.

Kindley Field Rd.

Bermuda Airport

The Causeway

Bermuda Perfumery

57

St. David's Island

St. David's Lighthouse

55

Crawl Hill North

Crystal Caves

Blue Hole

Leamington Caves

Castle Harbour

Harrington Sound Rd.

TUCKER'S TOWN

Aquarium, Museum, and Zoo

Harrington Sound

North Shore Rd.

53

Harrington Sound Rd.

54

56

SMITH'S

John Smith's Bay

52

DEVONSHIRE

South Shore Rd.

51

N

KEY

Cruise Ship Dock

Ferry

Railway Trail

| 0 | | | 2 miles |

| 0 | | | 3 km |

$$$ ⊡ **Grotto Bay Beach Resort.** This beachside resort completed major refurbishment in 2000, bringing traditional Bermudiana character and warmth to the reception, lounge, and dining areas. Wooden floors, potted palms, a pastel palette, and natural lighting give the interior a grander feel. Set among 21 acres of gardens, a mile from the airport, this 200-room resort boasts an enclosed bay with a fish-feeding aquarium and two illuminated underground attractions: the Cathedral Cave and Prospero's Cave. The 11 three-story lodges each contain between 15 and 30 sunny rooms decorated with light woods and bright fabrics. All have private balconies or patios and water views. The lodges don't have elevators, but the ground-floor units and main building are accessible by wheelchair. There are also three two-bedroom suites. The hotel has its own excursion boat for sightseeing, and offers scuba diving and snorkeling from a private deepwater dock. The hotel offers an all-inclusive package in addition to regular rates. ⊠ *11 Blue Hole Hill, Hamilton Parish CR 04,* ☎ *441/293–8333 or 800/582–3190,* ꜰꜽ *441/293–2306. 198 rooms, 3 suites. Restaurant, 2 bars, air-conditioning, pool, 4 tennis courts, exercise room, shuffleboard, beach, dive shop, boating, motorbikes, video games, children's programs (ages 4–12), playground, concierge, business services, meeting room. AE, MC, V. BP, EP, FAP, MAP.* ✑

Small Hotels

$$$$ ⊡ **Harmony Club.** Nestled in lovely gardens, this two-story pink-and-white all-inclusive hotel was built in the 1930s as a private home. The base rate covers everything, including airport transfers, meals, alcohol, and even two-seat scooters. The hotel is adult-oriented and has a couples-only policy, but a couple can be two friends, two cousins, or any other combination. Refurbished annually, the building has a spacious reception area with Bermuda cedar paneling and a club lounge with a large-screen TV and an assortment of games. A complimentary bottle of champagne comes with all rooms, which are spacious and luxuriously decorated with Queen Anne furnishings. All but 12 of the rooms have a patio or balcony. The hotel is not on the water, but there is a heated pool and the south-shore beaches are about five-minutes away by moped. There is a host of activities in high season, from informal barbecues to formal dances. Entertainment changes nightly and features everything from calypso and limbo to solo singers to slide shows on Bermuda. ⊠ *Box PG 299, Paget PG BX,* ☎ *441/236–3500; 888/427–6664 in U.S.;* ꜰꜽ *441/236–2624. 68 rooms. Restaurant, bar, air-conditioning, pool, hot tub, sauna, putting green, 2 tennis courts, motorbikes. AE, DC, MC, V. AP.* ✑

$$$$ ⊡ **Newstead.** This charming renovated manor house and its guest cottages are in classic Bermudian colonial style, but have also happily changed with the times. A stone's throw from the Hamilton ferry at Hodson's Landing, Newstead features brick steps and walkways leading to poolside suites and cottages. The latest revamp includes four new business suites, two conference centers, a new gym, outside dining area and bar, refurbished kitchen and dining room, and high-speed Internet connections in each room. The spacious drawing room is traditionally and tastefully furnished, and live musicians entertain on the upstairs terrace. The large guest rooms have polished mahogany campaign chests and sliding glass doors opening onto balconies. The hotel has no beach, but it does have three private docks for deepwater swimming and boating. There is also access to the Coral Beach & Tennis Club facilities on the south shore, about 10 minutes away by taxi. ⊠ *Box PG 196, Paget PG BX,* ☎ *441/236–6060; 800/468–4111 in U.S.;* ꜰꜽ *441/236–7454. 38 rooms, 6 suites. Restaurant, bar, air-condition-*

ing, pool, barbershop, beauty salon, massage, putting green, 2 tennis courts, exercise room, dock, boating, concierge, business services, meeting rooms. AE, MC, V. BP, MAP.

$$$$ ⊞ **Pompano Beach Club.** Expect a friendly, personal welcome at this
★ informal seaside hotel that was a fishing club (the island's first) until 1956. Tucked away between the Port Royal Golf Course (☞ Participant Sports *in* Chapter 7) and attractive woodland, the south-shore views are spectacular, especially at sunset. The can-do attitude of staff is refreshing, catering to golfers, water-sports enthusiasts, families, and anyone in search of a remote getaway. The pink-and-white crescent-shaped main building houses the dining room (with alfresco tables), a small pub, a cozy lounge, and a fitness center, all with sea views. Spread across a hillside are the rooms and one-bedroom suites, all with balconies or patios and ocean views. The best value is the superior rooms, which are larger than the suites and have ocean views from the bedroom (suites have an ocean view through the living-room windows). More spacious (and only a few dollars extra) are the deluxe rooms. Two man-made sunbathing beaches hug the hillside, but the real boon is the low tide stroll 250 yards into waist-high crystal clear waters. ⊠ *36 Pompano Beach Rd., Southampton SB 03,* ☎ *441/234–0222; 800/ 343–4155 in U.S.;* 𝔽𝔸𝕏 *441/234–1694. 36 rooms, 20 suites. Restaurant, bar, air-conditioning, in-room safes, refrigerators, pool, wading pool, 2 outdoor hot tubs, tennis court, exercise room, 2 beaches, windsurfing, boating. AE, MC, V. BP, MAP.* ✧

$$$$ ⊞ **The Reefs.** This small, elegant, and relaxed resort hugs the cliffs that
★ wind into the sea around Christian Bay, giving it unparalleled south shore ocean and coastline views. A popular wedding and honeymoon getaway, the Reefs also welcomes families among its many repeat guests. A traditional pink Bermuda cottage clubhouse houses registration as well as a spacious, comfortable lounge bar where local entertainers play nightly. The main dining room is inside beyond the lounge, but be sure to try the less formal Coconuts (☞ The Parishes *in* Chapter 4). It's got the island's best waterfront dining setting, perfect for casual lunches or candlelight dinners. The guest rooms near the beach are the most expensive, but for seclusion and tranquility the cliffside deluxe and superior rooms perched above wave-washed boulders at the far end of the resort are best. Tiled floors, vibrant fabrics, and rattan predominate in the modestly sized but airy rooms (TVs and VCRs available on request). All have ocean views and balconies. There are also eight cottage accommodations, some with garden whirlpools. Guests have access to the spa at the neighboring Sonesta Beach Resort (☞ Resort Hotels, *above*) for a fee. ⊠ *56 South Rd., Southampton SN 02,* ☎ *441/238–0222; 800/742–2008 in U.S. and Canada;* 𝔽𝔸𝕏 *441/238– 8372. 58 rooms, 1 suite, 8 cottage suites. 3 restaurants, 2 bars, lounge, air-conditioning, fans, in-room data ports, in-room safes, refrigerators, pool, 2 tennis courts, exercise room, beach, motorbikes, piano, babysitting, laundry service. AE, MC, V. BP, MAP.* ✧

$$$$ ⊞ **Stonington Beach Hotel.** This training ground for students of the Hospitality and Culinary Institute of Bermuda has one of the friendliest and hardest-working staffs on the island. Situated 10 minutes from Hamilton on the south shore Bermuda College grounds, this hotel has access to the largest multimedia meeting space on the island, the college gym and sports field, and even lectures. The spa and sports facilities at the Elbow Beach Hotel (☞ Resort Hotels, *above*) are also open to guests. The guest rooms, set in two-story terraced lodges, face one of the island's best beaches. The identical rooms are decorated with handsome wood furniture and elegant drapes and bedspreads. All have balconies or patios, ocean views, Internet access, and refrigerators. Rooms nearest the ocean are in a beach-front cottage housing a one-bedroom and a three-bedroom apartment, both with kitchens. The spacious lobby looks out to the ocean. Regency furnishings, well-stocked bookshelves, a fireplace, and a large-screen TV in the adjoining library make it a comfortable place to relax. Creative dishes can be savored in the Norwood Room restaurant. ⊠ *Box HM 523, Hamilton HM CX,* ☎ *441/236–5416; 800/447–7462 in U.S. and Canada,* 𝖥𝖠𝖷 *441/236–0371. 64 rooms, 2 cottages. Restaurant, bar, air-conditioning, in-room safes, refrigerators, pool, 2 tennis courts, beach, snorkeling, motorbikes, library. AE, DC, MC, V. BP, MAP.* ✎

$$$$ 🛏 **Waterloo House.** This quiet Relais & Châteaux retreat, preferred
★ by business travelers from all over the world, has a long history. An archway and steps leading to the flower-filled patio from Pitts Bay Road were later additions to a house that predates 1815, when it was renamed in honor of the defeat of Napoléon. Facing the harbor, its spacious terrace, dotted with umbrellas and tables, is used for outdoor dining and entertainment—piano, jazz, and calypso. Beautiful flower arrangements fill the stately lounge, which is tastefully decorated with oil paintings, antiques, chintz drapes, and a large fireplace. Most rooms are in the main house. Some are in the two-story stone buildings beside the pool and patio. Terraces and water views complement the rooms' soothing antiques-filled decor. The luxurious bathrooms have whirlpools, heated towel racks, and adjoining dressing areas. All rooms have Internet access. Picnic cruises on the property's launch provide views of Bermuda's outer islands. In 1999 the hotel's Wellington Room won a *Wine Spectator* magazine award for having one of the world's outstanding restaurant wine lists. Waterloo's dining plan allows dine-around privileges at the sister properties of Horizons & Cottages (☞ Cottage Colonies, *below*) and the Coral Beach & Tennis Club. You can also use the short golf course at Horizons and all facilities at the Coral Beach. Transportation is provided. ⊠ *Box HM 333, Hamilton HM BX,* ☎ *441/295–4480; 800/468–4100 in U.S.;* 𝖥𝖠𝖷 *441/295–2585. 28 rooms, 6 suites. Restaurant, bar, air-conditioning, pool. AE, MC, V. BP, MAP.* ✎

$$$$ 🛏 **White Sands Hotel & Cottages.** Perched high above the south shore, this small hotel is a 3-minute walk from the white sands of Grape Bay Beach. The dining room, with bentwood chairs upholstered in plush fabrics, commands a dazzling view of the sea. The cozy lounge has a fireplace and a terrace with yet more stunning views. You can have lunch in the lounge or on the pool terrace, which has its own snack bar and barbecue grill. Guest rooms are in the three-story main house and in cottages, each of which has two or three bedrooms with bath, living room, and kitchen. The best rooms have both a balcony and an ocean view. The standard rooms in the main house are smaller and have no balcony, but do have a sea view. "Moderate" balconied rooms have sea glimpses, and standard rooms in the terrace wing have a balcony overlooking the gardens. All rooms are large and decorated in blond woods and pastels. Each has a phone with Internet access and coffeemaker. The modern, tiled bathrooms have tubs and showers. Tea is served each afternoon, and a full breakfast is included in the rate. ⊠ *Box PG 174, Paget PG BX,* ☎ *441/236–2023; 800/548–0547 in U.S.; 800/228–3196 in Canada;* 𝖥𝖠𝖷 *441/236–2486. 37 rooms, 3 housekeeping cottages. Restaurant, bar, air-conditioning, in-room data ports, in-room safes, refrigerators, pool. AE, MC, V. BP, EP, MAP.* ✎

$$$–$$$$ 🛏 **Rosedon.** Notable for its spacious veranda and majestic garden approach, this stately Bermuda manor house attracts a diverse clientele for its ambience, service, and proximity to Front Street shops. The grand central staircase and communal rooms are particularly attractive. The spacious guest rooms in the main house retain the most character, but the other rooms, situated in two-story buildings around a large heated pool, enjoy an exotic garden setting. All the cheerfully decorated rooms have balconies or patios. There is no restaurant, but breakfast, sandwiches, and light meals are served either in your room or under umbrellas by the pool. Afternoon tea is offered in the large lounges in the main house, where films are shown nightly. The hotel has no beach, but guests have access to the Stonington Beach Hotel (☞ Small Hotels, *above*) and the Elbow Beach Hotel (☞ Resort Hotels, *above*) facilities with complimentary transport. ⊠ *Box HM 290, Hamilton HM AX,* ☎ *441/295–1640; 800/742–5008 in U.S. and Canada;* 𝔽𝔸𝕏 *441/ 295–5904. 43 rooms. Bar, 2 lounges, air-conditioning, in-room safes, refrigerators, pool, laundry service. AE, MC, V. BP, EP.* ✎

$$$–$$$$ 🏠 **Willowbank.** This former estate, located on six acres of landscaped gardens overlooking Ely's Harbour, was converted to a family-style hotel by a Christian trust. Morning devotions are held in a lounge and grace is said before meals, which are announced by an ancient ship's bell and served family style. But there is no proselytizing. Willowbank is simply a serene and restful alternative to the glitzy resorts, with wonderful views and marvelous beaches nonetheless. The two large lounges are the focal point for quiet conversations and afternoon tea. Guests also meet for fellowship in the library and the Loaves and Fishes dining room. You may have liquor in your room, but there is no bar. The guest rooms, many with an ocean or harbor view, are in one-story white cottages. They are large and simply furnished but have neither phones nor TVs. There is a free summer children's program including crafts and trips around the island. No service charge is added to the bill, and tipping is not expected, but the staff is friendly and helpful all the same. ⊠ *Box MA 296, Sandys MA BX,* ☎ *441/234–1616 or 800/752–8493,* 𝔽𝔸𝕏 *441/234–3373. 64 rooms. Restaurant, 2 lounges, air-conditioning, pool, 2 tennis courts, 2 beaches, dock, snorkeling, children's program (infants–14). MC, V. MAP.* ✎

$$$ 🏠 **Hamiltonian Hotel & Island Club.** High on Langton Hill overlooking Pembroke Parish and the city of Hamilton, this traditional hotel also offers stunning ocean views from all of its 32 suites. The well-kept rooms are decorated in summery pastel shades and have tiled hallways and living rooms and carpeted bedrooms. All have sofa beds, a balcony, and TV (no cable). Suites have a refrigerator, a microwave, a toaster, and a coffeemaker. Centrally located in a tropical garden setting on the outskirts of Hamilton, the hotel is a two-minute walk to a bus stop that will take you to the city center in about five minutes. A large outdoor pool and sun deck have great sea views. There's a golf course nearby. ⊠ *Box HM 1738, Hamilton HM GX,* ☎ *441/295–5608; 401/848– 7870 in the U.S.;* 𝔽𝔸𝕏 *441/295–7481. 32 suites. Air-conditioning, pool, 3 tennis courts. AE, MC, V. EP.*

$$$ 🏠 **Royal Palms Hotel.** The brother-and-sister team of Richard Smith and Susan Weare have transformed this grand home into a hotel with standards that are second to none. This aptly named 98-year-old Bermudian house is set in lush gardens of tall palms. Attention to detail and its closeness to Hamilton (it's a five-minute walk) makes it an excellent value for the money despite its distance from beaches. Many guests like to relax and read around the outdoor pool, and the mainhouse terrace is a favorite for outdoor summer dining. You can choose from cottages or mini-suites with kitchenettes. Some rooms can connect to others, ideal for families and groups. All rooms have Internet access, hair dryers, and irons. Ascots restaurant, situated on the premises, is very popular with locals. The complimentary breakfast is generous. ⊠ *Box HM 499, Hamilton HM CX,* ☎ *441/292–1854; 800/ 678–0783 in U.S.; 800/799–0824 in Canada;* 𝔽𝔸𝕏 *441/292–1946. 25 rooms. Restaurant, bar, lounge, air-conditioning, in-room data ports, pool, laundry service. AE, MC, V. CP.* ✎

$$$ 🔲 **Surf Side Beach Club.** This charming, relaxed, and affordable option is ideal for couples looking to share a space on the south shore. The bright and cozy reception area is sizable enough to work as a lounge. The cottages are tucked into cliffs and are built on terraced levels so they each have a view of the ocean and long stretch of beach below. The elevated studios and suites are all spacious. Each has a fully equipped kitchen, cable TV, phone, and porch. All are decorated with light-wood furnishings, bright island fabrics, and wall-to-wall carpeting or tile floors. You can cook on your own barbecue grill, or dine at the excellent poolside Palms restaurant, which offers thoughtful set-menu options from one of the island's most talented chefs (special diets, including celiac, are particularly well catered for). ⊠ *Box WK 101, Warwick WK BX,* ☎ *441/236–7100 or 800/553–9990,* 𝔽𝔸𝕏 *441/236–9765. 10 apartments, 23 studios, 3 suites, 2 penthouse units. Restaurant, bar, air-conditioning, room service, pool, beauty salon, massage, sauna, spa, beach, coin laundry. AE, MC, V. BP, MAP.* 🐌

Cottage Colonies

$$$$ 🔲 **Ariel Sands.** This most informal of the cottage colonies surrounds Cox's Bay in Devonshire Parish. The picturesque sandy beach spreads out behind a graceful statue of Ariel perched on a rock in the sea. The snorkeling is superb here, and there are two natural ocean-fed pools and a heated freshwater pool. The Bermudian cottage–style clubhouse has a cozy lounge and dining room with ocean view. Many locals enjoy the quiet atmosphere and come to sip cocktails in the bar after a game of tennis or before savoring the restaurant's international cuisine. Hardwood floors, straw mats, yellow walls, and white wicker and rattan furniture give the lobby a contemporary look. The three outdoor terraces are ideal for dining, dancing, and barbecuing in season. The sloping, tree-shaded grounds are home to two two-bedroom cottages, three one-bedroom suites, and 40 guest rooms. All rooms have ocean views and phones with voice mail. The Nirvana Spa is excellent. Ariel Sands, owned by actor Michael Douglas, is a member of the Bermuda Collection group, so MAP guests can dine elsewhere. ⊠ *Box HM 334, Hamilton HM BX,* ☎ *441/236–1010; 800/468–6610 in U.S.;* 𝔽𝔸𝕏 *441/236–0087. 40 rooms, 3 suites, 2 cottages. Restaurant, 2 bars, air-conditioning, in-room data ports, 2 saltwater pools, pool, spa, putting green, 3 tennis courts, exercise room, volleyball, beach, concierge, business services, meeting rooms. AE, MC, V. BP, MAP.* 🐌

$$$$ 🔲 **Cambridge Beaches.** This top resort near Somerset Village occupies
★   a beautiful peninsula edged with private coves and five pink-sand beaches. Bermuda's original cottage colony (it opened at the turn of the century), it remains a favorite among royals and celebrities. You register in a Bermuda-style clubhouse with large, handsomely furnished lounges. The Tamarisk restaurant and terrace have splendid views of Mangrove Bay. The range of accommodations and prices is varied. Pegem, on the high end, is a 300-year-old, two-bedroom Bermuda cottage with a cedar-beam ceiling, den, sunporch, and English antiques. The least expensive units have land views. Many rooms have whirlpools and fireplaces. Suites have bidets. The resort has a two-level leisure facility and a health and beauty spa staffed by European professionals. A complimentary shopping launch to Hamilton leaves three times a week during high season. The marina offers the largest selection of watersports equipment on the island—Windsurfers, Boston Whalers, three types of sailboats, snorkel equipment, canoes, and kayaks. Scuba instruction and dive trips are available. Children must be supervised at all times, and those under five are allowed in the dining room only by special arrangement. ⊠ *Somerset MA 02,* ☎ *441/234–0331; 800/*

When it Comes to Getting
Local Currency at an ATM,

Same Thing.

**Whether you're in Yosemite or Yemen, using your Visa® card or ATM card with
the PLUS symbol is the easiest and most convenient way to get local currency.**
For example, let's say you're in France. When you make a withdrawal, using your
secured PIN, it's dispensed in francs, but is debited from your account in U.S. dollars.
This makes it easy to take advantage of favorable
exchange rates. And if you need help finding one of
Visa's 627,000 ATMs in 127 countries worldwide, visit
visa.com/pd/atm. We'll make finding an ATM as easy
as finding the Eiffel Tower, the Pyramids or even the
Grand Canyon.

It's Everywhere You Want To Be.

PRETTY IN PINK: BERMUDA'S COTTAGE COLONIES

LONG BEFORE BERMUDA'S TOURISM heyday, in the golden age of cruise-ship travel, the seeds of the island's future economy base were being slowly sewn. Would-be hoteliers and innovative business minds could see potential in the well-lined pockets of the new cruise visitors. The beautiful people were transforming Bermuda into a chic getaway destination, and this exclusive clientele would want seclusion, colonial sophistication, and traditional Bermudian hospitality. And so the cottage colony was born: a purpose-built resort that left no comfort unexplored, no luxury ignored—a plush home-away-from-home for those who could afford it.

Since Cambridge Beaches, the first cottage colony, was built at the turn of the 20th century, six more official colonies have sprung up, many still frequented by a glamorous set. Jumping on the band-wagon has been a cornucopia of house-keeping apartments selling themselves under the tried-and-tested banner of "cottages" or "cottage suites." The result is confusing. Today it's hard to find anyone who really knows what a cottage colony is, but perhaps it's distinguishing what they are *not* that sparks the true debate.

The Bermuda Department of Tourism recognizes seven properties as cottage colonies: Ariel Sands, Cambridge Beaches, Fourways Inn, Horizons & Cottages, Pink Beach Club & Cottages, The St. George's Club, and Willowbank. Despite this demarcation, visitors are often baffled by the island's numerous lodgings that have the word cottages in their names or descriptions, and that's before realizing that there are even more cottages (often private homes) that have been converted into lodgings, and which *might not* have the word cottage in their title.

Confused? So are many locals. "What is a cottage colony, anyway?" asked a bemused Bermuda tourism official during a recent debate over how to attract more business. The definitive line over what does and does not qualify to earn the title continues to blur, but generally speaking it describes a purpose-built beachfront collection of Bermudian cottages, separated from a main building that often houses the front desk, restaurants, bars, and lounge areas. Originally the guest rooms were comprised of small detached cottages, a layout that survives in some of the island's colonies. Newer complexes, however, can include much larger guest houses, some of more modern design, which can contain up to five separate units. Rooms may be offered individually, or adjoining, in which case they are described as "cottage suites."

Whatever a cottage colony is, it certainly isn't basic or budget. The enduring properties reflect distinctive island architecture and interior design styles, such as gleaming white limestone ridged roofs, spacious living and dining areas, open fireplaces, terraces or balconies, often cedar-beamed ceilings and furniture, and British country-style fabrics and ornaments. The emphasis is on comfort, relaxation, and elegance. Many cottages are pink (Bermuda's trademark color) or other pastel shades, and most have either stunning water views or garden settings.

Bermuda's home-grown accommodations are some of the island's most exceptional—and expensive—and while many offer a unique holiday experience, they won't suit everyone. The emphasis is on peace and quiet, and they offer this admirably. Entertainment, children's programs, and other activities are not emphasized, so they may not be ideal for those seeking a lively, fun-packed vacation.

While the concept and reality of cottage colonies continues to evolve, the unabashed romance of these magical oases is alive and well. The pursuit of authentic Bermudian living, with a distinct British colonial tradition, still remains to transport guests into gracious lifestyle rather than simply a hotel room.

–Vivienne Sheath

468–7300 *in U.S.;* FAX *441/234–3352. 62 rooms, 20 suites. 2 restaurants, 2 bars, air-conditioning, in-room data ports, indoor pool, saltwater pool, spa, putting green, 3 tennis courts, croquet, exercise room, 5 beaches, dock, boating, marina. MC, V. MAP.*

$$$$ ⊞ **Horizons & Cottages.** Oriental rugs, polished wood floors, cathe-
★ dral ceilings, and knee-high open fireplaces are elegant reminders of
the 18th century, when the main house in this resort was a private home.
A Relais & Châteaux property, Horizons works continually to maintain its high standards. In 2000, three of its cottages were completely
renovated. Horizons, the outstanding restaurant (☞ The Parishes *in*
Chapter 4), is a chic place for intimate candlelight dining. In nice
weather, tables are set on the terrace. Menus are created under the guid-
ance of chef Jonathan Roberts, and the hotel has dine-around arrangements with sister properties Waterloo House (☞ Small Hotels,
above) and Coral Beach & Tennis Club. Guest cottages dot the terraced lawns. Most have two or three rooms and a large common room
with a fireplace, library, and shelves of board games, and all have terraces. Each has a distinct personality and decor. Some have white
wicker furnishings, while others have a traditional European flavor.
Most cottages also have a kitchen, where a maid prepares breakfast
before bringing it to your room. The hotel has no beach of its own,
but guests may use the facilities at Coral Beach, including a superb new
spa. ⊠ *Box PG 198, Paget PG BX,* ☎ *441/236–0048; 800/468–0022
in U.S.;* FAX *441/236–1981. 45 rooms, 3 suites. Restaurant, air-conditioning, in-room safes, pool, 9-hole golf course, 3 tennis courts, croquet. No credit cards. MAP (combination also available), BP.* ✎

$$$$ ⊞ **Pink Beach Club & Cottages.** With its two pretty pink beaches, this
secluded colony is Bermuda's largest and a favorite with celebrities.
The location is ideal. Ten minutes from the airport, 15 minutes by moped
from Hamilton's Front Street, and moments from nearby golfing.
Opened as a cottage colony in 1947, the main house has a clubby ambience reflected in its dark-wood paneling, large fireplace, and beam
ceilings. Paved paths wend their way through 16½ acres of gardens,
leading to the beaches and 25 pink cottages. Single or multiple cottage
units range from junior suites to two-bedroom executive suites with
two bathrooms and twin terraces. All are spacious and most have ocean
views. The decor is tasteful and conservative with muted colored fabrics and sliding glass doors that open onto a balcony or terrace. A full
breakfast is served in your room. Evenings can begin or end with
drinks in the bar or lounge while international dishes are available in
the formal dining room. Casual poolside dining with nightly entertainment is an alternative. ⊠ *Box HM 1017, Hamilton HM DX,* ☎
441/293–1666; 800/355–6161 in U.S. and Canada; FAX *441/293–8935.
91 suites. Restaurant, bar, air-conditioning, pool, massage, 2 tennis
courts, exercise room, 2 beaches. AE, MC, V. BP, MAP.* ✎

$$$$ ⊞ **St. George's Club.** Within walking distance of King's Square in St.
George's, this residential resort and hotel adjoins an 18-hole golf
course designed by Robert Trent Jones. The sleek, three-story main building contains the lobby, business center, cottages, Tillie's Restaurant and
pub, and a convenience store where you can buy everything from
champagne to suntan lotion. The individually decorated cottage units,
set in more than 18 acres of grounds, are huge and sunny. Each has a
fully equipped kitchen with microwave, dishwasher, china, and glassware. Bathrooms are large; some have double tubs. ⊠ *Box GE 92, St.
George's GE BX,* ☎ *441/297–1200,* FAX *441/297–8003. 71 cottages.
Restaurant, bar, air-conditioning, 3 pools (1 heated), 18-hole golf
course, putting green, 3 tennis courts. AE, MC, V. EP.* ✎

$$$–$$$$ 🏠 **Fourways Inn.** This small luxury inn and cottage colony has a formal, sedate ambience. Centrally located, Fourways is about a five-minute walk from the ferry landing and a five-minute bus ride to south-shore beaches. The architecture is typically Bermudian. The main building is a former family home that dates from 1727, and each of the five cottages, set in a profusion of greenery and flowers, has a poolside suite and a deluxe upper-floor room. Marble floors and marble bathrooms are common throughout, as are plenty of fresh flowers; each room also has a balcony or terrace and large closets paneled with full-length mirrors. Perks include bathrobes and slippers. You receive a complimentary fruit basket on arrival, and homemade pastries and the morning paper are delivered daily to your door. All of the suite kitchens were redesigned in 2000 by top kitchen designer Russ Pizzuto of Romano Gatland. Fourways' award-winning restaurant has around 8,000 bottles in its wine cellar and 650 selections. ⊠ *Box PG 294, Paget PG BX,* ☎ *441/236–6517; 800/962–7654 in U.S.;* ℻ *441/236–5528. 11 cottage suites. Restaurant, bar, air-conditioning, minibars, kitchenettes, heated pool, business services. AE, MC, V. CP.*

Housekeeping Cottages and Apartments

$$$$ 🏠 **Grape Bay Cottages.** These two almost-identical cottages sit within a whistle of the soft sands of Grape Bay Beach. Beach Crest and Beach Home are two-bedroom cottages with open fireplaces, hardwood floors, phones, and full-size kitchens. The comfortable furnishings include king-size beds. You can't step directly from door to beach, but the stroll down takes little more than two minutes. This is a very quiet, secluded location, ideal for beach lovers who like to cook, shift for themselves, and do serious sand-and-surf time. The cottages are a bit costly for one couple, but for two couples sharing expenses this is an eminently affordable choice. The beach house of the American consulate is right next door to Beach Home. A grocery store and cycle shop are nearby. ⊠ *Box HM 1851, Hamilton HM HX,* ☎ *441/296–0563; 800/ 637–4116 in U.S.;* ℻ *441/296–0563. 2 cottages. Air-conditioning, kitchenettes. AE, MC, V. EP.*

$$$–$$$$ 🏠 **Marley Beach Cottages.** Scenes from the films *Chapter Two* and *The Deep* were filmed here, and it's easy to see why. The setting is breathtaking. Near Astwood Park, on the south shore, the resort sits high on a cliff overlooking a private beach, stunning coastline, and dramatic reefs. A long path leads down to the sand and the sea. If you plan to stay here, pack light. There are a lot of steep steps. The price is hefty for one couple, but Marley Beach is excellent for two couples vacationing together. Each cottage contains a suite and a studio apartment, which can be rented separately or together. Some furnishings could benefit from modernization, but all accommodations have large sunny rooms, superb ocean views, private porches or patios, phones, and fully equipped kitchens with microwave and coffeemaker. The Heaven's Above and Seasong deluxe suites are spacious, and each has two wood-burning fireplaces. You can have groceries delivered, and there is daily maid service. If you're a pet lover, the resort's namesake—Marley, a pretty tabby cat—might keep you company. ⊠ *Box PG 278, Paget PG BX,* ☎ *441/236–1143 ext. 42; 800/637–4116 in U.S.;* ℻ *441/236– 1984. 6 studios, 4 suites, 3 executive suites. Air-conditioning, pool, hot tub, beach, snorkeling, fishing, baby-sitting. AE, MC, V. EP.*

$$$ 🏠 **Clear View Suites & Villas.** These spacious north-shore waterfront suites and villas offer breathtaking ocean views and quiet seclusion. One- to four-bedroom units are available; all units have kitchenettes and living and dining areas. The decor is modern, with carefully chosen fabrics and tasteful wooden furniture. If you don't want to cook,

Clear View's delightful clifftop Landfall Restaurant, designed with a mix of British colonial and Bermudian architecture, offers hearty breakfast, lunch, dinner, and Sunday brunch. The property is ideally located for walkers, who can take advantage of one of the most attractive coastal stretches of the Bermuda Railway Trail. Special packages such as the Learn and Leisure or Educational Focus programs incorporate field trips, museum visits, and local history and art. A conference room is available and maid service is included. ⊠ *Sandy Lane, Hamilton Parish CR 02,* ☎ *441/293–0484; 800/468–9600 in U.S.;* FAX *441/293–0267. 12 apartments. Restaurant, air-conditioning, pool, tennis, snorkeling, coin laundry, business services. AE, DC, MC, V. EP.*

$$$ 🏨 **Munro Beach Cottages.** Seclusion and privacy are the key words at this small group of cottages spread over five acres at Whitney Bay on the western end of the south shore. A beautiful palm-fringed beach is the view from the duplex cottages hidden away behind one of Bermuda's (and maybe the world's) most picturesque golf courses, Port Royal. What these cottages lack in facilities (there is no club room, restaurant, or activities provided) they make up for in stunning sunsets and tranquility. All standard units have a king-size bed or two twin beds and a double sofa bed and can accommodate up to four people. All have fully equipped kitchens, telephones, TVs, radios, and in-room safes, although some of the furnishings are a little dated. Barbecues are available and daily maid service is included. The resort is a 20-minute walk across the golf course to the nearest South Shore Road bus stop, so a moped is recommended for this location. ⊠ *Box SN 99, Southampton SN BX,* ☎ *441/234–1175,* FAX *441/234–3528. 9 cottages. Air-conditioning, kitchenettes, beach, fishing. AE, DC, MC, V. EP.*

$$$ 🏨 **Ocean Terrace.** Perched on top of "Scenic Heights," these self-contained studios enjoy spectacular all-round panoramic views of the island and ocean. The four spacious and modern units are well maintained. Each has a queen bed, sofa, full kitchen with dishwasher, private entrance and veranda, and cable TV. A roll-out bed can be arranged. Situated in a residential area, Ocean Terrace has views of the south and north shores and is well located for beaches. A five-minute walk to the bottom of the hill will bring you to Horseshoe Bay and the South Shore Road bus goes into Hamilton (a 30-minute ride) or toward Dockyard in the other direction. This traditional Bermudian coral-colored property, with a whitewashed roof and white shutters, has been owner-occupied for more than 20 years. There is a small pool and terrace dotted with tables, chairs, and sun loungers. ⊠ *Box SN 501, Southampton SN BX,* ☎ *441/238–0019; 800/637–4116 in U.S.;* FAX *441/238–4673. 4 apartments. Air-conditioning, pool, coin laundry. AE, MC, V. EP.*

$$$ 🏨 **Rosemont.** This modern family-owned hilltop complex of nearly 50 units was the first to corner Bermuda's self-catering niche, and it's not hard to see why. Ideally located a stone's throw from the capital, ferries, shops, and restaurants, these poolside or garden units are set in a quiet residential area with excellent views of Hamilton Harbour and the Great Sound. Units comprise bedroom, sitting area, kitchen, full bathroom, and private entrance and are simply but attractively decorated. Each has its own private patio or balcony. A recent expansion added three new penthouse suites with panoramic views, balconies, and whirlpools. ⊠ *Box HM 37, Hamilton HM AX,* ☎ *441/292–1055,* FAX *441/295–3913. 44 self-catering units, 3 penthouse suites. Air-conditioning, kitchenettes, in-room data ports, pool. No credit cards. EP.* ✎

$$–$$$ 🏨 **Angel's Grotto.** Some 30 years ago, this was a swinging nightclub
★ and one of the hottest spots on Bermuda. It's now a quiet residential apartment house on the south shore of Harrington Sound. Proprietor Helene Hart and her hardworking staff have won top Department of Tourism honors four years running for these charmingly decorated, im-

maculately maintained flats. Rooms have cable TVs, radios, phones, and fully equipped kitchens. There is no beach, but the pink sands of John Smith's Bay, on the south shore, are a five-minute walk away. Most guests are couples. The secluded Honeymoon Cottage is particularly appealing if you want privacy. The two-bedroom, two-bath apartment in the main house is a good buy for two couples traveling together. The large patio is ideal for cocktails, and there is also a barbecue. Deepwater swimming is available in Harrington Sound. ✉ *Box HS 81, Smith's HSG BX,* ☎ *441/293–1986; 800/550–6288 in U.S.;* FAX *441/236–1984. 7 apartments. Air-conditioning, kitchenettes. AE, MC, V. EP.*

$$–$$$ ⌂ **Paraquet Guest Apartments.** These apartments (pronounced "parakeet") have an ideal location—a five-minute walk from Elbow Beach, five minutes to Hamilton by moped, and a short walk to the grocery store. Good for cost-conscious travelers, rooms are spartan but spacious, sunny, and spick-and-span. Nine of the units have kitchenettes, the rest have refrigerators and coffeemakers. Ask for a higher unit to enjoy inland views and a private patio. Efficiency units have full baths, the others have showers only. A swimming pool on the adjacent property is available to guests 10–4 daily. Telephones cost $2.50 per day extra. The fine restaurants at Horizons & Cottages (☞ Cottage Colonies, *above*) and the Stonington Beach Hotel (☞ Small Hotels, *above*) are within walking distance. ✉ *Box PG 173, Paget PG BX,* ☎ *441/236–5842,* FAX *441/236–1665. 12 rooms. Restaurant, air-conditioning. No credit cards. EP.*

$$–$$$ ⌂ **Sky Top Cottages.** This aptly named hilltop property has spectacu-
★ lar views of the island's southern coastline and the azure ocean beyond. Runners and walkers will appreciate their proximity to Elbow Beach, one of Bermuda's best stretches of sand for a workout. Neat, sloping lawns and carefully tended gardens with sun loungers and paved walks provide a pleasant setting for studios and one-bedroom apartments. Owners John and Andrea Flood refurbish the properties annually. The individually decorated units have attractive prints and carefully coordinated colors. Studios have shower baths, and one-bedrooms have full baths. The very private one-bedroom Frangipani apartment is furnished in white wicker and rattan and has an eat-in kitchen, a king-size bed, and a sofa bed. All units have good kitchenette facilities, phones, and cable TVs. Barbecue grills are available. ✉ *Box PG 227, Paget PG BX,* ☎ *441/236–7984,* FAX *441/232–0446. 11 apartments. Air-conditioning, kitchenettes, volleyball. MC, V. EP.* ❧

$$–$$$ ⌂ **Valley Cottages & Apartments.** These pretty, informal Bermuda cottages and apartments are perfect for beach lovers, with one of the island's top stretches of sand—Elbow Beach—a short walk away. Choose from modern self-contained studio apartments or a larger one-bedroom cottage suite that can house up to four guests. The units are set in three attractive and traditional pink buildings. Palm trees and lush greenery surround the property. Most apartments have an accompanying patio or garden area and all have kitchens or kitchenettes, phones, and cable TVs. There is also a peaceful sun terrace and spa pool set in a secluded area. Guests also have the use of the tennis courts at the Harmony Club (☞ Small Hotels, *above*). ✉ *Box PG 173, Paget PG BX,* ☎ *441/236–0628; 800/637–4116 in U.S.;* FAX *441/236–3895. 9 apartments. Air-conditioning, pool. AE, MC, V. EP.*

$–$$$ ⌂ **Brightside Guest Apartments.** This attractive property with verandas overlooking picture-postcard Flatts inlet combines great views with good local amenities in the village. Ideal for an informal and relaxing vacation, these nine fully equipped housekeeping apartments are moments from the Bermuda Aquarium, Museum & Zoo. The newly built two-floor cottage is the most spacious. All rooms are clean and modern. There is no beach but guests can enjoy the patio and huge pool. Brightside is 15 minutes by bus from Hamilton and also well located for a visit to historic St. George's about 25 minutes away by bus. ✉ *Box FL 319, Flatts FL 07,* ☎ *441/292–8410,* ℻ *441/295–6968. 9 apartments. Air-conditioning, pool. No credit cards. EP.*

$$ ⌂ **Astwood Cove.** Set on terraced orchards across the road from the south shore's Astwood Park, these gleaming white apartments are a boon for beach-loving budget travelers. Guests have access to the south-shore beaches nearby and a good smattering of restaurants within a 2-mi radius. Standard and superior studios and suites have either a full kitchen or a microwave and refrigerator, the poolside rooms are a favorite with families, and the upstairs suites offer excellent value with views over Astwood Park and sea glimpses. Rooms are spanking clean, with whitewashed walls, and wicker and rattan furnishings. There are no TVs apart from the communal one in the barbecue pavilion, but each apartment has a phone. Bathrooms have showers only, but they do have heated towel racks. There are barbecue grills as well as a coin-operated laundry room and sauna (at extra charge). Guests can help themselves to the fruits of the orchard: grapefruit, loquats, peaches, and bananas. ✉ *49 South Rd., Warwick WK 07,* ☎ *441/236–0984,* ℻ *441/236–1164. 20 housekeeping apartments. Air-conditioning, pool. No credit cards. EP.*

$$ ⌂ **Barnsdale Guest Apartments.** Budget travelers who want to be near south-shore beaches and the Hamilton ferry should consider the small apartments in this two-story, terra-cotta house. On the bus route in a residential neighborhood and close to a grocery store, the apartments are set in a garden with an orchard of loquat, banana, and peach trees—all of whose fruits you are encouraged to sample. Barnsdale treats couples to every seventh night free. All apartments are neat and clean efficiencies, each with a private entrance. Rooms are tastefully decorated, annually spruced-up, and sleep up to four guests. Each has an iron and an ironing board. An outdoor barbecue gives you a chance to enjoy those balmy Bermuda nights. ✉ *Box DV 628, Devonshire DV BX,* ☎ *441/236–0164,* ℻ *441/236–4709. 7 efficiency studio apartments. Air-conditioning, fans, kitchenettes, pool. AE, MC, V. EP.* ✍

$$ ⌂ **Dawkins Manor.** These homey but modern housekeeping apartments tucked away in the rural lanes of Paget enjoy an idyllic garden setting. The friendly and informal atmosphere ensures you will get a taste of real Bermuda life here. The six attractively decorated apartments have private patios, modern bathrooms, cable TVs, clock radios, and phones. Units without kitchens have king-size beds, refrigerator, a hot pot for drinks, and some dishes. The apartments are well located for south-shore beaches, shops and restaurants, and cycle rentals. Hamilton is 10 minutes away by bus. There's good disabled access. ✉ *Box PG 34, Paget PG BX,* ☎ *441/236–7419,* ℻ *441/236–7088. 6 apartments. Air-conditioning, in-room data ports, in-room VCRs, pool, coin laundry, business services. AE, MC, V. EP.*

$$ ⌂ **Garden House.** Hospitable owner and manager Rosanne Galloway will make sure you feel at home at her beautiful harborside Bermudian property. Set in the Somerset Bridge area, in the West End, you can choose from a studio, a one-bedroom cottage with separate living room and kitchen, or a two-bedroom cottage with a huge living room that leads to a separate kitchen. Beds are either kings or two twins, but in the larger cottage there is an antique four-poster. All rooms have phones and kitchens. Living rooms are furnished in British country-house style with some Bermudian cedar furniture pieces. All units have patios where you can sit in a traditional Bermudian garden setting. A stroll to the end of the lawn will lead you onto Elys Harbour where deepwater swimming is possible. Children under 12 stay free. Maid service included daily. ✉ *4 Middle Rd., Sandys SB 01,* ☎ *441/234–1435,* ℻ *441/234–*

3006. 5 apartments. Air-conditioning, kitchenettes, no-smoking rooms, pool. AE, MC, V. Closed December through February. EP.

$$ ▦ **Greenbank Cottages.** On a quiet lane less than a minute's walk from the Salt Kettle ferry landing, these single-story cottages nestle among tall trees next to Hamilton Harbour. They're small and family-oriented rather than grand, but they come with plenty of personal attention from the Ashton family. The lounge in the 200-year-old main house has hardwood floors, a TV, and a grand piano. There are four units with kitchens in the main house. All other units are self-contained, with kitchens, private entrances, and shaded verandas. Only two have breakfast included in the rate. The waterside cottages are the best, especially Salt Winds. The harbor views from the bed, dining table, and kitchen are lovely. Rooms are simply furnished. There is a private dock for deepwater swimming, and the beaches are less than 10 minutes away by taxi or moped. One of the island's best water-sports operators—Salt Kettle Yacht Charters (☞ Participant Sports *in* Chapter 7)—is on the property. ⊠ *Box PG 201, Paget PG BX,* ☎ *441/236–3615; 800/637–4116 in U.S.;* FAX *441/236–2427. 3 rooms, 8 apartments. Air-conditioning, kitchenettes, dock. AE, MC, V. CP, EP.* ☙

$$ ▦ **La Casa Del Masa.** Set high on a hill with panoramic views of the north shore and the Great Sound, these three attractive units are a cozy find for a relaxing getaway close to the capital. The self-contained apartments are decorated with modern tables and chairs, and fully equipped kitchens include microwaves. All units have a private entrance, two double beds, cable TV, and phone. If you want to combine great views with proximity to Bermuda's best shops, then this accommodation is ideal. Hamilton is a short walk away, as are bus stops and grocery stores. You can round off a hard day's shopping with a soak in the outdoor whirlpool. Tennis and golf can be arranged. ⊠ *Box HM 2494, Hamilton HM GX,* ☎ *441/292–8726; 800/637–4116 in U.S.;* FAX *441/295–4447. 3 apartments. Air-conditioning, pool. AE, MC, V. EP.*

$$ ▦ **Mazarine by the Sea.** These cozy efficiencies perched on the water's edge a mile from Hamilton are ideal for couples on a budget. Six of the seven apartments have ocean views. Each has a bedroom, bathroom, kitchenette, and small patio or balcony overlooking gardens and sea. All have phones and TVs (but not cable). The whitewashed rooms are clean and well maintained. There is no beach, but there is deepwater swimming and good reef snorkeling at the doorstep. Those who are not strong swimmers can use the pool overlooking the sea. A grocery store and bus stops are a short walk away. ⊠ *Box HM 91, Hamilton HM AX,* ☎ *441/292–1659,* FAX *441/292–6891. 7 apartments. Air-conditioning, kitchenettes, pool, snorkeling, fishing. AE, MC, V. EP.* ☙

$$ ▦ **Robin's Nest.** Tucked away in its own valley in a residential area off the North Shore Road, this is a real find for those who like to cook for themselves and enjoy true garden tranquility. All apartments are spacious and modern and have kitchens. Three of the four open onto lush, intimate gardens. Units have cable TVs and phones. The small number of rooms means you are more than likely to enjoy the good-size pool and patio all to yourself. There is only one elevated apartment, which has sea views from its small rooftop patio. Repeat guests and business travelers alike enjoy the proximity to Hamilton, Admiralty Park, and snorkeling on the north shore. ⊠ *10 Vale Close, Pembroke West HM 04,* ☎ *441/292–4347. 4 apartments. Air-conditioning, in-room safes, kitchenettes, pool. No credit cards. EP.*

$$ ▦ **Sandpiper Apartments.** These spacious, simple, cheerfully decorated apartments in Warwick parish are ideally located for south-shore beaches and bus routes. The 14 whitewashed units include five one-bedroom apartments and nine studios. Most can accommodate up to four people, and all have balconies or patios, radios and cable TVs.

Tiled floors and bold floral-print curtains and bedspreads predominate. Situated on the main South Road and Hamilton bus route (a 15- to 20-minute bus ride into town), Sandpiper is set in lush gardens with a pool and whirlpool. There is a restaurant within walking distance, and guests can use the nearby beach and bar at Surf Side Beach Club (☞ Small Hotels, *above*). All units have a full kitchen with microwave and dining area and full bath. Daily maid service is included. ✉ *Box HM 685, Hamilton HM CX,* ☎ *441/236–7093,* ℻ *441/236–3898. 14 apartments. Air-conditioning, kitchenettes, pool, hot tub, coin laundry. AE, MC, V. EP.*

$$ 🖬 **Syl-Den.** These well-located guest apartments are an affordable option for the budget-minded beach lover who wants a place near the south shore. Set back on a hill from the South Shore Road, Syl-Den is a 5- to 10-minute walk to Warwick Long Bay and minutes by bus to Horseshoe Bay and the other beaches. It takes about 25 minutes to reach Hamilton by bus. Most of the spacious rooms have tiled floors and are clean but simply decorated. Each unit has cable TV, phone, bath and shower, and full kitchen. Three have a private patio or garden. Guests can also take advantage of a large pool and small sun terrace. ✉ *8 Warwickshire Estate, Warwick WK 02,* ☎ *441/238–1834,* ℻ *441/238– 3205. 12 apartments. Air-conditioning, in-room safes, kitchenettes, pool, coin laundry. AE, MC, V. EP.*

$$ 🖬 **Whale Bay Inn.** If peaceful, uncrowded beaches are your penchant, make a beeline for this inn. Whale Bay Park and Beach are a short walk away and the beaches at Church Bay (with some of Bermuda's best snorkeling), Horseshoe Bay, and Somerset Long Bay are easily reached by moped. Ocean views, a rolling lawn, and pretty flower beds are the setting for this pink Bermuda-style lodging, which is next to the beautiful Port Royal Golf Course (☞ Participant Sports *in* Chapter 7). The attractive guest rooms are modern and well-maintained. All five ground-floor units have a separate bedroom, phone, cable TV, and private entrance. Four of the five have a double and a single bed. One has a double bed and a sofa bed. The small kitchens have microwaves, two-burner stoves, refrigerators, coffeemakers, and cutlery. The two end units have larger bathrooms and are better for families. ✉ *Box SN 544, Southampton SN BX,* ☎ *441/238–0469,* ℻ *441/238–1224. 5 apartments. Air-conditioning, kitchenettes, beach. No credit cards. EP.* 🐾

$–$$ 🖬 **Clairfont Apartments.** These clean and quiet apartments perched on a hill close to the south-shore beaches offer excellent value for money. The six spacious one-bedroom apartments and two studios are simply decorated, and all have fully equipped kitchens, phones, radios, and TVs (cable is an extra $2 per day). Daily maid service is included. The four sunny upstairs units have balconies and lovely views across the valley toward the south shore. Downstairs apartments have patios leading onto a communal lawn. Children are welcome and can take advantage of a good playground that's a five-minute walk away and the use of Clairfont's new pool area. Cheap monthly off-season rates start from $1,000. Early booking is advised. ✉ *Box WK 85, Warwick WK 02,* ☎ *441/238–0149,* ℻ *441/238–3503. 8 apartments. Air-conditioning, kitchenettes, pool. AE, MC, V. EP.*

$–$$ 🖬 **Glenmar Holiday Apartments.** These are informal self-catering apartments offering value to travelers who want beaches, buses, and shops at their doorstep. Just off of the main South Shore Road, Glenmar is two minutes from bus stops (it's a 10-minute ride to Hamilton), a five-minute moped or bus ride from the south-shore beaches, and virtually next door to a grocery store and a branch of a leading department store—Trimingham's (☞ Department Stores *in* Chapter 8). Set in a residential area, the units are housed in a pale-green private Bermudian house. The self-contained budget efficiencies can accommodate two people. There are also two larger, more expensive cottage suites, one of which can sleep three to four people. All apartments have kitchens, cable TV, and phones. There is also a well-kept lawn with table, chairs, and sun loungers. ✉ *Box PG 151, Paget PG BX,* ☎ *441/236–2844,* FAX *441/236–7888. 5 apartments. Air-conditioning, kitchenettes. AE, MC, V. EP.*

$–$$ **Marula Apartments.** Spacious grounds on the water's edge of Mills Creek in Pembroke Parish make an idyllic setting for these apartments. The hustle and bustle of Hamilton may seem miles away while you're lounging by the pool overlooking the ocean, but in fact it's just a five-minute bus ride into town. There are five housekeeping units and a two-bedroom self-contained cottage. All accommodations are comfortable and roomy, with separate bedrooms, phones, cable TV, and ceiling fans as well as air-conditioning. Marula is also good for walks in nearby Admiralty House Park and only a stone's throw from Clarence Cove where you can sunbathe or swim. All apartments have full kitchens, and microwaves are available on request. ✉ *Box HM 576, Hamilton HM CX,* ☎ *441/295–2893; 800/637–4116 in U.S.;* FAX *441/292–3985. 6 apartments. Air-conditioning, fans, kitchenettes, pool, laundry service. AE, MC, V. EP.*

$ **Burch's Guest Apartments.** Panoramic views over the north shore make this property a good value for those wanting views and a central location. This smart-looking whitewashed house with red shutters is situated right in the middle of the island, set on the main North Shore Road in a residential area. Hamilton is a five-minute bus ride away, and there is a small grocery store within walking distance. Units are basically furnished, but all have kitchenettes, phones, and cable TV. The most spacious of the five units is at the front of the building and has the best views of the ocean. Three beds make it ideal for families with small children. The four smaller units have twin beds. Studios 6 and 7 have sea glimpses. There is a small garden at the back of the building with a pool. ✉ *110 North Shore Rd., Devonshire FL 03,* ☎ *441/292–5746. 5 apartments. Air-conditioning, kitchenettes, pool. No credit cards. EP.*

$ **Serendipity.** These two studio guest apartments tucked away in a residential area in Paget offer some of the best value on the island. They are part of the family residence of Albert and Judy Corday, and guests staying here have use of the owners' large family pool and benefit from a flat rate with no tax (an exemption applies to properties accommodating up to 5 people). Both ground-floor apartments are clean and pleasantly decorated. They have fully equipped kitchenettes, bathrooms with showers only, TVs (no cable), phones, and small private patios. One unit has a queen-size bed with a love seat sofa bed while the other has two single beds. There is no view, but a 15-minute walk will take you to Elbow Beach. It's a stone's throw from two grocery stores, a take-out restaurant, pharmacy, beauty parlor, dry cleaners, and vegetable stand. A bus stop is located just outside the front gate. There is maid service included Monday, Wednesday, and Friday mornings if required. ✉ *6 Rural Dr., Paget PG 06,* ☎ *441/236–1192,* FAX *441/232–0010. 2 studio apartments. Air-conditioning, kitchenettes, no-smoking rooms, pool, laundry service. No credit cards. EP.*

$ **Sound View Cottage.** This Bermudian cottage with three housekeeping apartments is set in an elevated residential area overlooking the Great Sound. All rooms are tastefully decorated and have full kitchen facilities. The cottage also has a pool, patio, and barbecue and is very convenient to the south-shore beaches. The winner of the Hospitality Professionals Association Sunshine Award in 2000, the cottage has enviable views of both the south shore and Great Sound. ✉ *9 Bowe La.,*

Southampton SN 04, ☎ 441/238–0064. 3 rooms. Air-conditioning, kitchenettes, pool. No credit cards. EP.

Guest Houses/Bed & Breakfasts

$$$ ▦ **Oxford House.** This elegant Bermuda-style town house is a five-minute
★   walk from the capital's shops, ferries, and buses. The family-owned
and -operated two-story establishment, recipient of the Department of
Tourism's highest award in its category for four years running, is pop-
ular with business travelers as well as tourists. It is an excellent choice
for shoppers, too. Polished cedar-wood floors, a fireplace, and hand-
some Chippendale chairs lend warmth and class to the breakfast room,
where you can sample scones, English muffins, fresh fruit, boiled eggs,
and cereal each morning. The bright, airy rooms (doubles, triples, and
quads) are individually decorated with bold fabrics, whitewashed
walls, and some with antique furniture. A small bookcase in the up-
stairs hall is crammed with paperbacks that you're welcome to bor-
row. ⊠ *Box HM 374, Hamilton HM BX, ☎ 441/295–0503; 800/548–
7758 in U.S.; 800/272–2306 in Canada; ℻ 441/295–0250. Breakfast
room, air-conditioning, laundry service. AE, MC, V. CP.* ✑

$$–$$$ ▦ **Aunt Nea's Inn at Hillcrest.** This truly enchanting inn is one of
★   Bermuda's coziest, most romantic getaways. Tasteful decor and attention
to detail has transformed this charming 18th-century house into more
of an experience than a lodging. The crowning glory of each of the 11
individually decorated rooms are the first-class beds. From handsome
oak canopy four-posters to wicker sleigh beds, each one is a work of
art. A new suite will have a fantastic wrought-iron Corsican designed
bed, a living room with open fireplace, and access to the public bal-
cony that overlooks a lawn and the waters of St. George's. A Conti-
nental breakfast buffet is enjoyed family style at a large communal table.
Your enthusiastic hosts, Delaey Robinson and Andrea Dismont, will
give new guests a tour of the property. Available for 2001 will be a
sauna, exercise room, and four new self-catering suites and a cottage
opposite the inn—ideal for families. Aunt Nea's, nestled in the historic
town of St. George's, is about 45 minutes from Hamilton by bus.
Nearby Tobacco Bay Beach and the adjoining secluded coves have good
snorkeling. The St. George's golf course is almost within putting dis-
tance. ⊠ *Box GE 96, St. George's GE BX, ☎ 441/297–1630, ℻ 441/
297–1908. 10 rooms, 1 suite, 1 cottage, 4 apartments. Breakfast room,
lounge, air-conditioning, refrigerators. AE, MC, V. CP.* ✑

$$ ▦ **Edgehill Manor.** Atop a high hill surrounded by gardens and shrubs,
this large colonial house is easy walking distance from Hamilton and
less than 15 minutes by moped from the best south-shore beaches. The
welcoming staff are attentive and add to the cozy feel. In the morning
you can feast on home-baked muffins and scones in the cheery breakfast room. The guest rooms, which are individually decorated with French
provincial furniture and colorful quilted bedspreads, have large windows and terraces, and benefit from recent bathroom upgrades. There's
a large poolside room with a kitchen that's suitable for families. All
rooms have cable TV. If you're traveling alone on a tight budget, ask
for the small ground-level room with a kitchen and private terrace. ⊠
*Box HM 1048, Hamilton HM EX, ☎ 441/295–7124, ℻ 441/295–
3850. 9 rooms. Breakfast room, air-conditioning, in-room safes, refrigerators, pool. No credit cards. CP.*

$$ ▦ **Greene's Guest House.** Set in the quiet western end of Southamp-
ton Parish on part of the Bermuda Railway Trail, this family-run guest
house is a tranquil retreat with beautiful views of the Great Sound. All
rooms are clean and modern, and each has a refrigerator, coffeemaker,
cable TV, VCR, radio, and phone. There is a breakfast room, spacious

lounge, and a large swimming pool at the back of the house with lovely views over Jennings Bay and the ocean. Greene's is a two-minute walk to bus stops on the main Middle Road for south-shore beaches (it's a five-minute ride). Hamilton is 30 minutes away. Port Royal Golf Course (☞ Participant Sports *in* Chapter 7) and moped hire can be reached in minutes by bus, and it is just a short walk to the Golf Academy where you can practice your technique. A full breakfast is included. ⊠ *Box SN 395, Southampton SN BX,* ☎ *441/238–0834,* ℻ *441/238– 8980. 6 rooms. Breakfast room, lounge, air-conditioning, in-room VCRs, refrigerators, pool. No credit cards. BP.*

$$ 🏠 **Little Pomander Guest House.** In a quiet residential area on Hamil-
★ ton Harbour, the Little Pomander is a find if you're seeking affordable accommodation near the capital. The rooms, in a charming waterside cottage, are decorated with plump, pastel comforters and coordinated fabrics. All units have microwaves, phones, refrigerators, and cable TV. Guests congregate at sunset on the waterside lawn to enjoy views of Hamilton Harbour and often stay to cook dinner on the barbecue grill. For a $10 fee you can play tennis across the road at the Pomander Tennis Club. Continental breakfast is served in a sunny room. ⊠ *Box HM 384, Hamilton HM BX,* ☎ *441/236–7635,* ℻ *441/236–8332. 5 rooms. Air-conditioning, refrigerators. AE, MC, V. CP.*

$$ 🏠 **Loughlands Guest House & Cottage.** This stately white mansion has seen grander days, but it still retains a charm and character accessible to the budget traveler. Set in spacious grounds above the South Shore Road, this 1920 house is loaded with fine antiques and European china. Lladro figurines grace the mantelpiece in the formal parlor, antique grandfather clocks stand in corners, and handsome breakfronts display Wedgwood china and Baccarat and Waterford crystal. Less than a five-minute walk from Elbow Beach, this guest house offers a Continental breakfast of cereals, fruit juice, prunes, croissants, Danishes, and coffee. The economical guest rooms tend to be somewhat worn, but most have large, comfortable chairs and cotton bedspreads. Singles, doubles, triples, and quads are available, and a large cottage near the main house has additional rooms. ⊠ *79 South Rd., Paget PG 03,* ☎ *441/236–1253. 18 rooms with bath, 6 with shared bath. Air-conditioning, pool, tennis court. No credit cards. CP.*

$$ 🏠 **Royal Heights Guest House.** This charming guest house has views of Gibbs Hill Lighthouse and the fantastic panorama of the Great Sound. Guests enjoy breathtaking sunsets in the spacious, carpeted living room or by the pool. The rooms are large, each with private entrance, big windows, and a terrace. While all rooms benefit from great views, numbers 3 and 6 are popular for their overlooks of the Great Sound. Pastel colors, with matching drapes and quilted spreads in good-quality fabrics, give rooms a fresh feel, and there is ample closet space. Room number 5, with its double bed and daybed, is good for families. All rooms have cable TVs and two have microwaves. Breakfast includes pastries, muffins, fruit, and sometimes egg dishes. Special honeymoon packages are available. The Fairmont Southampton Princess's golf course (☞ Resort Hotels, *above*) and some of the island's finest dining are within walking distance. ⊠ *Box SN 144, Southampton SN BX,* ☎ *441/238–0043,* ℻ *441/238–8445. 7 rooms. Air-conditioning, refrigerators, saltwater pool. AE, MC, V. CP.*

$ 🏠 **Salt Kettle House.** Set behind a screen of palm trees on a bay ad-
★ joining Hamilton Harbour, only a quick walk from the Hamilton ferry, this small, secluded guest house is a gem for the budget traveler looking for the best of British hospitality. Just left of the entrance is a cozy lounge with a fireplace where guests gather for cocktails and conversation. A hearty English breakfast is served family style in the dining room, which has water views. The main house has two guest rooms

and an adjoining apartment has a bedroom, bathroom, living room, and kitchen. The best accommodations are in the four waterside cottages that have shaded patios and lounge chairs, bedrooms, sitting rooms, and kitchens. Guest rooms are small but well-kept and the decor is charming. The owner, Hazel Lowe, makes improvements every year. You can swim in a cove nearby. ⊠ *10 Salt Kettle Rd., Paget PG 01,* ☎ *441/236–0407,* FAX *441/236–8639. 3 rooms in main house, 4 cottages. Lounge, air-conditioning. No credit cards. BP.*

6 NIGHTLIFE AND THE ARTS

This relatively small island has a surprisingly diverse cultural scene. A lively dance community, talented local painters and musicians, and sophisticated nightclubs all contribute to Bermuda's recent cultural renaissance. With three major festivals—film, jazz, and performing arts—and countless parish cultural activities, this mid-Atlantic island is definitely a happening place.

NIGHTLIFE

Updated by
Ron Bernthal

Because Bermuda has no casinos and only a few nightclubs, you'll find most of the action in pubs, lounges, hotel bars, and local hangouts. Some places close in the off season, so check *This Week in Bermuda* and *Preview of Bermuda,* free publications available in all hotels and tourist-information centers, for the latest information. As a general rule, men should wear a jacket and tie to clubs. For women the dress code is casual chic. Pubs and clubs begin to fill up around 9:30 or 10.

The music scene is dominated by local bands playing the island's hotel and pub circuits. Outside performers are billed occasionally, particularly during the **Bermuda Festival** (☞ The Arts, *below*). The island's longtime superstar, **Gene Steede**—a guitarist, singer, and comedian who has been described as Tony Bennett, Harry Belafonte, and Johnny Carson rolled into one—can usually be found, with his band, at the airport arrivals hall greeting visitors with bouncy island music. He also appears at some private island functions. Try for an invitation if you can. Other popular entertainers to seek out are the **Coca-Cola Steel Band** and the **Bermuda Strollers. Sharx** is a rock band, heard at many conventions and private parties, and the **Travellers** straddle country and rock, although they don't perform as often as they used to.

A band that has been around a few years, but is just now getting the recognition it deserves, is **The Kennel Boys,** who perform at The Oasis. **Tropical Heat,** with a reggae/calypso/soca/Latin sound, is a regular at Hawkins Island's "Don't Stop the Carnival Show." Some of the Bermuda bands list their performance dates and venues on a Web site at www.bermuda.com.

Around 3 AM, when bars and clubs close, head for the **Ice Queen** (✉ Middle Rd., Paget, ☎ 441/236–3136). It's like a drive-in movie without the movie. The parking lot is just jammed with cars and mopeds. The main attraction is the $2.75 burgers, which taste terrific after a night on the town. Order them from the take-out window and head for the beach, where drunk and disorderly crowds won't bother you. The Ice Queen opens at 11 AM, which also makes it a good stop for an ice-cream break.

As the name indicates, **After Hours** (✉ 117 South Rd., past intersection with Middle Rd., Paget, ☎ 441/236–8563) is another late-night spot. It opens at midnight and serves good curries, hamburgers, and sandwiches until 4 AM.

Bars and Lounges

Hamilton

Casey's (✉ Queen St. across from the Little Theatre, Hamilton, ☎ 441/293–9549). If you like to toss a few back in a hard-core bar, consider Casey's, a narrow room with a jukebox and a few tables. It's by no means fancy or touristy, and it really packs them in, especially on Friday nights. Casey's is open 10–10 every day except Sunday.

Coconut Rock (✉ 20 Reid St., Hamilton, ☎ 441/292–1043).With a trendy Bermudian restaurant on one level, and an even trendier sushi bar called Yashi in the back, this place is filled with music, good feelings, and Hamilton's young and beautiful. It's interesting and fun, and open daily for lunch and dinner (Sunday dinner only). Don't confuse this place with Coconuts, the upscale restaurant in Southampton parish.

Colony Pub (✉ The Princess, 76 Pitts Bay Rd., Hamilton, ☎ 441/295–3000). The Colony, where the lights are low and the piano music soft and soothing, is a popular meeting place for young professionals. This pub boasts a true Cuban cigar selection along with a martini bar and aged ports. There's live entertainment every night except Sunday, mostly jazz and blues. Dress is casual, and the atmosphere typical Bermudian.

Docksider (⊠ Front St., Hamilton, ☎ 441/292–4088). This Front Street pub attracts a mixed crowd of visitors and locals with a new sports-and-entertainment big-screen TV. If the activity at the long cedar bar is too noisy, opt for the wine bar, which is quieter and more intimate. A third section, the pool room, offers yet another environment. Docksider is open daily, and pub grub is served (☞ Hamilton & Environs *in* Chapter 4).

Flanagan's Irish Pub & Restaurant (⊠ 69 Front St., Hamilton, ☎ 441/295–8299). On the second floor of the Emporium Building, this pub run by Irishman Thomas Gallagher is a favorite for folks who like to dance and talk over drinks. Local groups entertain nightly after 10, and there's a giant TV screen for sporting events. Lots of exotic, fun drinks, like frozen mudslides, are on offer. It's open year-round, 10 AM to 1 AM.

Fresco's Wine Bar & Restaurant (⊠ 2 Chancery La., Hamilton, ☎ 441/295–5058). A great place for a bottle or glass of wine and some excellent desserts. Formerly the Chancery Wine Bar, Fresco's has enclosed the European-style patio for year-round use. Open daily for lunch, dinner, or drinks at the upstairs bar.

The Pickled Onion (⊠ 53 Front St., Hamilton, ☎ 441/295–2263). This restaurant and bar caters to a well-heeled crowd of locals and tourists. There's live music—usually jazz and pop—nightly 9:30 PM to 1 AM in the high season and irregularly off-season. Dress is casual smart, and reservations are taken but not required for dinner (☞ Hamilton & Environs *in* Chapter 4).

Robin Hood (⊠ Richmond St., Hamilton, ☎ 441/295–3314). Casual and friendly Robin Hood is popular at night for pub fare, pizza, and patio dining under the stars. Sporting events are shown on the main TV screen.

The Spinning Wheel (⊠ 33 Court St., Hamilton, ☎ 441/292–7799). This has been a favorite among locals for more than 30 years. There's a cocktail lounge with an outdoor pool and disco area. The bar is open noon to 3 AM, with happy hour 5 to 7.

Ye Olde Cock & Feather (⊠ 53 Front St., Hamilton, ☎ 441/295–2263). This bar draws both locals and travelers, has a happy hour Monday through Saturday from 5 to 7, live music Friday and Saturday nights, and a jam session on Sunday.

Outside Hamilton

Henry VIII (⊠ South Shore Rd., Southampton, ☎ 441/238–1977). There's always local or visiting entertainment at this ever-popular watering hole. The dark pub is decorated with rich oak paneling and polished brass, and the waitresses are attired in period garb. The bar serves a large assortment of English draft ales. A competent menu of English and Bermudian fare is also offered (☞ The Parishes *in* Chapter 4). All in all, a great speakeasy.

Neptune Club (⊠ South Shore Rd., Southampton, ☎ 441/238–8000). Located at the Southampton Princess Hotel, the Neptune Club gained its reputation thanks to British comedian-pianist Jimmy Keys, a Bermudian legend who, alas, moved to Miami recently. But no worries. Musician Irving Witter keeps customers happy in the lobby lounge and a new band, Exotique, is expected to maintain the Neptune Club's reputation. It's open nightly except Sunday.

Swizzle Inn (⊠ 3 Blue Hole Hill, Hamilton Parish, ☎ 441/293–1854, ✒). "Swizzle Inn, swagger out" is the motto at this watering hole catering to a young crowd. It comes with a dartboard, a jukebox that plays soft and hard rock, and business cards from all over the world tacked on the walls, ceilings, and doors. Food is also served (☞ The Parishes *in* Chapter 4). It's located in the Bailey's Bay area, between Hamilton and St. George's.

Wharf Tavern (⊠ Somers Wharf, St. George's, ☎ 441/297–1515). The yachting crowd gathers here for rum swizzling and nautical talk. There's also a moderately priced pub-style menu (☞ The Town of St. George *in* Chapter 4).

The Club Scene

Calypso

Clayhouse Inn (⊠ North Shore Rd., Devonshire, ☎ 441/292–3193). Both locals and visitors pack in here for a rowdy show starring limbo dancers, the Bermuda Strollers, the Coca-Cola Steel Band, and an occasional big name. Shows are at 10:15 Monday through Thursday. About $23 covers the entry fee plus two drinks. A range of entertainment is laid on for the weekend. Calypso bands from the Clayhouse Inn often entertain at the various hotels during high season.

Folk

The only folk-music venue is the **Bermuda Folk Club**'s monthly get-togethers, which usually take place at 8:15 on the first and third Saturday of the month at the Old Colony Club (⊠ Trott Rd., Hamilton, ☎ 441/293–9241). Local and visiting musicians provide the entertainment and cover any number of musical styles besides folk. Drinks have happy-hour prices, and the cover is $5.

Jazz

The **Bermuda Jazz Festival,** which celebrates its sixth year in 2001, kicks off each fall at the Royal Naval Dockyard, usually during a long weekend in September. Local and internationally known jazz artists pump out the tunes, and tickets go fast for this popular event. For schedule and performance information, contact Track Entertainment (⊠ 485 Madison Ave., New York, NY, 10022 ☎ 212/921–2100, FAX 212/921–2290). Tickets are available from TicketWeb (☎ 510/704–4448, FAX 510/649–9218, ✆).

Hubie's Bar (⊠ Angle St., Hamilton, ☎ 441/293–9287). Hubie's, located off Court Street, attracts jovial locals and visitors who appreciate good live jazz at a weekly session on Friday from 7 to 10 PM. It's best to take a cab. The area can be dangerous at night. There is no cover charge.

Nightclubs

The Club (⊠ Bermudiana Rd., Hamilton, ☎ 441/295–6693). At press time this popular Hamilton night spot was closed for renovation. Plans call for it to become a new restaurant/club. It had been a popular place for comfort, elegance, and dancing every night until the wee hours. Stop by and see what the place is offering.

The Oasis (⊠ Emporium Bldg., Front St., Hamilton, ☎ 441/292–4978 or 441/292–3379, ✆). A hot dance spot for rock and disco, The Oasis draws a somewhat younger crowd who gladly pay the $15 cover charge. In high season, there's dancing nightly from 9 PM to 3 AM; in low season, Thursday–Sunday. One of Bermuda's top bands, The Kennel Boys, plays on Tuesday, Wednesday, Friday, and Saturday nights, beginning at midnight.

THE ARTS

The Bermuda Department of Tourism and all of its Visitors Service Bureaus (☞ Visitor Information *in* Smart Travel Tips A to Z) give away the "Bermuda Calendar of Events" brochure. The informative *Bermuda* ($3.95), a quarterly magazine, describes upcoming island events and runs feature articles on how visitors can amuse themselves. The glossy monthly magazine *The Bermudian* ($4) also has a calendar of events. Some hotels carry a **TV station** that broadcasts a wealth of information about sightseeing, restaurants, cultural events, and nightlife on the island. **Radio VSB**, FM 1450, gives a lineup of events daily at 11:15 AM. Or you can **dial 974** for a phone recording with information on nature walks, tours, cultural events, afternoon teas, and seasonal events. The island is so small, however, that virtually everyone knows what's going on, so you won't have to do much research. Another good resource for meeting Bermuda musicians and songwriters, and to scout out local gigs, is the **Bermuda Songwriters Association** (⊠ Box HM 2857, Hamilton, HM LX, ☎ 441/BDA–SONG, ✎).

Because the arts scene in Bermuda is so casual, many of the events and performing groups listed below operate on a seasonal or part-time basis. If you see a bulletin board, inspect it for posters advertising upcoming events. **City Hall Theatre** (⊠ City Hall, Church St., Hamilton) is the major venue for a number of top-quality cultural events each year. Contact the **Box Office** (⊠ Visitors Service Bureau, ☎ 441/295–1727) for reservations and for information about all cultural events on the island. American Express, MasterCard, and Visa are accepted at the theater and the box office.

In January and February, the **Bermuda Festival** brings internationally renowned artists to the island. The two-month program includes theater and classical and jazz concerts. In 2000 the Bermuda Festival celebrated its 25th anniversary with a list of performers that included soloists from the Bolshoi Ballet, Cuban jazz pianist Chucho Valdes, the English Chamber Orchestra with Pinchas Zuckerman, and the American dance troupe Pilobolus. Most shows take place in City Hall, with additional "lunchtime" and "cocktail" concerts at various venues. Ticket prices range from $15 to $35. For information and reservations, contact Bermuda Festivals Ltd. (⊠ Suite 480, 48 Par-la-Ville Rd., Hamilton HM 11, ☎ 441/292–8572 Dec.–Feb.; 441/295–1291 Mar.–Nov.; ℻ 441/295–7403 Dec.–Feb.; 441/295–7403 Mar.–Nov., ✎) or the Bermuda Department of Tourism.

Debuting in 2000, the **The Festival Fringe** was designed to complement the annual Bermuda Festival. The Fringe, whose dates coincide with those of the Bermuda Festival, offers visitors an opportunity to enjoy smaller, more avant-garde performances by local and visiting artists. Schedules and ticket information is available from the Bermuda Department of Tourism in the United States or Bermuda, or from the Bermuda Department of Cultural Affairs (☎ 441/292–9447).

If you want to meet local painters and see some of their work, members of the **Bermuda Society of Arts** (⊠ Front St. W, Hamilton, ☎ 441/292–3824, ℻ 441/296–0699, ✎) will welcome you to the top floor of City Hall, the venue for exhibits of members' works. During the past 40-plus years, the society has grown into one of Bermuda's leading organizations supporting art-oriented activities.

Concerts

The **Beat Retreat Ceremony** and **Regimental Musical Display** are separate performances by the Bermuda Regiment Band and the Bermuda Isles Pipe Band with Dancers, arranged by the Bermuda Department of Tourism once or twice a month except in August. They perform on

Front Street in Hamilton, King's Square in St. George's, or the Royal Naval Dockyard on Ireland Island.

The **Bermuda Philharmonic Society** (✉ Box HM 552, Hamilton, ☎ 441/291–6690, 𝔽𝔸𝕏 441/295–3770), now in its 40th season, presents several programs throughout the year featuring both the full orchestra and various soloists. Students of the Menuhin Foundation, established in Bermuda by the late violin virtuoso Yehudi Menuhin, sometimes perform with the orchestra. Visiting musicians often participate in these events. Concerts take place in the Cathedral of the Most Holy Trinity in Hamilton (☞ Hamilton *in* Chapter 3), King's Square in St. George's, or at the Royal Naval Dockyard.

The **Gilbert & Sullivan Society of Bermuda** (✉ Box HM 3098, Hamilton, HM NX, ☎ 441/295–3218, 𝔽𝔸𝕏 441/295–6812), devoted to performing the works of Sir W. S. Gilbert and Sir Arthur Sullivan, began in 1972 under the name Warwick Players. The society puts on a musical each year, usually in October. In addition to Gilbert and Sullivan operettas, the group occasionally stages Broadway shows.

The **Bermuda Conservatory of Music** (✉ Colony Club, Trott Rd., Hamilton, ☎ 441/296–5100) was formed in 1997 by merging the two leading music schools. The BCM is now the largest music school on the island. Concerts are presented periodically during the academic year at various venues.

Dance

One of the many Bermuda Gombey troupes performs each week as part of the off-season (November–March) festivities organized by the Bermuda Department of Tourism. Gombey (pronounced "gum-bay") dancing is a blend of African, West Indian, and Caribbean Indian influences. The Gombey tradition in Bermuda dates from the mid-18th century, when costumed slaves celebrated Christmas by singing and marching through the streets. The masked male dancers move to the accompaniment of skin-covered drums and the shrill, whistle-blown commands of the troupe's captain. The ritualistic, often frenetic movements of the dancers, the staccato drum accompaniment, and the whistle commands are passed from generation to generation. The dancers' colorful costumes include tall headdresses decorated with peacock feathers and tiny mirrors. On all major holidays different troupes of Gombeys dance through the streets to many of the hotels, attracting crowds of followers. It's traditional to toss coins at the dancers' feet. Performance times and locations vary, but check out the No. 1 shed on Front Street on Tuesdays. Here, at the large building where the cruise ships dock, troupes perform at 3 PM.

The **Bermuda Civic Ballet** performs classical ballet at various venues during the academic year. Internationally known artists sometimes appear as guests. The group is affiliated with the Bermuda School of Russian Ballet (☞ *below*).

The **National Dance Theatre of Bermuda** (✉ P.O. Box 1759, Hamilton HM HX) began in 1980 and has enjoyed much success in Bermuda and abroad. Several years ago the group performed its first full-length classical ballet, *The Nutcracker,* with guest artists from the American Ballet Theater. The company continues to present a blend of classical, modern, and jazz dance throughout the academic year.

The **Bermuda School of Russian Ballet** (✉ Pembroke Sunday School Bldg., Pembroke, ☎ 441/293–4147 or 295–8621) has been around for half a century and presents unique ballet and modern dance performances. Some shows are held at the City Hall Theatre. Chosen students may participate in the Civic Ballet productions at Government House. Show times and venues vary, so call for details.

If the **Jackson School of Performing Arts** (✉ Arcade Bldg., Burnaby St., Hamilton, ☎ 441/292–5815 or 292–2927) is a weather vane for Bermuda's direction in the performing arts, then this sunny island will soon rival major U.S. cities in the number of talented young artists. The school enrolls more than 1,000 and includes an innovative gymnastics program, run at local schools, that brings students from preschool activities to competitive levels. The dance department is still the backbone of the school, however, and it would behoove any visitor to seek out a performance schedule.

Movies

Bermuda has four cinemas showing first-run movies: two in Hamilton, one in St. George's, and another in the West End. Check the listings in the *Royal Gazette* for movies and show times.

Neptune Cinema (✉ The Cooperage, Dockyards, ☎ 441/291–2035) is a 118-seat cinema that typically shows feature films at 7:30 and 9:30 nightly, with matinees at 2:30 Friday, Saturday, and Sunday.
The Little Theatre (✉ Queen St., Hamilton, ☎ 441/292–2135) is a 173-seat theater across the street from Casey's Bar. Show times are usually 2:15, 7, and 9:30.
Liberty Theatre (✉ Union and Victoria Sts., Hamilton, ☎ 441/291–2035) is a 270-seat cinema in an unsavory section of Hamilton. The area immediately outside the theater is safe during the day, but you should not loiter in this neighborhood after dark. Show times are usually 2:30, 5:30, 7:30, and 9:30 Monday to Saturday; and 2:30 and 7:30 on Sunday.
New Somers Theatre (✉ York St., St. George's, ☎ 441/297–2821) is a 248-seat cinema at the entrance to the town of St. George's, just below the St. George's Club. Show times are usually 7 and 9 Monday through Thursday, with an additional show Friday through Sunday.
The **Bermuda International Film Festival** (✉ Box HM 2963, Hamilton, ☎ 441/293–3456, ℻ 441/293–7769, ✍) is a relatively new (2000 was the the third year) festival celebrating independent films from many countries. Films are screened for a full week during late April or early May at the cinemas in Hamilton. Directors and stars mingle with a congenial audience of visitors and locals. Tickets are sold for individual films as well as for workshops and seminars on topics that include screen writing, camera techniques, and marketing independent films. Festival parties are also popular as Hamilton mimics—for a few days at least—the Hollywood-style glamour of Sundance, minus stretch limos.

Theater

Bermuda is the only place outside the United States where Harvard University's **Hasty Pudding Theatricals** performs. For almost 30 years this satirical troupe has entertained the island during Bermuda College Weeks (March–April). Produced by the Bermuda Musical and Dramatic Society, each of these Bermuda-based shows incorporates political and social issues of the past year. They're all staged at the City Hall Theatre (☞ *above*). Tickets are about $20.

The **Bermuda Musical & Dramatic Society** (✉ Box DV 631, Devonshire DV BX, ☎ 441/292–0848 or 441/295–5584) has some good amateur actors on its roster. Formed in 1944, this active theater society stages performances throughout the year in the society's Daylesford headquarters, one block north of City Hall. The Christmas pantomime is always a sellout, as are most other performances. Visit or call the box office at Daylesford, on Dundonald Street, for reservations and information. Tickets are about $10.

Visual Arts

In addition to the well-known Bermuda National Gallery and the Bermuda Society of Arts Gallery (☞ Hamilton *in* Chapter 3), and the always popular Bermuda Arts Centre at Dockyard, Bermuda is filled with wonderful little art galleries along sun-splashed beach roads and down narrow shady lanes. You'll want to see the watercolors, oils, and color lithographs by Bermuda artist Joan Forbes at **The Art House Gallery** (✉ Waterloo House, Hamilton, ☎ 441/236–6746), and the interesting prints at the **Pegasus Print & Book Shop** (✉ Pitts Bay Rd., Hamilton, ☎ 441/295–2900). For sculpture, visit the **Desmond Fountain Sculpture Gallery** at the Fairmont Southampton Princess (☞ Specialty Stores *in* Chapter 8). The best stop to see ceramic art, much of it Bermuda-inspired, is the **Omax Ceramics Studio** (✉ Admiralty House, Pembroke Parish, ☎ 441/292–8478).

The two **Michael Swan Galleries** (✉ Butterfield Pl., Front St., Hamilton, ☎ 441/296–5650; ✉ Clock Tower Centre at Royal Naval Dockyard, ☎ 441/234–3128) are worth noting. Swan uses pastels to capture Bermuda's houses in a very special way. His depiction of the local architecture, in galleries and exhibitions all over the world, has made him one of the island's favorite artists.

Bridge House Art Gallery (✉ 1 Bridge St., St. George's, ☎ 441/297–8211) is housed in Bridge House, a good example of late-17th-century Colonial-style architecture. Original oils and watercolors by local artists are on display. For information about other galleries, *see* Specialty Stores *in* Chapter 8.

The **Gumba Trail and Outdoor Museum** (✉ Cockburn Rd., Sandys Parish, ☎ 441/293–7330) is an interesting little museum that specializes in 16th through 18th century Bermudian art. A specialty is the Gombey, whose masks are a key to ancient traditions. The museum is on the Gumba Trail, near the T. S. Ventrue Sea Cadet Building. Admission is $5. Call for hours. For information about other galleries, *see* Specialty Stores *in* Chapter 8.

7 BEACHES, OUTDOOR ACTIVITIES, AND SPORTS

Bermuda's beaches—fine-grain sand tinted pink with shells, marine invertebrates, and crushed coral—are surrounded by dramatic cliff and rock formations, shaded with coconut palms, or complemented by dunes that slope gently toward the shimmering turquoise and purple tones of the Atlantic Ocean. Climate, more than anything else, makes Bermuda ideal for sports—both in the water and out.

L ONG BEFORE YOUR JET TOUCHES DOWN in Bermuda, the island's greatest asset becomes breathtakingly obvious—the crystal-clear, aquamarine water that frames the tiny, hook-shape atoll. So clear is the seawater that in 1994 the Bermuda government nixed a plan by local scuba-diving groups to create a unique dive site by sinking an abandoned American warplane in 30 ft of water off the island's East End, fairly close to the end of the airport's runway. The government feared that the plane would be easily visible from above—to arriving passengers—and could cause undue distress. That clarity makes Bermuda one of the world's greatest places for exploratory scuba diving and snorkeling. Yet clear as it is, the water wasn't quite lucid enough to make Bermuda's treacherous reefs visible to the hundreds of ship captains who have smashed their vessels on them through the centuries.

Updated by
Dexter E. Smith

Thanks to Bermuda's position near the Gulf Stream, the water stays warm year-round. Bermudians consider anything below 60°F frigid. In summer the ocean is usually above 80°F, and even warmer in the shallows between the reefs and shore. In winter the water temperature only occasionally drops below 70°F, but it seems cooler because the air temperature is usually in the mid-60s. Lack of business, more than a drop in water temperature, is responsible for the comparative dearth of water-sports activity from December through March. Winter does tend to be windier, which means that water conditions can be less than ideal. Rough water creates problems anchoring or stabilizing fishing and diving boats, and underwater visibility is often clouded by sand and debris. Look into wearing a wet suit if you plan to spend an extended period of time in the water.

In high season, which runs from April through October, fishing, diving, and yacht charters fill up quickly. Most boats carry fewer than 20 passengers, so it's advisable to sign up as soon as you arrive on the island. The shoulder seasons are March through April and October through November. The off season is December through February, a period when many operators close to make repairs and perform routine maintenance. A few operators stay open on a limited basis during these months, scheduling charters only when there are enough people to fill a boat; if too few people sign up, a charter is usually canceled. Thus, water-sports enthusiasts need to be flexible in winter.

Bermudians take their sports seriously. The daily newspaper's sports section is full of local coverage. Cricket and soccer grab most of the headlines, but road running, golf, field hockey, rugby, and a host of other island activities also get their share of space. Elite soccer players have delighted crowds in English and United States leagues through the years, and Bermudian sailors hold their own in world competition, as do runners, equestrians, and swimmers. The island is a golf and tennis paradise. With eight courses and more than 70 courts packed into these 22 square mi, it's hard to believe there's room left for horseback riding, cycling, running, and playing squash.

Take advantage of your hotel's activities director or your ship's cruise director, who can make sports arrangements for you long before you arrive. For extensive details on the island's sports and leisure facilities, pick up **"What to Do in Bermuda"** and **"What to Do: Information and Prices,"** both available free from the Bermuda Department of Tourism (☞ Visitor Information *in* Smart Travel Tips A to Z).

BEACHES

Most people would agree that Bermuda's south-shore beaches are more scenic than those on the north side—fine, pinkish sand; coral bluffs topped with summer flowers; gentle, pale-blue surf slipping past the barrier reefs offshore. The water at south-shore beaches does get a little rougher when the winds are from the south and southwest, but waves continuously roll in and break on this sandy shoreline even when breezes are gentle. Many travelers join locals in the popular pastime of body surfing. Most Bermudian beaches are relatively small compared with ocean beaches in the United States, ranging from about 15 yards to half a mile or so in length. In winter, when the weather is more severe, beaches may erode—even disappear—only to be replenished as the wind subsides in the spring.

The Public Transportation Board publishes "Bermuda's Guide to Beaches and Transportation," available free in all visitor centers and most hotels. A combination map and bus and ferry schedule, the guide shows locations of beaches and how to reach them.

Few Bermudian beaches offer shade, but some have palm trees and thatched shelters. The sun can be intense, so bring a hat and plenty of sunscreen. You can rent umbrellas at some beaches. Here, we review the major beaches open to the public. South-shore hotels with private beaches are reviewed in Chapter 5.

North-Shore Beaches

Shelly Bay Beach. As at Somerset Long Bay, the water at this beach near Flatts is well protected from strong southerly winds. In addition, a sandy bottom and shallow water make this a good place to take small children. Shelly Bay also has shade trees, a rarity at Bermudian beaches. There is also a children's playground behind the beach, which attracts hoards of youngsters on weekends and during school holidays. A drawback can be the traffic noise from nearby North Shore Road. ⊠ *North Shore Rd., Hamilton Parish. Bus 10 or 11 from Hamilton.*

Somerset Long Bay. Popular with Somerset locals, this beach is on the quiet northwestern end of the island, far from the bustle of Hamilton, and major tourist hubs. In keeping with the area's rural atmosphere, the beach is low-key. Undeveloped parkland shields the beach from the light traffic on Cambridge Road. The main beach is crescent-shape and long by Bermudian standards—nearly ¼ mi from end to end. In contrast to the great coral outcroppings common on the south shore, the main backdrops here are grass and brush. Although exposed to northerly storm winds, the bay water is normally calm and shallow—ideal for children. The bottom, however, is rocky and uneven. ⊠ *Cambridge Rd., Sandys. Bus 7 or 8 from Hamilton.*

Tobacco Bay Beach. The most popular beach near St. George's—about 15 minutes northwest on foot—this small north-shore beach is huddled in a coral cove. Its beach house has a snack bar, equipment rentals, toilets, showers, and changing rooms. From the bus stop in the town of St. George's, the beach is a 10-minute hike, or you can flag down one of St. George's Minibus Service's vans and ask to be taken to the beach ($2 per person). ⊠ *Coot Pond Rd., St. George's,* ☎ *441/297–8199. Bus 1, 3, 10, or 11 from Hamilton.*

South-Shore Beaches

Chaplin and Stonehole Bays. In a secluded area east of Horseshoe Bay Beach (☞ *below*), these tiny adjacent beaches almost disappear at high tide. Stonehole's most distinguishing feature is a high coral wall

Beaches and Outdoor Activities

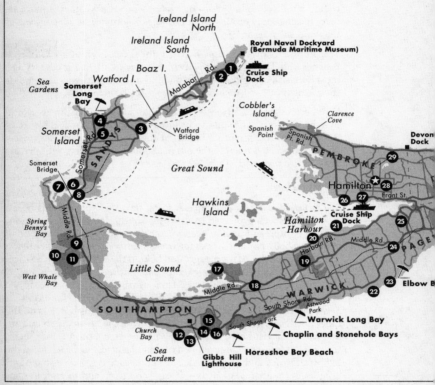

ATLANTIC OCEAN

Ireland Island North

Ireland Island South

Boaz I.

Malabar Rd.

Watford I.

Watford Bridge

Sea Gardens

Somerset Long Bay

Somerset Island

Somerset Bridge

SANDYS

Somerset Rd.

Middle Rd.

Spring Benny's Bay

West Whale Bay

Little Sound

SOUTHAMPTON

Church Bay

Sea Gardens

Gibbs Hill Lighthouse

Horseshoe Bay Beach

Chaplin and Stonehole Bays

Warwick Long Bay

South Shore Park

Middle Rd.

WARWICK

Astwood Park

South Shore Rd.

Elbow B

Harbour Rd.

Middle Rd.

PAGET

Great Sound

Hawkins Island

Hamilton Harbour

Cruise Ship Dock

Hamilton

Front St.

Cobbler's Island

Spanish Point

Spanish Pt. Rd.

Clarence Cove

PEMBROKE

Devon Dock

Royal Naval Dockyard (Bermuda Maritime Museum)

Cruise Ship Dock

Bicycling

Eve's Cycle Livery 24

Oleander Cycles 9

Wheels Cycles 27

Golf Courses

Belmont Golf & Country Club 19

Castle Harbour Golf Club 38

Mid Ocean Club 39

Ocean View Golf & Country Club 30

Port Royal Golf Course 11

Princess Golf Club 15

Riddell's Bay Golf and Country Club 17

St. George's Golf Club 41

Horseback Riding

Spicelands Riding Centre 18

Tennis and Squash Courts

Bermuda Squash Club 33

Coral Beach & Tennis Club 22

Elbow Beach Hotel 23

Fairmont Southampton Princess Hotel 16

Government Tennis Stadium 29

Pomander Gate Tennis Club 25

Port Royal Course 10

Sonesta Beach Hotel & Spa 12

Spectator Sports

Bermuda Equestrian Federation 31

Bermuda Football Association 28

National Sports Club 32

St. George's Cricket Club 40

Somerset Cricket Club 5

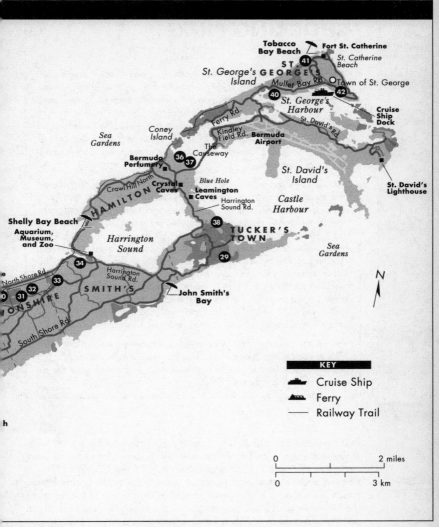

Tobacco
Bay Beach
Fort St. Catherine
41
St. Catherine
Beach
ST. GEORGE'S
St. George's
Island
Mullet Bay Rd.
Town of St. George
40
42
St. George's
Harbour
Cruise
Ship
Dock
Ferry Rd.
St. David's Rd.
Coney
Island
Kindley
Field Rd.
Bermuda
Airport
Sea
Gardens
The
Causeway
36
37
Bermuda
Perfumery
St. David's
Island
Blue Hole
Crawl Hill North
Crystal
Caves
Leamington
Caves
Harrington
Sound Rd.
Castle
Harbour
St. David's
Lighthouse
HAMILTON
Shelly Bay Beach
Aquarium,
Museum,
and Zoo
38
TUCKER'S
TOWN
Harrington
Sound
29
Sea
Gardens
34
North Shore Rd.
33
Harrington
Sound Rd.
SMITH'S
0
31
32
DEVONSHIRE
John Smith's
Bay
South Shore Rd.

N

KEY

🚢 Cruise Ship

⛴ Ferry

— Railway Trail

| 0 | | 2 miles |
| 0 | | 3 km |

h

SHOCKING PINK!

THE SANDS OF THE WORLD come in many hues, from basaltic black to gleaming quartz white, with a rainbow of red, green, yellow, and brown thrown in—and yes, even pink. Pink sand is considered choice by many beach connoisseurs, and Bermuda's south shore has plenty of it. You'll find the rosy tint of the island's sand most intense in the bright sun of midday, but in the gentler light of early morning and late afternoon the hue can appear darker, tending toward mauve.

In only a few regions where tropical coral reefs flourish offshore do pink-sand beaches form. What makes the sand pink is an amalgam of calcium-rich shells and fragments of invertebrate sea creatures, from minute, single-cell protozoa to spiny sea urchins. Chiefly responsible are foraminifera ("foram" for short), a type of protozoan that lives in great profusion in reef environments. The microscopic red *Homotrema rubrum* (red foram) variety is numerous both on the reefs and in the ocean sediments that surround Bermuda, and their persistent red pigment remains even in the microscopic "skeletons" these animals leave behind when they die. The red gets mixed in with other (predominantly white) reef debris—broken clam and snail shells, fragments of coral—and, when washed ashore, forms the island's signature pink sand.

The beaches most visited to view—and collect—pink sand are Warwick Long Bay Beach and Horseshoe Bay Beach in Southampton. But just about any beach you visit on the South Shore will have the famous sand in abundance.

that reaches across the beach to the water, perforated by a 10-ft-high, arrowhead-shape hole. Like Horseshoe Bay, the beach fronts South Shore Park. ⊠ *Off South Rd., Southampton. Bus 7 from Hamilton.*

Elbow Beach. Swimming and body surfing are great at this beach, which lies adjacent to the prime strand of sand reserved for guests of the Elbow Beach Hotel. As pleasant as the setting is, however, it can get very noisy and crowded on summer weekends. A nearby lunch wagon offers fast food and cold soft drinks. ⊠ *Off South Rd., Paget. Bus 2 or 7 from Hamilton.*

Horseshoe Bay Beach. Horseshoe Bay has everything you would expect of a Bermudian beach: clear water, a ⅓-mi crescent of pink sand, a vibrant social scene, and the uncluttered backdrop of South Shore Park. This is one of the island's most popular beaches. Lifeguards in summer (the only other beach with lifeguards is John Smith's Bay (☞ *below*), a variety of rental facilities, a snack bar, and toilets add to the beach's appeal. In fact, it can become uncomfortably crowded here on summer weekends. Parents should keep a close eye on their children in the water, as the undertow can be strong. ⊠ *Off South Rd., Southampton,* ☏ *441/238–2651. Bus 7 from Hamilton.*

John Smith's Bay. Backed by houses and South Road, this beach consists of a pretty strand of long, flat, open sand. The presence of a lifeguard in summer makes it an ideal place to bring children. As the only public beach in Smith's Parish, John Smith's Bay is also popular with locals. Groups of young folks like to gather here for parties, especially on weekends and holidays, so if you're not in the mood for a festive bunch with loud radios, this may not be the place for you. ⊠ *South Rd., Smith's. Bus 1 from Hamilton.*

Warwick Long Bay. Very different from covelike Chaplin, Stonehole, and Horseshoe bays, Warwick Long Bay has the longest stretch of sand—about ½ mi—of any beach on the island. Its backdrop is a combination of very steep cliffs and low grass- and brush-covered hills. The beach is exposed to some strong southerly winds, but the waves are usually moderate because the inner reef is close to shore. An interesting feature of the bay is a 20-ft coral outcrop less than 200 ft offshore. It looks like a sculpted boulder balancing on the surface of the water. South Shore Park, which surrounds the bay, is often empty, a fact that only heightens the beach's appealing isolation and serenity. ⊠ *Off South Rd., Southampton. Bus 7 from Hamilton.*

PARTICIPANT SPORTS

Remember that you can arrange your own sporting activities (tee times, for example) through your hotel or ship activities director.

Bicycling

Bermuda is not the easiest place in the world to bicycle. Be prepared for some tough climbs—the roads running north–south across the island are particularly steep and winding—and the wind can sap even the strongest rider's strength, especially along South Road in Warwick and Southampton parishes. Bermudian roads are narrow, with heavy traffic (especially near Hamilton during rush hours) and no shoulders. Most motorists are courteous to cyclists and stay within 10 mph of the 20-mph speed limit. Despite the traffic, bicycle racing is a popular sport in Bermuda, and club groups regularly whir around the island on evening and weekend training rides. Bermudian roads are no place for novice riders, however. Helmets are strongly recommended, and parents should think twice before allowing preteen children to bike.

Bermuda's premier cycling and walking route, the Railway Trail, requires almost no road riding. Restricted to pedestrian and bicycle traffic, the trail is mostly paved, and it runs intermittently for almost the length of the island along the route of the old Bermuda Railway. The free pamphlet "The Bermuda Railway Trail Guide," published by the Bermuda Department of Tourism (☞ Visitor Information *in* Smart Travel Tips A to Z), outlines a series of short exploring tours along the trail.

Tribe roads—small side roads, often unpaved—also make for good exploring, but don't be surprised if many of these roads, which date back to the earliest settlement of Bermuda, are dead ends. Well-paved South Road has relatively few climbs and some excellent ocean views, but it's one of Bermuda's most heavily traveled thoroughfares. The "Bermuda Handy Reference Map," also available at Visitors Service Bureaus, is quite good, but the highly detailed "Bermuda Islands" map, available at the Bermuda Book Store in Hamilton, is even better.

In Bermuda, bicycles are called pedal or push bikes to distinguish them from the more common, motorized two-wheelers. Some of the cycle liveries around the island also rent pedal bikes. If you can, reserve bikes a few days in advance. Rental rates are $10 to $20 a day (the longer you rent, the more economical your daily rate becomes). You may be charged an additional $15 for a repair waiver and you may be required to pay by credit card or to leave a refundable deposit. Contact **Eve's Cycle Livery** (⊠ Middle Rd., Paget, ☎ 441/236–6247), **Oleander Cycles** (⊠ Middle Rd., Southampton, ☎ 441/234–0629), or **Wheels Cycles** (⊠ Front St., Hamilton, ☎ 441/292–2245).

Boating and Sailing

In Bermuda you can either rent your own boat or charter one with a skipper. Rental boats, which are 18 ft at most, range from sailboats (typically tiny Sunfish) to motorboats (13-ft Boston Whalers), in addition to kayaks and pedal boats. Some of these vessels are ideal for exploring the coves and harbors of the sounds, or, in the case of motorboats, dropping anchor and snorkeling around the shorelines, which teem with various coral and colorful fish. In **Great Sound,** several small islands, such as **Hawkins Island** and **Darrell's Island,** have tiny secluded beaches and coves that are usually empty during the week. If the wind is fresh, and is blowing in the right direction, the islands are about half an hour's sail from Hamilton Harbour or Salt Kettle. The beaches are wonderful places to picnic, although some are privately owned and do not always welcome visitors. Check with the boat-rental operator before planning an island trip.

The trade winds pass well to the south of Bermuda, so the island does not have predictable air currents. Channeled by islands and headlands, the wind direction around **Hamilton Harbour,** the **Great Sound,** and **Mangrove Bay** changes regularly. This variability has undoubtedly aided the education of Bermuda's racing skippers, who are traditionally among the world's best. To the casual sailor, however, wind changes can be troublesome, though you can be fairly confident that you won't be becalmed. The average summer breeze is 7–10 knots, often out of the south or southwest. Mangrove Bay, often protected, is the ideal place for novice sailors and pedal boaters. A range of boats is available at **Mangrove Marina** (☞ Boat Rentals, *below*). If you want a taste of open water in summer, head for Pompano Beach Club Watersports Centre, on the western ocean shore. For Great Sound and Somerset shoreline boating, go to the Royal Naval Dockyard.

Boat Rentals

Rates for small powerboats start at about $65 for two hours and go up to $185 for a full day. Sailboat rentals begin at $60 for four hours and go up to $170 for a full day. A credit card number is usually required. You can rent sailboats and powerboats at **Blue Hole Water Sports,** within the Grotto Bay Beach Hotel & Tennis Club (✉ 11 Blue Hole Hill, Hamilton Parish, ☎ 441/293–2915 or 441/293–8333 ext. 37), **Windjammer Water Sports** (✉ Royal Naval Dockyard, ☎ 441/234–0250; ✉ Cambridge Beaches, Sandys, ☎ 441/234–3082), **Mangrove Marina** (✉ Somerset Bridge, Sandys, ☎ 441/234–0914 or 441/234–3145), **Pompano Beach Club** (✉ 36 Pompano Rd., Southampton, ☎ 441/234–0222), and **Salt Kettle Yacht Charters** (✉ Off Harbour Rd., Salt Kettle Rd., Paget, ☎ 441/236–4863, ℻ 441/236–2427).

Charter Boats

More than 20 large power cruisers and sailing vessels, piloted by local skippers, are available for charter. Ranging from 30 ft to 60 ft long, charter sailboats can carry up to 30 passengers, sometimes overnight. Meals and drinks can be included on request, and a few skippers offer dinner cruises for the romantically inclined. Rates generally range between $300 and $450 for a three-hour cruise, or $650 to $1,500 for a full-day cruise, with additional per-person charges for large groups. Where you go and what you do—exploring, swimming, snorkeling, cruising—is up to you and your skipper. Most charter companies pick up passengers from various locations around Bermuda, and most cruises travel to and around the islands of Great Sound. Several charter skippers advertise year-round operations, but the off-season (December through February) schedule can be haphazard. Skippers devote periods of the off-season to maintenance and repairs, or close altogether if bookings lag. Be sure to book well in advance; in the high season do so before you arrive on the island.

Sailboat charter firms include **Adventure Enterprises** (☎ 441/297–1459), Capt. Kirk Ward's **Native Tours** (☎ 441/297–1459, 441/234–8149, or 441/234–1434), David Ashton's **Salt Kettle Yacht Charters** (☎ 441/236–4863), Capt. Ed Williams's **Starlight Sailing Cruises** (☎ 441/292–1834), Percy Smith's **Perrah Yacht Charters** (☎ 441/295–0060, FAX 441/296–1688), and Michael Voegeli's **Wind Sail Charters** (☎ 441/238–0825 or 441/234–8547, FAX 441/238–1614).

Charter a powerboat through Capt. Douglas Shirley's **Bermuda Barefoot Cruises** (☎ 441/236–3498), **Tam Marina** (☎ FAX 441/236–0127), or **Salt Kettle Yacht Charters** (☎ 441/236–4863).

Kayaks

Good kayaking areas in Bermuda range from protected coves to open ocean. Hourly rates begin at about $20 for a single kayak and $25 for a double. For a full day, plan to spend about $75 for a single and $80 for a double.

Rent a kayak through **Blue Hole Water Sports** (✉ Grotto Bay Beach Hotel & Tennis Club, 11 Blue Hole Hill, Hamilton Parish, ☎ 441/293–2915 or 441/293–8333 ext. 37), **Mangrove Marina** (✉ Somerset Bridge, Sandys, ☎ 441/234–0914), or **Windjammer Water Sports** (✉ Royal Naval Dockyard, Sandys, ☎ 441/234–0250; ✉ Cambridge Beaches, Sandys, ☎ 441/234–3082).

Diving

Bermuda has all the ingredients for classic scuba diving—reefs, wrecks, underwater caves, a variety of coral and marine life, and clear, warm water. Although you can dive year-round (you will have to bring your own gear in winter, when dive shops are closed), the best months are May through October, when the water is calmest and warmest. No prior certification is necessary. Novices can learn the basics and dive in water up to 25 ft deep on the same day. Three-hour resort courses ($95–$110), which teach the basics in a pool, on the beach, or off a dive boat and culminate in a reef or wreck dive, are offered by **Fantasea Diving** (✉ Darrell's Wharf, Harbour Rd., Paget, ☎ 441/236–6339), **Nautilus Diving** (✉ Princess Hotel, Hamilton, ☎ 441/295–9485, FAX 441/296–4006; ✉ Southampton Princess Hotel, off South Rd., Southampton, ☎ 441/238–2332, FAX 441/234–5180), **Scuba Look** (✉ Grotto Bay Beach Hotel, 11 Blue Hole Hill, Hamilton Parish, ☎ 441/293–7319, FAX 441/295–2421), **South Side Scuba** (✉ Sonesta Beach Hotel, Southampton, ☎ 441/238–1833, FAX 441/236–0394), and **Blue Water Divers Ltd.** (✉ Elbow Beach Hotel, Paget, ☎ 441/232–2909, FAX 441/234–3561; ✉ Robinson's Marina, Somerset Bridge, Sandys, ☎ 441/234–1034, FAX 441/234–3561).

The easiest day trips, offered by Nautilus Diving, involve exploring the south-shore reefs that lie inshore. These reefs may be the most dramatic in Bermuda. The ocean-side drop-off exceeds 60 ft in some places, and the coral is so honeycombed with caves, ledges, and holes that opportunities for discovery are pretty much infinite. Despite concerns about dying coral and dwindling fish populations, most of Bermuda's reefs are still in good health. No one eager to swim with multicolored schools of fish or the occasional barracuda will be disappointed. In the interest of preservation, however, the removal of coral is illegal.

Dive shops around Bermuda prominently display a map of the outlying reef system and its wreck sites. Only 38 of the wrecks from the past three centuries are marked. They are the larger wrecks that are still in good condition. The nautical carnage includes some 300 wreck sites in all—an astonishing number—many of which are well preserved. As a general rule, the more recent the wreck or the more deeply submerged it is, the better its condition. Most of the well-preserved wrecks are to the north and east, and dive depths range between 25 ft and 80 ft. Several wrecks off the western end of the island are in relatively shallow water, 30 ft or less, making them accessible to novice divers and even snorkelers. The major dive operator for wrecks on the western side of the island is Blue Water Divers at Somerset Bridge. From this company's Elbow Beach Hotel location, in Paget, you can ride a diver propulsion vehicle (DPV), which is like an underwater scooter, past a wreck and through caves and canyons. A one-tank dive costs $40–$55; for introductory divers the price range is $95–$110. Two-tank dives for experienced divers cost $75–$80. With two tanks you can explore two or more wrecks in one four-hour outing. For all necessary equipment—mask, fins, snorkel, scuba apparatus, and wet suit (if needed)—plan to spend about $40 more. Some operators also offer night dives.

Helmet Diving

A different, less technical type of diving popular in Bermuda is "helmet diving," offered between April and mid-November. Although helmet-diving cruises last three hours or more, the actual time underwater is about 25 minutes, during which time underwater explorers walk along the sandy bottom in about 10–12 ft of water (depending on the tide), wearing helmets that receive air through hoses leading to the surface. Underwater portraits are available for an extra charge. A morning or afternoon tour costs about $50 for adults, $40 for children 12 and under, and includes wet suits when the water temperature is less than 80°F. Contact **Bermuda Bell Diving** (⊠ Flatts Village, Smith's, ☎ 441/292-4434, FAX 441/295-7235), **Greg Hartley's Under Sea Adventure** (⊠ Watford Bridge, Sandys, ☎ 441/234-2861, FAX 441/234-3000), or **Adventure Enterprises** (⊠ Ordnance Island, St. George's, ☎ 441/297-1459), which does not take children.

Fishing

Fishing in Bermuda falls into three basic categories: shore or shallow-water fishing, reef fishing, and deep-sea fishing. No license is required, although some restrictions apply, particularly regarding the fish you can keep (for instance, only Bermudians with commercial fishing licenses are allowed to take lobsters) and the prohibition against spear guns. Some have expressed concern about the decline in the number of reef and shore fish in Bermudian waters. Government measures to restore fish populations have had an adverse impact on some commercial operations, but sportfishing has been largely unaffected.

Reef Fishing

Three major reef bands lie at various distances from the island. The first is anywhere from ½ mi to 5 mi offshore. The second, the Challenger Bank, is about 12 mi offshore. The third, the Argus Bank, is about 30 mi offshore. As a rule, the farther out you go, the larger the fish—and the more expensive the charter.

Most charter fishing captains go to the reefs and deep water to the southwest and northwest of the island, where the fishing is best. Catches over the reefs include snapper, amberjack, grouper, and barracuda. Of the most sought after deepwater fish—marlin, tuna, wahoo, and dolphinfish—wahoos are the most common, dolphinfish the least. Trolling is the usual method of deepwater fishing, and charter-boat operators offer various tackle setups, with test-line weights ranging from 20 pounds to 130 pounds. The boats, which range between 31 ft and 55 ft long, are fitted with a wide array of gear and electronics to track fish, including depth sounders, global positioning systems, loran systems, video fish finders, radar, and computer scanners.

Half-day or full-day charters are offered by most operators, but full-day trips offer the best chance for a big catch because the boat has time to reach waters that are less often fished. Rates are about $600 per boat for half a day (four hours), $850 per day (eight hours). Many captains encourage clients to participate in the catch-and-release program to maintain the abundant supply of fish, but successful anglers can certainly keep fish if they like.

The Bermuda Department of Tourism (☞ Visitor Information *in* Smart Travel Tips A to Z) runs the free **Game Fishing Competition,** open to all anglers, throughout the year. Catches of any of 26 game varieties can be registered with the Department, and prizes are awarded. Charter trips are arranged through two organizations: the **Bermuda Sport Fishing Association** (✉ Creek View House, 8 Tulo La., Pembroke Parish, ☎ 441/295–2370) and the smaller **St. George's Game Fishing Association** (✉ Box 107GE, St. George's, ☎ 441/297–8093, speak with Capt. Joe Kelley). In addition, several independent charter boats operate out of Hamilton Harbour as well as harbors in Sandys, at the island's western end. For more information about chartering a fishing boat, pick up a copy of "What to Do: Information and Prices" at the Bermuda Department of Tourism (☞ Visitor Information *in* Smart Travel Tips A to Z).

Shore Fishing
The principal catches for shore fishers are pompano, bonefish, and snapper. Excellent sport for saltwater fly-fishing is the wily and strong bonefish, which hovers in coves, harbors, and bays. Among the more popular spots for bonefish are **West Whale Bay** and **Spring Benny's Bay,** which have large expanses of clear, shallow water protected by reefs close to shore. Good fishing holes are plentiful along the south shore, too. Fishing in the waters of the **Great Sound** and **St. George's Harbour** can be rewarding, but enclosed **Harrington Sound** is less promising. Ask at local tackle shops about the latest hot spots and the best baits.

Rod and reel rentals for shore fishing are available for about $15–$20 a day ($20–$30 deposit or credit card impression required) from **Mangrove Marina** (✉ Somerset Bridge, Sandys, ☎ 441/234–0914) and **Windjammer Water Sports** (✉ Royal Naval Dockyard, ☎ 441/234–0250; ✉ Cambridge Beaches, Sandys, ☎ 441/234–3082). Rental prices usually include bait and a tackle box. You can also make rental arrangements through hotel activities directors.

Golf

Bermuda is justifiably renowned for its golf courses. The scenery is spectacular, and the courses are challenging. However, you should not expect the soft, manicured fairways and greens typical of U.S. courses. Just as courses in Scotland have their own character, those in Bermuda are distinguished by plenty of sand, firm fairways and greens, relatively short par fours, and wind—*especially* wind. Most golf courses elsewhere are designed with the wind in mind—long downwind holes and short upwind holes. Not so on Bermuda's eight courses, where the wind is anything but consistent or predictable. Quirky air currents make a Bermudian course play differently every day. On some days a 350-yard par four may be drivable. On other days a solidly hit drive may fall short on a 160-yard par three. Regardless, the wind puts a premium on being able to hit the ball straight and grossly exaggerates any slice or hook.

The island's freshwater supply is limited, so irrigation is minimal and the ground around the green tends to be quite hard. For success in the short game, therefore, you need to run the ball to the hole, rather than relying on high, arcing chips, which require plenty of club face under the ball. Bermudian greens are normally elevated, and protected by sand traps rather than thick grass. Most traps are filled with the soft limestone sand and pulverized pieces of pink shell. Such fine sand may be unfamiliar to you, but it tends to be consistent from trap to trap and from course to course.

Greens are usually seeded with Bermuda grass and then over-seeded with rye, which means that you putt on Bermuda grass in warmer months (March through November) and on rye when the weather cools and the Bermuda grass dies out. Greens are reseeded anytime from late September to early November, according to the weather. (The greens at the Castle Harbour Golf Club are reseeded in early January.) Some courses use temporary greens for two to four weeks. Others keep the greens in play while reseeding and resurfacing. Greens in Bermuda tend to be much slower than the bent-grass greens prevalent in the United States, and putts tend to break less.

Another characteristic of Bermudian courses is the preponderance of rolling, hummocky fairways, making a flat lie the exception rather than the rule. Little effort has been made to flatten the fairways, because much of the ground beneath the island's surface is honeycombed with caves. Bulldozer and backhoe operators are understandably uneasy about doing extensive landscaping.

The "Golf Guide," published by the Bermuda Department of Tourism (☞ Visitor Information *in* Smart Travel Tips A to Z), has descriptions of all golf courses, including addresses, phone numbers, and prices.

How should golfers prepare for a Bermuda trip? In anticipation of the wind, practice hitting lower shots. Punching the ball or playing it farther back in the stance may be helpful. Working on chip-and-run shots (a seven iron is ideal for this), especially from close-cropped lies, should also help. You can also save yourself some strokes by practicing iron shots from awkward hillside lies. On the greens, a long, firm putting stroke may keep you from the bugaboo that haunts many first-time visitors—gently stroked putts dying short of the hole, or drifting off-line with the grain of the Bermuda grass. As Allan Wilkinson, the former professional at the Princess Golf Club, has said, "In Bermuda, ya gotta slam 'em into the back of the cup."

Lessons, available at all courses, usually cost $40–$60 for a half hour, and club rentals range between $15 and $40. Caddies are a thing of the past, except at the Mid Ocean Club. Below are reviews and ratings of Bermuda's eight golf courses. The ratings, devised and administered by the United States Golf Association (USGA), "represent the expected score of an expert amateur golfer based upon yardage and other obstacles." For example, a par-72 course with a rating of 68 means that a scratch golfer would hit a four-under-par round, and ordinary hackers would probably score a little better, too. Ratings are given for the blue tees (championship), white tees (men's), and red tees (women's).

Belmont Golf & Country Club

Length: 5,777 yards from the blue tees. Par: 70. Rating: blue tees, 68.9; white tees, 67.9; red tees, 69.1.

Among Bermuda's eight courses, the layout of the public Belmont Golf & Country Club is perhaps the most maddening. The first two holes, straight par fours, are a false preview of what lies ahead—a series of doglegs and blind tee shots. A newcomer may be able to trim six or more shots from a round by playing with an experienced Belmont player who knows where to hit drives on such blind holes as the 6th, 11th, and 16th, and how best to play a dogleg hole such as the 8th. Despite the layout, Belmont remains one of Bermuda's easier courses, and it's ideal for inexperienced players. The course is inland, with few ocean panoramas; instead, most holes overlook pastel houses with white roofs, a few of which have taken a beating from errant golf balls. An upgraded irrigation system has improved the course dramatically. Fairway grass tends to be denser—and the clay soil moister—than the grass on the close-cropped, sandy fairways typical of other Bermudian courses. The rough, too, is generally deeper, snaring any wild tee shots. For this reason, and because Belmont is a short course (only one par four is more than 400 yards), it makes sense to use a three or five wood, or even a low iron, from the tee. Belmont's chief drawback, especially on the weekend, is slow play. Weekend rounds of five hours or more are common. Note: the Belmont Hotel closed permanently in 1998, but the golf course remains open at press time. Elbow Beach Hotel has made a bid to purchase the course (and turn it into the Elbow Beach Golf Club), but government approval is still pending as of mid-2000. Be sure to get an update before making plans.

Highlight hole: The par-five 11th has a severe dogleg left, with a blind tee shot—Belmont in a nutshell. A short but straight drive is the key. Trying and failing to cut the corner can be disastrous. The approach to the green is straight, although a row of wispy trees on the left awaits hooked or pulled shots. ⊠ *Belmont Rd., Warwick,* ☎ *441/236–6400,* ℻ *441/236–6867.* 🖅 *Greens fees $86 per person, with cart. Shoe rentals $8. Club rentals $28.*

Castle Harbour Golf Club

Length: 6,440 yards from the blue tees. Par: 71. Rating: blue tees, 71.3; white tees, 69.2; red tees, 69.2.

The only flat areas on this course seem to be the tees. The first tee, a crow's-nest perch by the clubhouse, offers an indication of things to come: looking out over the fairway, with the harbor beyond, is like peering onto a golf course from a 20th-story window. Wind can make this course play especially long. Although most par fours feature good landing areas despite all the hills, holes such as the 2nd, 16th, and 17th require players to drive over fairway rises. A wind-shortened drive can mean a long, blind shot to the green. Carrying the rise, on the other hand, can mean a relatively easy short shot, especially on the 2nd and 17th holes. Elevated greens are a common feature of Castle Harbour. The most extreme example is the 190-yard, par-three 13th, with the green perched atop a steep, 100-ft embankment. Balls short of the green inevitably roll back down into a grassy basin between the tee and the green. On the other hand, sand traps at Castle Harbour are mercifully few and far between by Bermudian standards. Ten holes feature two or fewer bunkers around the green.

Castle Harbour is one of Bermuda's most expensive courses, but the money is clearly reinvested in the course. Greens are well maintained—firm, consistently cropped, and generally faster than most other Bermudian greens. The course also rewards golfers with several spectacular views, such as the hilltop panorama from the 14th tee, where blue water stretches into the distance on three sides.

Highlight hole: The 235-yard, par-three 18th is the most difficult finishing hole on Bermuda, especially when the wind is blowing from the northwest. On the right are jagged coral cliffs rising from the harbor, and on the left are a pair of traps. When the course was revamped a few years ago, a small, flower-lined pond was added on the front right of the green, making this hard hole even harder. ⊠ *Paynters Rd., Tucker's Town,* ☎ *441/293–2040 ext. 6869,* FAX *441/293–1051.* 🖾 *Greens fees $149 per person with cart Mar.–Nov., $99 per person Dec.– Feb. Shoe rentals $8. Club rentals $30.*

Mid Ocean Club
Length: 6,512 yards from the blue tees. Par: 71. Rating: blue tees, 72; white tees, 70; red tees, 73.6.

It isn't Bermuda's oldest course—that honor belongs to Riddell's Bay— and other Bermudian courses are equally difficult, but the elite Mid Ocean Club is generally regarded as one of the top 50 courses in the world. Quite simply, this course has charisma, embodying everything that is golf in Bermuda—tees on coral cliffs above the ocean, rolling fairways lined with palms and spice trees, doglegs around water, and windswept views. It's rich in history, too. At the dogleg fifth hole, for example, Babe Ruth is said to have splashed a dozen balls in Mangrove Lake in a futile effort to drive the green. The course rewards long, straight tee shots and deft play around the green, while penalizing—often cruelly—anything less. The 5th and 9th holes, for example, require that tee shots (from the blue tees) carry 180 yards or more over water. And whereas length is not a factor on two fairly short par fives, the 471-yard 2nd and the 487-yard 11th, accuracy is. Tight doglegs ensure that any wayward tee shot ends up in trees, shrubbery, or the rough. However, the course may have mellowed with age. Having lost hundreds of trees to a tornado in 1986, and again to Hurricane Emily in 1987, the tight, tree-lined fairways have become more open, and the rough is less threatening.

Highlight hole: The 433-yard fifth is a par four dogleg around Mangrove Lake. The elevated tee overlooks a hillside of flowering shrubbery and the lake, making the fairway seem impossibly far away. Big hitters can take a shortcut over the lake (although the green is unreachable, as the Babe's heroic but unsuccessful efforts attest), but anyone who hits the fairway has scored a major victory. To the left of the green, a steep embankment leads into a bunker that is among the hardest in Bermuda from which to recover. ⊠ *Mid Ocean Dr., off South Shore Rd., Tucker's Town,* ☎ *441/293–0330,* FAX *441/293–8837.* 🖾 *Greens fees $160 ($70 when accompanied by a member). Nonmembers must be introduced by a club member; nonmember starting times available Mon., Wed., and Fri., except public holidays. Caddies $25 per bag (tip not included). Cart rental $40.*

Ocean View Golf & Country Club
Length: 3,000 yards (nine holes) from the blue tees. Par: men, 35; women, 37. Rating: none.

Founded in the 1940s, the Ocean View Golf & Country Club has magnificent views of the island's north shore. The good restaurant and bar and excellent driving range enhance the club's popularity. Plan ahead for tee times. This nine-hole course is busy all week long. Several holes challenge and intrigue. The first is a tough par five that is a tight driving hole, with a 40-ft coral wall on one side and views of the north shore on the other. The sixth is a difficult par four because of its elevated green. The ninth is a par three with water guarding the front of the green, so shooting with accuracy is the key.

Highlight hole: The green on the 187-yard, par-three ninth hole is cut out of a coral hillside that's beautifully landscaped with attractive plants. This is a demanding tee shot, and club selection can be tricky, particularly when strong winds are blowing from the north or west. ⊠ *Off North Shore Rd., Devonshire,* ☎ *441/295–9092,* FAX *441/295–9097.* ✉ *Greens fees $33 for 9 or 18 holes, plus $9 for cart rental for 9 holes or $18 for 18 holes, or $6 for hand cart. Club rentals $20. (Fees reduced when playing with a member, or after 3:45.)*

Port Royal Golf Course

Length: 6,565 yards from the blue tees. Par: men, 71; women, 72. Rating: blue tees, 72; white tees, 69.7; red tees, 72.5.

Such golfing luminaries as Jack Nicklaus rank the Port Royal Golf Course among the world's best public courses. A favorite with Bermudians as well as visitors, the course is well laid out, and the greens fees are modest. By Bermudian standards, Port Royal is also relatively flat. Although there are some hills (on the back nine in particular), the course has few of the blind shots and hillside lies that prevail elsewhere, and those holes that do have gradients tend to run either directly uphill or downhill. In other respects, however, Port Royal is classically Bermudian, with close-cropped fairways, numerous elevated tees and greens, and holes raked by the wind, especially the 8th and the 16th. The 16th hole, one of Bermuda's most famous, is often pictured in magazines. The green sits on a treeless promontory overlooking the blue waters and pink-white sands of Whale Bay, a popular boating and fishing area. When the wind is blowing hard onshore, as it frequently does, you may need a driver to reach the green, which is 163 yards away. One complaint often raised about Port Royal is the condition of the course, which sometimes gets chewed up by heavy usage—more than 55,000 rounds a year.

Highlight hole: Like the much-photographed 16th hole, the 387-yard, par-four 15th skirts the cliffs along Whale Bay. As of 1995, par-three holes 8 and 16 are longer. Hole 11 doglegs to the right. And hole 13 plays a light dogleg to the left, with mounds and bunkers down the left-hand side. In addition to the ocean view, the remains of Whale Bay Battery, a 19th-century fortification, lie between the fairway and the bay. Only golf balls hooked wildly from the tee have any chance of a direct hit on the fort. The wind can be brutal on this hole. ⊠ *Off Middle Rd., Southampton,* ☎ *441/234–0974; 441/295–6500 automated system to reserve golf time 4 days in advance;* FAX *441/234–3562.* ✉ *Greens fees $72 weekdays, $82 weekends and holidays, discount rates after 4. Cart rental $18 per person, $9 for hand cart. Club rentals $25. Shoe rentals $12.*

Princess Golf Club

Length: 2,684 yards from the blue tees. Par: 54. Rating: none.

The Princess Golf Club unfolds on the hillside beneath the Southampton Princess. The hotel has managed to sculpt a neat little par-three course from the steep terrain, and players who opt to walk around find their mountaineering skills and stamina severely tested. The vertical drop on the first two holes alone is at least 200 ft, and the rise on the fourth hole makes 178 yards play like 220. Kept in excellent shape by an extensive irrigation system, the course is a good warm-up for Bermuda's full-length courses, offering a legitimate test of wind and bunker play with a minimum of obstructions and hazards. Ocean views are a constant feature of the front nine, although the looming presence of the hotel does detract from the scenery.

Highlight hole: The green of the 174-yard 16th hole sits in a cup ringed by pink oleander bushes. The Gibbs Hill Lighthouse, less than a mile away, dominates the backdrop. ⊠ *Southampton Princess, South Rd.,* ☎ *441/238–0446,* FAX *441/238–8479.* ☞ *Greens fees $62 per person with mandatory cart ($56 for hotel guests). Shoe rentals $8. Club rentals $20.*

Riddell's Bay Golf and Country Club
Length: 5,588 yards from the blue tees. Par: men, 69; women, 71. Rating: blue tees, 66.9; white tees, 66.1; red tees, 70.6.

Built in 1922, the Riddell's Bay Golf and Country Club course is Bermuda's oldest. In design, however, it more nearly approximates a Florida course—relatively flat, with wide, palm-lined fairways. You don't need to be a power hitter to score well here, although the first four holes, including a 427-yard uphill par four and a 244-yard par three, might suggest otherwise. The par fours are mostly in the 360-yard range, and the fairways are generously flat and open. Despite the course's position, on a narrow peninsula between Riddell's Bay and the Great Sound, water comes into play only on holes 8 through 11. With the twin threats of wind and water, these are the most typically Bermudian holes on the course, and accuracy off the tee is important. This is especially true of the par-four eighth, a 360-yard right dogleg around the water. With a tail wind, big hitters might try for the green, but playing around the dogleg on this relatively short hole is the more prudent choice. A few tees are fronted with stone walls—an old-fashioned touch that harks back to the old courses of Great Britain. Like Mid Ocean's, Riddell's is private, and opens to the public only at certain times, but the clubby atmosphere is much less pronounced here.

Highlight hole: The tees on the 340-yard, par-four 10th are set on a grass-top quay on the harbor's edge. The fairway narrows severely after about 200 yards, and a drive hit down the right side leaves a player no chance to reach the green in two. Two ponds guard the left side of a sloped and elevated green. The hole is rated only the sixth most difficult on the course, but the need for pinpoint accuracy probably makes it the hardest to par. ⊠ *Riddell's Bay Rd., Warwick,* ☎ *441/ 238–1060,* FAX *441/238–8785.* ☞ *Greens fees $70 weekdays, $90 weekends ($40 weekdays, $50 weekends and holidays when accompanied by a member). Cart rental $40 (for 2 people), $5 for hand cart. Club rentals $25.*

St. George's Golf Club
Length: 4,043 yards from the blue tees. Par: 63. Rating: blue tees, 62.8; white tees, 61.4; red tees, 62.8.

Built in 1985, St. George's Golf Club dominates a secluded headland at the island's northeastern end. The 4,043-yard course is short, but it makes up for its lack of length with sharp teeth. No course in Bermuda is more exposed to wind, and no course has smaller greens. Some are no more than 25 ft across. To make matters trickier, the greens are hard and slick from the wind and salty air. Many of the holes have commanding views of the ocean, particularly the 8th, 9th, 14th, and 15th. Wind—especially from the north—can turn these short holes into club-selection nightmares. Don't let high scores here ruin your enjoyment of some of the finest views on the island. The course's shortness and its relative emptiness midweek makes it a good choice for couples or groups of varying ability.

Highlight hole: Pause to admire the view from the par-four 14th hole before you tee off. From the elevated tee area, the 326-yard hole curls around Coot Pond, an ocean-fed cove, to the green on a small, treeless peninsula. Beyond the neighboring 15th hole is old Fort St. Catherine, and beyond it the sea. With a tail wind, it's tempting to hit for the green from the tee, but Coot Pond leaves no room for error. ⊠ *1 Park Rd., St. George's,* ☎ *441/297–8067; 441/295–5600 (tee times and information); 441/297–8148 (pro's office); 441/297–8353 (pro shop);* FAX *441/297–2273.* ⌨ *Greens fees $45; $23 after 3* PM*, Apr.–Oct.; $18 after 2* PM*, Nov.–Mar. Cart rental $36, $8 for hand cart.*

Horseback Riding

Because most of the land on Bermuda is residential, opportunities for riding through the countryside are few. The chief exception is **South Shore Park,** between South Road and the Warwick beaches. Sandy trails, most of which are open only to walkers or riders, wind through stands of dune grass and oleander and over coral bluffs. (Horses are not generally allowed on the beaches.)

Spicelands Riding Centre (⊠ Middle Rd., Warwick, ☎ 441/238–8212 or 441/238–8246) leads riders on trails along the dunes above the south shore beaches at 7 AM, 10 AM, and 11:30 AM daily. These one-hour jaunts cost $50 per person, with a maximum of 10 people in each group (and no one under age 12). From December through March, Bermuda's off season, you can ride along the beach. Afternoon rides are also offered on weekdays. Spicelands gives private lessons in its riding ring for $30 per half hour. Beginners are required to take a series of at least three lessons. On Saturdays, children ages 12 and under can take 15-minute pony rides for $10.

Jet Skiing

If riding a moped on terra firma isn't enough for you, consider mounting a jet ski. In Bermuda you can ride these high-speed aqua-cycles only if you do so in the company of a guide. Rates are about $90–$100 an hour for a single jet ski and $110–$125 for a double. At **Mangrove Marina** in Somerset, you can arrange to take a "speed tour" at the western end of the island, in the Great Sound, Ely's Harbour, Mangrove Bay, and above the visible Sea Gardens coral formations. Groups are kept small—no more than four jet skis per guide.

Contact **Mangrove Marina** (⊠ Somerset Bridge, Sandys, ☎ 441/234–0914), or try **Windjammer Water Sports** (⊠ Royal Naval Dockyard, Sandys, ☎ 441/234–0250; ⊠ Cambridge Beaches, Sandys, ☎ 441/234–3082).

Jogging and Running

Many of the difficulties that cyclists face in Bermuda—hills, traffic, and wind—also confront runners. The presence of sidewalks and roadside footpaths, however, does make the going somewhat easier. Runners who like firm pavement are happiest on the Railway Trail (☞ Bicycling, *above*) or on South Road, a popular route. For those who like running on sand, the trails through **South Shore Park** are relatively firm, although the island's beaches obviously present a much softer surface. **Horseshoe Beach** and **Elbow Beach** are frequented by a large number of serious runners in the early morning and after 5 PM. Another beach for running is ½-mi **Warwick Long Bay,** the longest uninterrupted stretch of sand on the island. But the sand is softer here than at Horseshoe and Elbow, so it's difficult to get a good footing, particularly at high tide.

By using South Shore Park trails to skirt coral bluffs, runners can create a route that connects several beaches, although trails can be winding and uneven in some places.

Parasailing

Parasailing outfits operate in the **Great Sound** and in **Castle Harbour** from May through October. The cost is about $45 per person for an eight-minute flight. Try **Bermuda Island Parasail Co.** (✉ Darrell's Wharf, Paget, ☎ 441/232–2871). Couples who want to sail through the sky under a single parachute should call **Skyrider Bermuda** (✉ Royal Naval Dockyard, ☎ 441/234–3019) or **Adventure Enterprises** (✉ Ordnance Island, St. George's, ☎ 441/297–1459). A two-person trip costs about $80.

Snorkeling

The clarity of the water, the stunning array of coral reefs, and the shallow resting places of several wrecks make snorkeling in the waters around Bermuda—both inshore and offshore—particularly rewarding. You can snorkel year-round, although a wet suit is advisable for anyone planning to spend a long time in the water in winter, when the water temperature can dip into the 60s. The water also tends to be rougher in winter, often restricting snorkeling to the protected areas of Harrington Sound and Castle Harbour. Underwater caves, grottoes, coral formations, and schools of small fish are the highlights of these areas. When Bermudians are asked to name a favorite snorkeling spot, however, they invariably rank **Church Bay** in Southampton (at the western end of the south-shore beaches) at or near the top of the list. A small cove cut out of the coral cliffs, this picturesque bay is full of nooks and crannies, and the reefs are relatively close to shore. Snorkelers should exercise caution here (as they should everywhere along the south shore), as the water can be rough. Other popular snorkeling areas close inshore are the beaches of **John Smith's Bay** at the eastern end of the south shore, and **Tobacco Bay** at the eastern end of the north shore. Despite its small size, **West Whale Bay** is also worth a visit.

Some of the best snorkeling sites are accessible only by boat, and others would require long swims. You can rent small boats by the hour, half day, or day (☞ Boat Rentals *in* Boating and Sailing, *above*). As the number of wrecks attests, navigating around Bermuda's reef-strewn waters is no simple task, especially for inexperienced boaters. If you rent a boat yourself, stick to the protected waters of the sounds, harbors, and bays, and be sure to ask for an ocean-navigation chart. (These point out shallow waters, rocks, and hidden reefs.) For trips to the reefs, let someone else do the navigating—a charter-boat skipper or one of the snorkeling-cruise operators. Some of the best reefs for snorkeling, complete with shallow-water wrecks, are to the west, but where the tour guide or skipper goes often depends on the tide, weather, and water conditions. For snorkelers who demand privacy and freedom of movement, a boat charter (complete with captain) is the only answer, but the cost is considerable—$650 a day for a party of 18. By comparison, half a day of snorkeling on regularly scheduled cruises generally costs $40–$65, including equipment and instruction.

Snorkeling equipment is available for rental at most major hotels. The **Grotto Bay Beach Hotel & Tennis Club, Sonesta Beach Hotel & Spa,** and **Southampton Princess** have dive operators on site. Rates for mask, flippers, and snorkel are usually $15–$20 a day, with the price per day decreasing when a rental is longer. A deposit or credit-card impression is required. You can also rent equipment, including small boats and underwater cameras, at several marinas. To rent equipment at the island's western end, go to **Mangrove Marina** (⊠ Somerset Bridge, Sandys, ☎ 441/234–0914), **Pompano Beach Club Watersports Centre** (⊠ Pompano Beach Club Rd., Southampton, ☎ 441/234–0222), or **Windjammer Water Sports** (⊠ Dockyard Marina, Royal Naval Dockyard, ☎ 441/234–0250), all of which also rent small boats. In the central part of the island, rent boats and gear at **Salt Kettle Yacht Charters** (⊠ Off Harbour Rd., Salt Kettle Rd., Paget, ☎ 441/236–4863 or 441/236–3612). **Horseshoe Bay Beach** (⊠ Southampton, ☎ 441/238–2651) also rents equipment.

Snorkeling Cruises

Snorkeling cruises, offered from April to November, may be too touristy for many visitors. Some boats carry up to 40 passengers to snorkeling sites, but focus mostly on their music and bars (complimentary beverages are usually served on the trip back from the reefs). Smaller boats, which limit capacity to 10–16 passengers, offer more personal attention and focus more on the beautiful snorkeling areas themselves. To make sure you choose a boat that's right for you, ask for details before booking. Many of the boats can easily arrange private charters for groups. Half-day snorkeling tours cost between $40 and $65.

Two of the best half-day snorkeling trips (or longer for special charters) are offered by **Hayward's Snorkeling & Glass Bottom Boat Cruises** (⊠ Dock adjacent to Hamilton Ferry Terminal, ☎ 441/292–8652; 441/236–9894 after hours) and **Pitman's Snorkeling** (⊠ Robinson's Marina, Somerset Bridge, ☎ 441/234–0700). Both relate interesting historical and ecological information about the island in addition to visiting pristine offshore snorkeling areas, often at shipwreck sites.

Captain Kirk Ward's **Native Tours** (⊠ Dockyard, Sandys, ☎ 441/234–8149 or 441/234–1434) offers regularly scheduled sailing-snorkeling trips to the outer reefs on a 38-ft trimaran and a 48-ft catamaran. Half-day cruises are also available from **Salt Kettle Yacht Charters** (⊠ Off Harbour Rd., Salt Kettle Rd., Paget, ☎ 441/236–4863) and **Jessie James Snorkeling & Sightseeing Cruises** (⊠ 48 Par-la-Ville Rd., Suite 366, Hamilton, ☎ 441/296–5801).

Squash

The **Bermuda Squash Club** (⊠ Middle Rd., Devonshire, ☎ 441/292–6881) makes its four courts available to nonmembers of all ages and standards between 11 AM and 11 PM by reservation. A $10 per-person guest fee (plus $4–$6.50 court fees, depending on the time of day) buys 40 minutes of play, and you can borrow rackets and balls. Temporary memberships are available, if you plan to play several times. Visitors can even be teamed up with a local partner, and participate in timed matches and competitions. To play on the two courts at the **Coral Beach & Tennis Club** (⊠ South Rd., Paget, ☎ 441/236–2233), you must be introduced by a member.

Swimming

There are no public swimming pools on the island, but most hotels and some guest houses have their own pools. The Fairmont Southampton Princess and the Sonesta Beach Hotel & Spa are the top of the heap as far as pools go. Whaler Inn is the Fairmont's beach property, situated a few hundred yards away from the main hotel. The pool holds in the region of 100 in a relaxed setting, and those seeking a little wilder swim can slip across to Horseshoe Bay Beach.

Of the island's bays and beaches, Horseshoe Bay is one of the most recommended for swimmers. If you find it a little on the busy side, John Smith's Bay, Chaplin Bay, and Achilles Bay are great alternatives. John Smith's Bay, in the Devil's Hole area, has waters that are calmer and without the undertow usually associated with the south shore beaches. Chaplin Bay, next to Warwick Long Bay, is one of the cosier spots along the south shore and is ideal for anyone who wants to get away from it all. Similarly cosy is Achilles Bay, which is just off Fort St. Catherine in St. George's. Calmer waters, as is the nature of the north shore, are the prevailing condition here.

Tennis

Bermuda has one tennis court for every 600 residents, a ratio that even the most tennis-crazed countries would find difficult to match. Many are private, but the public has access to more than 70 courts in 20 locations island-wide. Courts are inexpensive and seldom full. Hourly rates for nonguests are about $10–$16. You might want to consider bringing along a few fresh cans of balls, because balls in Bermuda cost $6–$7 per can—two to three times the rate in the United States. Among the surfaces used in Bermuda are Har-Tru, clay, cork, and hard composites, of which the relatively slow Plexipave composite is the most prevalent. Despite Bermuda's British roots, the island has no grass court.

Wind, heat (in summer), and humidity are the most distinct characteristics of Bermudian tennis. From October through March, when daytime temperatures rarely exceed 80°F, play is comfortable throughout the day. But in summer, the heat radiating from the court (especially hard courts) can make play uncomfortable between 11 and 3. At such times, the breezes normally considered a curse in tennis can be a real blessing. Early morning or evening tennis presents players with an entirely different problem, when tennis balls grow heavy with moisture from Bermuda's humid sea air, always at its wettest early and late in the day. On clay courts the moist balls become matted with clay, making them even heavier.

Most tennis facilities offer lessons, ranging from $25–$30 for 30 minutes of instruction, and racket rentals for $4–$6 per hour or per play. There are no "public" or free courts on the island.

Coral Beach & Tennis Club
Introduction by a member is required to play here. This exclusive club houses eight clay courts, three of which are floodlit, and is open daily from 8 AM to 8 PM. Coral Beach is the site of the annual Bermuda Open tournament each April. ⊠ *Off South Rd., Paget,* ☎ *441/236–6495 or 441/236–2233.*

Elbow Beach Hotel
This facility is fortunate to have as its Director of Tennis David Lambert, who is also President of the Bermuda Lawn Tennis Association. Serving under Mr. Lambert as a teaching pro is Ricky Mallory, the Island's top-ranked men's player. There are five Plexipave courts on hand, two with lights, and hours of play are from 8 AM to 6 PM throughout the week. Courts are rented for $14 per hour by day and $20 per hour at night. In addition to lessons, match play can be arranged for visitors. ⊠ *South Shore, Paget,* ☎ *441/236–3535.*

Fairmont Southampton Princess Hotel
Despite their position at the water's edge, the Plexipave hard courts here are reasonably well shielded from the wind, although the breeze can be swirling and difficult. Six courts are at hand with fees ranging from $12 per hour to $16 per hour on any of the three courts, which

have lighting. Hours of service are from 8 AM to 6 PM, until 8 PM in summer. The tennis shop features the Bermuda Mixer, a popular round-robin get-together that's a great place for meeting new people. ⊠ *South Rd., Southampton,* ☎ *441/238–1005.*

Government Tennis Stadium

These are the busiest of Bermuda's tennis courts, their inland location ideal for combating strong winds. Of the eight all-weather courts available, five are Plexi-Cushion and three are Har-Tru. Floodlight capacity is featured on three courts in the main stadium. Hours run from 8 AM to 10 PM on weekdays and 8 AM to 6 PM on weekends. Rates are $8 per hour during the day and $16 per hour at night. ⊠ *2 Marsh Folly, Pembroke,* ☎ *441/292–0105.*

Grotto Bay Beach Hotel and Tennis Club

This is the most easterly of the island's feature facilities, situated a little more than a stone's throw from the Bermuda International Airport. There are four Plexipave cork-based courts, two lighted, with an hourly rate of $12. Lessons are available upon request. ⊠ *North Shore Rd., Hamilton Parish,* ☎ *441/293–8333, ext. 1914.*

Pomander Gate Tennis Club

There are five hard courts available (four with lighting) at this scenic establishment located off Hamilton Harbour. It's known for its strong membership. For visitors, temporary membership is available for $30 per couple per week. Hours of play are 7 AM to 11 PM on weekdays, until 10 PM on weekends. ⊠ *Pomander Rd., Paget,* ☎ *441/236–5400.*

Port Royal Golf Course

This club offers four hard courts, two of which are floodlit. A host of pros are on hand to offer instruction to juniors and seniors. Rates for court play are $10 per hour in the day and $14 per hour at night until 10 PM. Arrangements can be made through the golf club from 10 AM. ⊠ *Off Middle Rd., Southampton,* ☎ *441/238–9430.*

Sonesta Beach Hotel & Spa

The Sonesta offers players one of the more spectacular settings on the island, but the courts are exposed to summer winds from the south and southwest. The hotel has six Plexipave courts, two lighted for night play. Rates are $8 per hour, with lessons also available from the resident pro. ⊠ *Off South Rd., Southampton,* ☎ *441/238–8122.*

Waterskiing

Winds on Bermuda vary considerably, making it difficult to predict when the water will be calmest. But early morning and evening breezes are often the lightest. The best season for waterskiing is May through October. Head for the Warwick, Southampton, or Somerset shoreline of the **Great Sound** when the winds are coming from the south or southwest. In the event of northerly winds, stick to the protected areas in **Hamilton Harbour** and **Harrington Sound. Castle Harbour** and **Ferry Reach** are also good areas, depending on wind strength and direction.

If possible, befriend a Bermudian who has a boat; otherwise, contact **Blue Hole Water Sports** (⊠ Grotto Bay Beach & Tennis Club, 11 Blue Hole Hill, Hamilton Parish, ☎ 441/293–2915). Rates fluctuate with fuel costs but average $40 for 15 minutes, $60 per half hour, and $100 per hour, instruction included.

Windsurfing

The **Great Sound, Elbow Beach, Somerset Long Bay, Shelly Bay,** and **Harrington Sound** are the favorite haunts of board sailors in Bermuda.

For novices, the often calm waters of Mangrove Bay and Castle Harbour are probably best. The Great Sound, with its many islands, coves, and harbors, is good for board sailors of all abilities, although the quirky winds that sometimes bedevil yachts in the sound obviously affect sailboards as well. The open bays on the north shore are popular among wave enthusiasts when the northerly storm winds blow. Only experts should consider windsurfing on the south shore. Wind, waves, and reefs make it so dangerous that rental companies are prohibited from renting boards there. Experienced board sailors who want to meet local windsurfers can call former Olympic competitor Hubert Watlington at **Sail On** (✉ Old Cellar, off Front St., Hamilton, ☎ 441/295–0808). He's an integral part of this sailing circuit.

Even the most avid board sailors should rent sailboards rather than bring their own. Transporting a board around Bermuda is a logistical nightmare. There are no rental cars, and few taxi drivers are willing to see their car roofs scoured with scratches in the interest of sport. Rental rates range from $25 to $35 an hour, and from $60 to $90 a day. Some shops negotiate special long-term rates. Contact **Blue Hole Water Sports** (✉ Grotto Bay Beach Hotel & Tennis Club, 11 Blue Hole Hill, Hamilton Parish, ☎ 441/293–2915), **Windjammer Water Sports** (✉ Royal Naval Dockyard, ☎ 441/234–0250; ✉ Cambridge Beaches, Sandys, ☎ 441/234–3082), or **Pompano Beach Club** (✉ 36 Pompano Rd., Pompano Beach Club, Southampton, ☎ 441/234–0222).

SPECTATOR SPORTS

Bermuda is a great place for sports fans seeking a change of scenery from baseball, football, and basketball—sports that mean little to Bermudians. In addition to golf and tennis, the big spectator sports here are cricket, rugby, soccer, field hockey, and yacht racing.

The **World Rugby Classic,** in the fall, brings erstwhile top players, now retired, to the island for a week of top play and parties. At this time of year, the fabled Mid Ocean Club hosts a two-day golf tournament, the **Tour Challenge,** that has featured such top names as Corey Pavin, Tom Watson, Ray Floyd, and Se Ri Pak in a perfectly relaxed setting. Top runners flock to the island in January for the **Bermuda International Marathon, Half Marathon and 10K Race.** And prestigious summer and fall sailing events include the Newport–to–Bermuda race and the Omega Gold Cup. The Bermuda Department of Tourism (☞ Visitor Information *in* Smart Travel Tips A to Z) can provide exact dates and details for all major sporting events.

Cricket

Cricket is the big team sport in summer, and **Cup Match** in late July or early August is *the* summer sporting event played over two days. The top players from around the island compete at the **Somerset Cricket Club** (✉ Broome St. off Somerset Rd., ☎ 441/234–0327) or the **St. George's Cricket Club** (✉ Wellington Slip Rd., ☎ 441/297–0374). Although the cricket is taken very seriously, the event itself is a real festival, attended by thousands of picnickers and partyers. There is an entry fee of $10 per day. The regular cricket season runs from April through September. For more information, contact the **Bermuda Cricket Board of Control** (☎ 441/292–8958, ℻ 441/292–8959).

Equestrian Events

Events are held throughout the year at the **Bermuda Equestrian Federation** (✉ Vesey St., Devonshire, ☎ 441/234–0485, ℻ 441/234–

3010). In October the horsey set turns out in full force for the FEI/Samsung Dressage Competition and Show Jumping events. For more information, write to the Bermuda Equestrian Federation (✉ Box DV 583, Devonshire DV BX).

Golf

Tournaments for pros, seniors, juniors, women, and mixed groups fill Bermuda's golfing schedule from February through December. The highlight of the golf year is October's **Bermuda Open,** which attracts a host of professionals and amateurs.

Handicap limits are usually imposed for the more serious tournaments, and entry fees range from $150 to $275 (not all events are open to non-Bermudian participants). A schedule with entry forms is available from the **Bermuda Golf Association** (✉ Box HM, Hamilton HM BX, ☎ 441/238–1367, ℻ 441/238–0983).

In January, February, and March, tournaments for seniors, couples, and women are held at **Port Royal Golf Course** in Southampton. The adjacent **Pompano Beach Club,** which cosponsors these events, offers special golf-hotel packages. Contact the Pompano (☞ Small Hotels *in* Chapter 5) for more information.

Rugby

Bermuda's rugby season runs from September to April. November brings the World Rugby Classic, held at the **National Sports Club** (✉ Middle Rd., Devonshire, ☎ 441/236–6994). The competition attracts teams from the United States, Great Britain, France, New Zealand, and Australia as well as Bermuda. Tickets cost about $12. During the rest of the season you can watch matches between local teams.

Running

The big running event on the island is the **Bermuda International Marathon, Half Marathon and 10K Race (International Race Weekend),** held in mid-January. The race attracts world-class distance runners from several countries, but it's open to everyone. For information, contact the Race Committee (✉ Box DV 397, Devonshire DV BX, ☎ 441/236–6086). The committee can also provide information on other races held throughout the year. It may be second to International Race Weekend in worldwide appeal, but the **Bermuda Marathon Derby** captures the imagination of the island like no other race. A public holiday, **Bermuda Day,** is celebrated with thousands of locals and visitors alike lining the edges of the 13.3-mi course. The race, which begins in Somerset and finishes near the Government Tennis Stadium, is open to residents only. Fitness fanatics can also enter the **Bermuda Triathlons,** held about once a month from April to October. The events combine a swim, a cycling leg, and a run. Contact the Bermuda Triathlon Association (✉ 48 Parla-Ville Rd., Suite 547, Hamilton HM 11, ☎ 441/293–2765).

Less competitive—and certainly less strenuous—events are the 2-mi "fun runs" sponsored by the **Mid-Atlantic Athletic Club** (✉ Box HM 1745, Hamilton HM BX, ☎ 441/293–8103, ℻ 441/293–4089). They're held every Tuesday evening from April through October. Runs begin at 6 PM near the Berry Hill Road entrance to the Botanical Gardens. There is no entry fee. Additional information on races is available from the **Bermuda Track & Field Association** (✉ Box DV 397, Devonshire DV BX, ☎ 441/296–0951).

Soccer

Football (soccer) season runs from September through April in Bermuda. You can watch local teams in various age divisions duke it out on fields around the island. For details, contact the **Bermuda Football Association** (⌷ Cedar Ave., Hamilton, ☎ 441/295–2199).

Tennis

Tennis tournaments are played year-round, although most of the major ones are in the fall and winter. Several welcome visitors as competitors. Top events include: the March and April **All Bermuda Tennis Club Members' Tournament** (⌷ Government Tennis Stadium, Pembroke Parish, ☎ 441/292–0105), a closed, clay-court competition to which visitors are welcome; April's **Bermuda Open,** an ATP Tour, USTA-sanctioned event of the world's top professionals played on clay courts at the Coral Beach & Tennis Club (☎ 441/236–2233), another closed competition to which visitors are welcome; May's **Heineken Open,** played at the Government Tennis Stadium (☞ *above*) and open to visitors; June's **Pomander Gate Tennis Club Open** (⌷ Pomander Rd., Paget, ☎ 441/236–5400), a hard-court competition open to visitors; September's **Grotto Bay Open,** an 11-day hard-court tournament open to visitors, played at the Grotto Bay Beach Hotel & Tennis Club (⌷ Hamilton Parish, ☎ 441/293–8333 ext. 1914); and October's **All Bermuda Tennis Club Open,** played at the Government Tennis Stadium (☞ *above*) and open to visitors.

Every November there is back-to-back tournament activity at the Coral Beach & Tennis Club (☞ *above*), which attracts numerous visitors and a host of the top local players. The action begins with the **Bermuda Lawn Tennis Club Invitational** followed by the **Coral Beach Club Invitational.** For more information about these and other tournaments, contact the **Bermuda Lawn Tennis Association** (⌷ Box HM 341, Hamilton HM BX, ☎ 441/296–0834, ℻ 441/295–3056).

Yachting

Bermuda has a worldwide reputation as a center of yacht racing. Spectators, particularly those on land, may find it difficult to follow the intricacies of a race or regatta, but the sight of the racing fleet, with brightly colored spinnakers flying, is always striking. The racing season runs from March to November. Most races are held on weekends in the Great Sound, and several classes of boats usually compete. You can watch the racing from a distance at Spanish Point and along the Somerset shoreline. Anyone who wants to get a real sense of the action should be on board a boat near the race course.

In June in alternating years, Bermuda serves as the finish for ocean-going yachts in three major races beginning in the United States: the **Newport–Bermuda Ocean Yacht Race,** the **Marion to Bermuda Race,** and the **Bermuda Ocean Race** from Annapolis, Maryland. Of these, the Newport–Bermuda Race (next held in 2002) usually attracts the most entries, but all fill the island's harbors and yacht-club docks with yachts, which usually range in length from about 30 ft to 80 ft—a spectacular sight. For those more interested in racing than gawking at expensive yachts, the **Omega Gold Cup International Match Race Tournament** is the event of choice. Held in October in Hamilton Harbour, the tournament hosts many of the world's top sailors—some of whom are America's Cup skippers—and includes the elite among the Bermudians in a lucrative chase for thousands in prize money.

8   SHOPPING

If you're looking for colorful street markets where you can haggle over the price of low-cost goods and souvenirs, find another island. Bermuda's sophisticated department stores and boutiques purvey top-notch, top-price merchandise. The quality of wares is quite good, and if you keep that in mind, you'll find that Bermuda does offer substantial savings on many items, particularly jewelry and British-made clothing.

By Honey
Naylor

Updated by
Vivienne
Sheath

IF YOU'RE ACCUSTOMED TO SHOPPING in Saks Fifth Avenue, Neiman Marcus, and Bergdorf Goodman, the prices in Bermuda's elegant shops won't come as a surprise. In fact, the prices on many items in Bermuda's stores are discounted, but a $600 dress or suit discounted by 20% is still $480. Bermuda shopkeepers have felt the effect of the growing number of discount stores in the United States. It would be wise to check discount prices before you leave home and to compare them with Bermudian prices on items that interest you. Remember that Bermuda, unlike most U.S. states, has no sales tax, which means that the price on the tag is the price you pay.

Woolens and cashmere are good buys, especially after Christmas and in January when many stores offer substantial discounts. Naturally, Bermuda shorts are hot items, as are kilts, but bargains on these are a rarity. Only products actually made in Bermuda (and antiques more than 100 years old) can be sold duty-free.

European-made crystal and china—Wedgwood, Royal Crown Derby, Villeroy & Boch, Waterford, and Orrefors, to name a few—are available at prices at least 25% lower than those in the United States. Figurines from Lladró, Royal Doulton, and Hummel are also sold at significantly discounted prices. European fragrances and cosmetics are priced about 25%–30% less than in the United States, as are Rolex, Tissot, Patek Philippe, and other watches.

Bermuda has a thriving population of artists and artisans, whose work ranges from sculpture and paintings to miniature furniture, hand-blown glass, and dolls. Other Bermuda-made specialties include delicious local honey, which you can find in most grocery stores. Outerbridge's Sherry Peppers condiments add zip to soups, stews, drinks, and chowders. The original line has been expanded to include Bloody Mary mix, pepper jellies, and barbecue sauce.

Bermuda rum is another popular item, and a variety of rum-based liqueurs is available, including Bermuda Banana, Banana Coconut Rum, and Bermuda Gold. Gosling's Black Seal Rum is excellent mixed with ginger beer to make a Dark and Stormy, a famous Bermuda drink that should be treated with respect and caution. Rum is also found in quantity in Fourways Dark and Stormy cakes, which are made in Bermuda and can be mailed home.

U.S. citizens age 21 and older who have been out of the country for 48 hours are allowed to bring home 1 liter of duty-free liquor each (☞ Customs & Duties *in* Smart Travel Tips A to Z). In an odd catch-22, however, Bermuda requires a minimum purchase of 2 liters or five 75-centiliter bottles to qualify for in-bond (duty-free) prices. There is now duty-free shopping at the airport, but you can order duty-free liquor at any store, and the management will make arrangements to deliver your purchase to the airport departure lounge or your cruise ship. If you choose to shop in town rather than at the airport, it is best to buy the liquor at least 24 hours before your departure, or by 9:30 AM on the day of an afternoon departure, in order to allow enough time for delivery. With liquor, it pays to shop around, because prices vary. Grocery stores usually charge more than liquor stores. Some stores allow customers to create their own mixed packs of various liquors at in-bond prices, while others offer a selection of prepackaged sets (the five-pack is most common). Below are some sample prices at press time for 1 liter bottles: Tia Maria, $16.35; Grand Marnier, $27.50; Chivas Regal (12-year-old), $31.45; J & B Rare, $14.70; Johnnie Walker Black, $31.85;

Stolichnaya vodka, $10.30; Beefeater gin, $14.20; and Gosling's Black Seal rum, $11.

For products other than liquor, comparison shopping within Bermuda is usually a waste of time, because the merchants' association keeps prices almost identical island-wide. Again, it is worth checking the price of items at home—especially crystal and china—before you embark on a shopping spree in Bermuda. Ask your local department store if any sales are scheduled and check the prices of designer and name-brand products at local factory outlets.

Although the numbering of houses is becoming more common—houses have traditionally been known only by their picturesque names rather than numbers—buildings in Hamilton are still numbered rather whimsically. If you check the phone directory for a store address, you may find a listing on Front Street or Water Street, for example, but no street number. In fact, some Front Street buildings have two numbers, one of them an old historic address that has nothing to do with the building's present location. Fortunately, almost all Bermudians can give you precise directions.

In general, shops are open Monday–Saturday 9–5 or 9–5:30, closed on Sunday (although some supermarkets remain open) and public holidays. Some Hamilton shops stay open late on Wednesday for Harbour Night festivities from April through October. From late November through Christmas Eve, stores often stay open until 9 on Friday. In the two weeks before Christmas, many stores stay open until 9 most nights. Between April and October, some of the smaller Front Street shops open on Sunday. The shops in the Clocktower Centre at the Royal Naval Dockyard are usually open Monday–Saturday 10–5 from April through October (11–5 in winter) and Sunday 11–5. Some extend their hours around Christmas. Almost all stores close for public holidays.

In most cases in this chapter, if a store has several branches or outlets, only the main branch phone number has been listed.

Shopping Districts

Hamilton has the greatest concentration of shops in Bermuda, and **Front Street** is its pièce de résistance. Lined with small, pastel-color buildings, this most fashionable of Bermuda's streets houses sedate department stores and snazzy boutiques, with several small arcades and shopping alleys leading off it. A smart canopy shades the entrance to the **55 Front Street Group,** which houses several upmarket boutiques. **The Emporium** on Front Street, a renovated old building that encloses an open atrium, is home to an eclectic collection of antiques, jewelry, souvenir, and low-quality art shops. The statue on top of the atrium fountain is of Bermudian Gina Swainson, who ruled as Miss World in 1979–80. **Butterfield Place** is a modern mall on Front Street with boutiques selling, among other things, Louis Vuitton leather goods, as well as art galleries displaying the works of local artists.

In St. George's, **Water Street, Duke of York Street, Hunters Wharf, Penno's Wharf,** and **Somers Wharf** are the sites of numerous renovated buildings that house branches of Front Street stores, as well as studios of local artisans. Historic **King's Square** offers little more than a couple of T-shirt and souvenir shops. In the West End, **Somerset Village** has a few shops, but they hardly merit a special shopping trip. However, the historic **Clocktower Centre at Royal Naval Dockyard** has a few more shopping opportunities, including branches of Front Street shops and specialty boutiques. The Dockyard is also home to the **Craft Market,** the **Bermuda Arts Centre,** and **Bermuda Clayworks,** where local artisans display their wares and visitors can sometimes watch them at work. Several other small plazas are sprinkled around the island. They typically contain a few shops and often a grocery store.

Department Stores

Bermuda's three leading department stores are A. S. Cooper & Son, Trimingham's, and H. A. & E. Smith's, the main branches of which are on Front Street in Hamilton. The third or fourth generations of the families that founded them now run these elegant, venerable institutions, and customers stand a good chance of being waited on by a Cooper, a Trimingham, or a Smith. In addition, many of the salespeople have worked at the stores for two or three decades. They tend to be unobtrusive, but polite and helpful when you need them.

A. S. Cooper & Son (✉ 59 Front St., Hamilton, ☎ 441/295–3961; other branches in all major hotels, the Clocktower Building at Dockyard, and in St. George's at 22 Water St.). This store is best known for its extensive inventory of Waterford and Swarovski crystal; china, including Wedgwood, Royal Doulton, Belleek, Villeroy & Boch, and Royal Copenhagen; and Lladró figurines. A five-piece place setting of the Wedgwood Countryware pattern costs $64.20 (add 25% for shipping to the United States, with duty, freight, and insurance). Prices on the stock of china and crystal are similarly attractive. A free home-delivery service with up to 40% savings (without affecting the $400 duty-free allowance) is available to U.S. customers who order Waterford chandeliers; tableware by Royal Doulton, Royal Crown Derby, Minton, Wedgwood, Villeroy & Boch, Royal Copenhagen, and French Quimper; and stemware by Orrefors, Kosta Boda, and Atlantis Crystal. A. S. Cooper & Son's private-label collection of clothing can be found in the well-stocked men's, women's, and children's departments. The gift department on the Front Street level carries a large selection of tasteful Bermudian gifts and souvenirs.

H. A. & E. Smith's (✉ 35 Front St., Hamilton, ☎ 441/295–2288; branches in the Southampton Princess hotel and at 18 York St. in St. George's). Founded in 1889 by Henry Archibald and Edith Smith, this is arguably the best men's store in Bermuda—and exclusive agents for Burberry, William Lockie cashmeres, and Church shoes. Men's Burberry raincoats are priced from $495 to $595, and William Lockie cashmeres sell from $248 to $448. Men's 100% cashmere topcoats go for $425, and Italian silk ties for $26 and up. There is a large selection of Shetland woolen and cotton sweaters, which go for about $35–$49 each. Smith's is also a good place to buy kilts.

Women can find Fendi handbags here (the only place in Bermuda) for about $500 for a medium size, as well as cashmere-lined leather gloves for $58 and $65 (unlined $42 and $45). The women's department also has an extensive selection of formal and casual wear. William Lockie cashmere turtleneck sweaters are priced from $278. Burberry raincoats range from $575 to $695. The women's shoe department offers a broad choice of fine Italian styles, both classic and contemporary.

The Front Street–level china department carries a large selection of patterns from Royal Doulton, Royal Crown Derby, Royal Worcester, and Rosenthal, and crystal of all types is sold. French perfume sells for 20%–30% less than in the States. As with many of the island's older buildings, the store has a confusing layout that makes it easy to get lost. The staff here is especially genteel, however, and they will help orient you.

Marks & Spencer (✉ 18 Reid St., Hamilton, ☎ 441/295–0031). A franchise of the large British chain, it's called Marks and Sparks by every-

BERMUDA SHORTS

HOWEVER MANY IMAGES of Bermudian businessmen in shorts and long socks the books and brochures depict, nothing quite prepares visitors for the first sighting. Tourists can be spotted snickering in shop doorways after discovering the bottom half of a blazer-and-tie-clad executive on his cell phone. After all, where else in the world could he walk into the boardroom wearing bright-pink shorts without so much as a batting of an eyelid? Only in Bermuda. These unique all-purpose garments, however flamboyantly dyed, are worn with complete seriousness and pride. Bermudians would go so far as to say it is the rest of the world that is peculiar, and they have a point—particularly in the steaming humidity of the summer months, when full-length trousers are unthinkable to any self-respecting local.

What is surprising is how the original khaki cutoffs evolved into formal attire. They were introduced to Bermuda in the early 1900s by the British military who adopted the belted, baggy, cotton-twill version to survive the sweltering outposts of the Empire. By the 1920s Bermudian pragmatism and innovation was at play as locals started chopping off their trousers at the knees to stay cool. Tailors seized on the trend and started manufacturing a smarter pair of shorts, and men were soon discovering the benefits of a breeze around the knees.

But for an island that has a love affair with rules there was always going to be a right and a wrong way to wear this new uniform. Bermudas had to be worn with knee-high socks, and a jacket and tie was the only acceptable way of dressing them up for business. But it didn't stop there. Obsession with detail prevailed, fueled by gentlemen who were disturbed at the unseemly shortness of other men's shorts. A law was passed to ensure propriety, and the bizarre result was patrolling policemen, armed with tape measures and warning tickets, scouring the capital for men showing too much leg. Officially, shorts could be no more than 6 inches above the knee, while 2 to 4 was preferable.

Other rigid but unwritten rules made it unheard of to wear them in hotel dining rooms after 6 PM or in churches on Sunday mornings, and even to this day they are out of bounds in the Supreme Court and the House of Assembly. They are, however, viewed as conservative and respectable men's wear for almost any other occasion, and can even be seen paired with tuxedo jackets and are even acceptable (providing they are black) at funerals.

If you're planning on joining in the local tradition, however, play by the rules. Don't expect to be allowed in a restaurant with a pair of check-patterned American interpretations. Real Bermudas are characterized by their fabric and styling—linen or wool blends and a 3-inch hem. The official shorts season is May to November. Take your cue from the local policemen who drop their full-length navy blues at the start of summer.

But if Bermudas are practical, smart dress for men, where does that leave the island's women during the sticky summer months? Wearing skirts, it would seem. Shorts are not considered ideal business wear for women, and are only really acceptable on the beach and while shopping (but again, not if they're skimpy). In a country where pink is a man's color and men's bare legs are all but mandatory for six months of the year, perhaps the men feel the need to stamp their masculine pride on their pants. Whatever the motives, men have truly claimed Bermudas as their own and look set to be showing leg well into the 21st century.

—Vivienne Sheath

one in Bermuda and England. This large store is usually filled with locals attracted by its moderate prices for men's, women's, and children's clothing. Summer wear, including swimsuits, cotton jerseys, and polo shirts, is a good buy. High-quality men's and women's cashmere and woolen sweaters are also sold at substantial discounts.

Trimingham's (⊠ 37 Front St., Hamilton, ☎ 441/295–1183). A Hamilton fixture since 1842, this is Bermuda's largest department store— home of Daks Bermuda shorts ($47.50) and tailored-for-Trimingham's sportswear. Famous women's designers, such as Liz Claiborne, Tommy Hilfiger, and Calvin Klein, have complete lines here, and fine tableware by Lenox, Mikasa, Noritake, Aynsley, Portmeirion, Waterford, Royal Worcester, and Spode is sold for up to 25%–40% less than in the United States. The store has an impressive display of perfumes and cosmetics, and it is Bermuda's exclusive distributor of Christian Dior, Estée Lauder, and Yves Saint Laurent. Shoppers will also find a potpourri of fine leather, jewelry, children's fashions, and gift items. Trimingham branches—10 in all—can be found all over the island, including at Somers Wharf in St. George's, South Shore Road in Paget, and in Somerset Village.

Specialty Stores

Antiques
The Bermuda Railway Museum (⊠ 37 North Shore Rd., Hamilton Parish, ☎ 441/293–4753). If you're in the area near Flatts, be sure to take in this den of treasures. As well as an extensive collection of historic artifacts from Bermuda's short-lived railway, it also sells photos, maps, books, prints, and antiques, and collectibles from jewelry and coins to stamps, books, and china. If you take the bus here, get off at the first stop after the Bermuda Aquarium. The shop is open Tuesday to Friday from 10 to 4 or by appointment with Rose Hollis.

Pegasus (⊠ 63 Pitts Bay Rd., Hamilton, ☎ 441/295–2900). This Dickensian place in an old house with creaky wood floors is a few minutes' walk from downtown Hamilton on Front Street West, near the Princess. The store has bins and bins of antique prints and a small selection of antique maps. In particular, look for the original Leslie Ward (Spy) Vanity Fair caricatures that were published between 1869 and 1914 (from $70) and the Curtis botanicals ($50). Topographical engravings of America, Canada, Ireland, and Scotland by Bartlett start at $50. French fashion scenes and early lithographs of fruit, butterflies, and shells are priced from $50. There is a huge selection of greeting cards and wrapping paper from England, and you can order beautifully crafted ceramic house signs from England here. The shop provides certificates of antiquity for buyers to show to U.S. and Canadian customs (antiques are duty-free and do not affect the $400 allowance). You can browse here to your heart's content from 10 to 5, but never on Sunday.

Portobello (⊠ Emporium Bldg., 9 Front St., Hamilton, ☎ 441/295– 1407). This small, charming shop is an oasis of antiquity tucked away in the modern Emporium Building shopping complex just off Front Street. It is the perfect haunt for stamp and coin collectors with the best collection of 19th- and 20th-century stamps on the island. They also sell a small range of antique prints and ornaments.

Thistle Gallery (⊠ 7 Park Rd., Hamilton, ☎ 441/292–3839). A must for antique furniture lovers. Porcelain, china, glassware, and silver are also on sale.

Art Galleries

Buying artwork by someone you know is always more satisfying than buying it blind, and a number of Bermuda's resident artists—some of whose works are in the collections of famous collectors worldwide—encourage visits to their studios. Call ahead first, however, to find out if it's convenient to stop by. Be sure to check about payment before going. Although commercial shops that sell original art usually accept credit cards, most artists on the island do not. Remember that there are no duties levied on Bermudian arts and crafts.

PAINTINGS, PRINTS, AND SCULPTURE

Diana Amos (⊠ Studio at Hunter's Wharf, St. George's, ☎ 441/297–2354). An art teacher at Bermuda College, Ms. Amos has a discerning eye that is revealed in her Bermudian scenes. She uses pastel watercolor tones to render the beauty of the island's unique architecture, landscapes, and seascapes. Her work is in galleries throughout the island and costs between $500 and about $2,000. She can be found in her studio Monday through Friday.

Bermuda Arts Centre at Dockyard (⊠ Museum Row, Dockyard, Ireland Island, ☎ 441/234–2809). Sleek and modern, with well-designed displays of local art, this gallery is housed in one of the stone buildings of the former British naval dockyard. The walls are adorned with paintings and photographs, and glass display cases contain exquisitely crafted quilts as well as costume dolls, jewelry, and wood sculpture. Exhibits change frequently. Several artists' studios inside the gallery are open to the public. The Centre is open daily from 10 to 5.

Bermuda Society of Arts (⊠ West Wing, City Hall, Hamilton, ☎ 441/292–3824). Many highly creative Society members sell their work at the perennial members' shows and during a revolving series of special group exhibits. You will find watercolor, oil, and acrylic paintings and pastel and charcoal drawings, as well as occasional photographs, collages, and pieces of sculpture. The Society's second gallery, Harbour Gallery, is on Front Street West.

Birdsey Studio (⊠ "Rosecote," 5 Stowe Hill, Paget, ☎ 441/236–6658). Alfred Birdsey died in 1996, and the island mourned his loss. His studio, operated by his daughter, Jo Birdsey Linberg, remains open. Renowned on the island, Mr. Birdsey received the Queen's Certificate of Honour and Medal in recognition of "valuable services given to Her Majesty for more than 40 years as an artist of Bermuda." New works continue the tradition admirably. Watercolors cost from $50 and lithographs from $15 at the studio, which is usually open weekdays 10:30 to 1, and by appointment. Call before going because hours vary.

Bridge House Gallery (⊠ 1 Bridge St., St. George's, ☎ 441/297–8211). Housed in part of a Bermuda home that dates from 1700, this gallery is of historical and architectural interest in its own right. During the 18th century the two-story white building was the home of Bermuda's governors. Today it is maintained by the Bermuda National Trust. Original works by local artists, inexpensive prints, and souvenirs are for sale.

Stephen Card (⊠ Scaur Hill, Somerset, ☎ 441/234–2353). A native Bermudian, this fine marine artist was for many years a captain in the British merchant marine. He relinquished full-time life at sea some years ago to devote himself to painting. Many of his ships from yesteryear are painted only after careful research. Mr. Card's work hangs in private collections in the United States and can be seen aboard major cruise passenger ships. He often travels, but you can also find his work at Heritage House (☞ *below*). His prices are based on detail and size, and range from $2,000 to $20,000.

Will Collieson (⊠ 18 York St., St. George's, ☎ 441/297–0171). One of the island's most talented and versatile artists, Mr. Collieson works in many mediums, and his sense of humor shines in many of his zany three-dimensional contemporary collages, made with materials found around the island. His creations can be seen daily in the window displays at H. A. & E. Smith's department store. Prices vary, depending on the medium used, but a collage costs between $200 and $800.

Joan Forbes (⊠ Art House, 80 South Shore Rd., Paget, ☎ 441/236–6746). Ms. Forbes's watercolors and lithographs of local architecture, horticulture, and seascapes are made for visitors as inexpensive mementos. Her lithographs sell for under $50. She also produces cards, notepaper, and envelopes.

Desmond Fountain (☎ 441/238–8840). This award-winning sculptor's works are on display all over the island, whether it's a life-size bronze statue perched beside a lagoon or a lolling figure seated in a garden chair. Fountain created the *Land Ho!* statue of Sir George Somers on Ordnance Island in St. George's, and other works of his can be seen in the Sculpture Gallery on the mezzanine of the Southampton Princess. Prices start at about $4,500 for a small bronze and soar to dizzying heights.

Sheilagh Head (☎ 441/238–0173). One of the island's finest painters, Mrs. Head, schooled in Italy and England, works with colors better than any other local painter. Her oils stand apart because she explores light and shadow, illuminating the soft hues of the surroundings. Whether it is an abstract, an old Bermudian chimney, a cluster of buildings, or the sky rising above a swath of foliage or the ocean, this artist's sensitivity shines forth in every canvas. Mrs. Head's work hangs in private collections in the United States, Europe, and Britain. Her paintings are sold through the Bermuda Society of Arts (⊠ West Wing, City Hall, Church St., Hamilton). Prices range from about $1,000 to $3,500.

Heritage House (⊠ 2 W. Front St., Hamilton, ☎ 441/295–2615). This gallery regularly displays original works by the island's leading artists including Sheilagh Head, Maria Smith, Kathy Zuill, Diana Amos, and internationally known marine artist Stephen Card. A large selection of local and foreign prints is also available. An on-site framing department has a computerized system that allows for less expensive production. Throughout the store you will find quality reproduction furniture from Great Britain and many interesting and tasteful Bermudian souvenirs.

Carole Holding Print & Craft Shops (⊠ King's Sq., St. George's, ☎ 441/297–1373; ⊠ Clocktower Centre, Dockyard, ☎ 441/297–1373; ⊠ 81 Front St., Hamilton, ☎ 441/297–1373 or 800/880–8570, FAX 441/297–8374). Commercial artist Ms. Holding mass-produces watercolors of Bermuda's scenes and flowers; many of the same works are sold as signed prints and limited editions. Crafts, both imported and by local artists, are also available. Prices range from $15 (small prints) to $200 (framed watercolors).

John Kaufmann (⊠ 16 Tranquillity Hill, Sandys, ☎ 441/234–4095 or 441/235–2232). Mr. Kaufmann works solely with oils to execute his well-known seascapes and landscapes. The Bermuda National Gallery has done a retrospective of his work, and he has had successful one-man shows at the Windjammer Gallery, which is the only gallery that carries his work. Prices range from $1,500 for an 8×10 to about $2,500 for a 12×16.

Masterworks Foundation Gallery (⊠ 97 Front St., Hamilton, ☎ 441/295–5580). Formed in 1987, the foundation exhibits well-known Canadian, British, French, and American artists, including Winslow Homer, whose works were inspired by Bermuda, and Georgia O'Keeffe. The Bermudiana Collection contains more than 400 works in watercolor, oil, pencil, charcoal, and other mediums. The Bermuda

National Gallery at City Hall, Camden House, and Waterloo House all display selected pieces from this collection.

Elmer Midgett (✉ Scaur Hill, Somerset, ☎ 441/234–1936). Using an uncompromising style in oils that employs bold strokes reminiscent of those of van Gogh, Mr. Midgett focuses on the island's unusual buildings and angles. He is also a master at stained glass. His paintings—priced from $600 to about $1,200—are often on display at the Bermuda Society of Arts Gallery (☞ City Hall *in* Chapter 3).

Ann Proctor (✉ Harbour Rd., Paget, ☎ 441/292–8339). This artist's delicate, beautifully executed, and much sought after watercolors of Bermuda plants and flowers have the quality of botanical drawings. Prices start at about $550.

Bruce Stuart (✉ Windjammer Gallery, Reid and King Sts., Hamilton, ☎ 441/292–7861). The island's unique architecture appears in Stuart's paintings, which have a near-photographic quality. Original works range in price from $1,100 to $5,000.

Otto Trott (✉ Clearview Art Gallery, Crawl Hill, Hamilton Parish, ☎ 441/293–4057). A Bermudian who is known for his sensitive use of light and shade, Mr. Trott renders beautiful oil paintings of landscapes and local characters. His work can be found at other island galleries, but he owns the Clearview Art Gallery, and often his best pictures are found there. Small watercolors are priced at $50, oils from about $200 to $2,000. Mr. Trott gives lessons to visitors.

Sharon Wilson (✉ Turtle Pl., Southampton, ☎ 441/238–2583). Ms. Wilson occupies a special place in the local art scene because she is one of the few artists who depict Bermuda's people. This talented woman has had many successful shows, and her work—priced between $5,500 and $7,000—sells well to visitors and locals alike. She employs a radiant range of pastels and often captures people absorbed in their own private world. She is also an illustrator of children's books.

Windjammer Gallery (✉ King and Reid Sts., Hamilton, ☎ 441/292–7861; ✉ 95 Front St., Hamilton, ☎ 441/292–5878). The island's largest selection of local and imported art is in a charming four-room cottage whose colorful garden has life-size bronze sculptures. Individual and group shows are held regularly, and work is exported to collectors worldwide. The knowledgeable staff can help with your selection and shipping arrangements. Prints and lithographs are also available. Prints Plus (✉ 95 Front St.) is Windjammer's print shop, where there is an extensive collection of local prints, cards, books, photographs, and art-related gifts as well as wearable art. All purchases may be shipped, and a catalog is available.

Dr. Charles Zuill (☎ 441/236–9000). One of the island's most innovative artists, Dr. Zuill is also the head of the art department at Bermuda College. His most recent exhibit at the Bermuda Society of Arts, consisting of "Earth Paintings" on square and rectangular canvases, employed a new medium that combined paint and sand from beaches in several parts of the world. His prices begin around $500.

Mary Zuill (✉ 10 Southlyn La., off South Shore Rd., Paget, ☎ 441/236–2439). In a tiny studio attached to her house, Ms. Zuill paints delightful watercolors of Bermuda's flowers, architecture, and seascapes. She accepts commissions and will either design a painting, or work from a photograph you've taken in Bermuda. Watercolors cost between $85 and $450. She welcomes visitors Tuesday through Friday 10 to noon and 2:30 to 5, from about mid-March to November only.

PHOTOGRAPHY

Mark Emmerson (✉ Belvedere Bldg., Hamilton, ☎ 441/292–6283). This photographer produces rich black-and-white prints on platinum and other specialized photographic papers. His portfolio is extensive, and he occasionally shows his work at the Arts Centre at Dockyard.

Ian MacDonald-Smith (⊠ 5 Clarendon La., Flatts, ☎ 441/292–3295). Bold, bright, and large Cibachrome prints—many images are priced at about $250—are this photographer's passion. Unusual angles and portions of the island's unique architecture are the subjects of many pictures. He has produced several books, which are available throughout the island and make a good substitute if his originals are more than your budget allows.

Graeme Outerbridge (⊠ Heritage House, 2 W. Front St., Hamilton, ☎ 441/295–2615; ⊠ Windjammer Gallery, corner of Reid and King Sts., ☎ 441/292–7861). A photographer who contributed to the acclaimed *Day in the Life* book series, Mr. Outerbridge captures Bermuda in original photographic prints, silk screens, and posters.

DeForest Trimingham (⊠ South Shore Rd., Paget, ☎ 441/236–2727). After he retired from working in the family's Front Street department store, Mr. Trimingham resumed working with his camera. He has traveled the world and produced numerous fine Cibachromes of remote places, but most visitors seem to prefer his sensitive Bermuda compositions, which are priced from about $650 for an 11×14.

Judith Wadson (⊠ Box 223, Hamilton, ☎ 441/232–2173). This photographer's specialty consists of hand-colored black-and-white prints as well as photographic prints of Bermuda's architecture and landscapes on archival watercolor paper and high-quality photographic papers. Ms. Wadson, who formerly was a staff photographer for *Yachting* magazine, focuses on the old-world side of Bermuda. Prices for her work range from about $200 to $400, depending on the size and whether the image is framed.

Bookstores

Bermuda Book Store (⊠ Queen St., Hamilton, ☎ 441/295–3698). Once you set foot inside this musty old place, you'll have a hard time tearing yourself away. Stacked on a long table is a host of books about Bermuda. The proprietor can probably answer any questions you have about the island.

The Book Cellar (⊠ Water St., St. George's, ☎ 441/297–0448). This small shop below the National Trust's Tucker House crams in a large selection of books about Bermuda and an interesting assortment of novels by English and American authors beyond the contemporary bestsellers. Coffee-table books cover a range of subjects, and there is a variety of British children's books that are hard to find in the United States. Owner Jill White and her well-read staff will be happy to help you search for an obscure title or let you browse at your leisure.

The Bookmart (⊠ The Phoenix Centre, 3 Reid St., Hamilton, ☎ 441/295–3838). The island's largest bookstore specializes in best-sellers and paperbacks. There is a complete selection of Bermuda titles, as well as a large children's section.

Buds, Beans & Books (⊠ 55 Front St., Hamilton, ☎ 441/292–1990). This handy new Front Street store, opened in 2000, is ideal for grabbing a fresh cup of coffee, cut flowers, or the latest best-seller. There is also a well-stocked selection of magazines and greeting cards.

The Children's Bookshop (⊠ International Centre, 26 Bermudiana Rd., Hamilton, ☎ 441/292–9078). A wonderful selection of hard-to-find British titles is geared to all ages.

Ship's Inn Book Gallery (⊠ Clocktower Centre, Dockyard, Ireland Island, ☎ 441/234–2807). Sherlyn Swan carries an ever-changing assortment of used books as well as some rare and antique titles. The only new books are about Bermuda.

Washington Mall Magazine (✉ Washington Mall, Reid St., Hamilton, ☎ 441/292–7420). Come here for Bermuda's best selection of magazines, including hard-to-find periodicals. This is also the place to find a best-seller for the beach or the journey home, children's books, and coffee-table publications about the island.

Children's Shopping

The Annex Toys (✉ 3 Reid St., Hamilton, ☎ 441/295–3838). This large toy department in the basement of The Phoenix Centre offers one of the best and most up-to-date selections of toys on the island, including Barbie dolls. A "Generation Girl" Barbie will cost you around $50.

Jack 'N' Jill's Toy Shop (✉ 7 Park Rd., Hamilton, ☎ 441/292–3769). At one of Bermuda's top toy retailers you'll find a good selection of traditional toys as well as more modern merchandise.

Toys 'N' Stuff (✉ corner of Queen and Church Sts., Hamilton, ☎ 441/292–6698). Popular with locals, this huge, centrally located store sells everything from children's furniture and prams to the latest toys and games for all ages.

Twiggy's Closet (✉ Washington Mall, Hamilton, ☎ 441/295–8228). Young customers will find it hard to leave Bermuda's only shop devoted entirely to children's clothing. It's decked out like a colorful nursery. The bright, fun clothes are sold at affordable prices and in sizes from infants to 16.

Cigars

Chatham House (✉ 63 Front St., Hamilton, ☎ 441/292–8422). The politically correct be warned that, not only is the air here thick with the aroma of cigar and cigarette smoke, but there is a life-size wooden Indian princess to greet customers. In business since 1895, this shop has the ambience of an old-time country store. It stocks not only top-quality cigars from Cuba (Romeo y Julieta, Bolivar, Partagas, and Punch), but Briar and Meerschaum pipes, Swiss Army knives, Dunhill lighters, sunglasses, gum, and postcards. A sign advises that it is illegal to bring Cuban cigars into the United States.

Tienda de Tabacs (✉ Emporium Bldg., 69 Front St., Hamilton, ☎ 441/295–8475). As sleek as the Chatham House is rustic, this store focuses almost exclusively on cigars, Cuban and otherwise. The hardwood floors are polished to a high sheen, and shelves and glass cases are lined with boxes of stogies. At the rear of the long room there are three huge soft leather armchairs grouped around a coffee table appropriately set with ashtrays. So even if you can't take the Cubans into the States, you're surely invited to smoke 'em right here in the store, along with the sales staff.

Clothing and Accessories

MEN'S CLOTHING

Archie Brown & Son (✉ 51 Front St., Hamilton, ☎ 441/295–2928; ✉ Clocktower Centre, Dockyard, ☎ 441/234–1017; ✉ York St., St. George's, ☎ 441/297–0036). Top-quality woolens, Pringle of Scotland cashmeres, Shetland and lambswool sweaters, and 100% wool tartan kilts are among the specialties here.

Aston & Gunn (✉ 2 Reid St., Hamilton, ☎ 441/295–4866). An up-market member of the English Sports Shops that dot the island, this handsome store carries men's and women's clothing and accessories. Men's European clothing, including Hugo Boss and Van Gils, costs up to 30% less than in the United States. Aston & Gunn cotton dress shirts sell for about $50. Women's wear, including designs by Calvin Klein and Anne Klein, is mainly from the United States, but because there's no sales tax it may be less expensive.

English Sports Shop (✉ 95 Front St., Hamilton, ☎ 441/295–2672; ✉ Water St., St. George's, ☎ 441/295–2672). This shop specializes in British woolens: Shetland woolen sweaters are priced at around $30. Cashmere sweaters start from $200. This store also sells women's sweaters.

MEN'S AND WOMEN'S CLOTHING

Bananas (✉ 93 W. Front St., Hamilton, ☎ 441/295–1106; ✉ 7 E. Front St., Hamilton, ☎ 441/292–7264; ✉ Princess Hotel, Hamilton, ☎ 441/295–3000; ✉ 3 King's Sq., St. George's, ☎ 441/297–0351; ✉ Sonesta Beach Resort, Southampton, ☎ 441/238–3409). Sportswear and T-shirts make this a teenager's dream. Brightly colored Bermuda umbrellas cost about $20.

Davison's of Bermuda (✉ 73 Front St., Hamilton, ☎ 441/292–7137; ✉ Water St., St. George's, ☎ 441/297–8363; ✉ Southampton Princess Hotel, South Shore Rd., Southampton, ☎ 441/238–1036; ✉ Clocktower Centre, Dockyard, ☎ 441/234–0959). High-quality cotton sportswear items include sweaters and slacks, tennis and sailing clothing, golf and tennis hats, and children's sportswear. They also carry gift packages of Bermuda fish chowder, clam chowder, and sherry peppers, and a collection of deliciously vicious-looking stuffed trolls. In the United States you'll find branches of this store in Baltimore and Myrtle Beach.

Upstairs Golf & Tennis Shop (✉ 26 Church St., Hamilton, ☎ 441/295–5161). This store stocks clubs and accessories from some of the best brands available, including Ping, Callaway, and Titleist. Tennis players can choose a racket by Yonex or Dunlop. Men's and women's sportswear is also sold.

SHOES AND HANDBAGS

Boyle, W. J. & Sons Ltd. (✉ Queen St., Hamilton, ☎ 441/295–1887; ✉ Mangrove Bay, Somerset, ☎ 441/234–0530; ✉ Water St., St. George's, ☎ 441/297–1922; ✉ Trends, The Walkway, Reid St., Hamilton, ☎ 441/295–8589; ✉ The Sports Locker, Windsor Place, 18 Queen St., Hamilton, ☎ 441/292–3300). Bermuda's leading shoe store chain, Boyle's sells a wide range of men's, women's, and children's shoes across the island. Trends on Reid Street has the most up-to-the-minute foot fashions.

Gucci (✉ 71 Front St., Hamilton, ☎ 441/295–2351). This small designer shop, tucked away at the back of Crisson's jewelry on Front Street, stocks a small range of fabulous women's sandals, shoes, and handbags and some men's shoes, too. Watch for frequent sales that often cut the tag price by as much as half.

Locomotion (✉ Upper Level, Washington Mall, Hamilton, ☎ 441/296–4030). A small shop with a modest range of very young, up-to-the-minute, affordable styles for women and children.

Louis Vuitton (✉ Butterfield Pl., Hamilton, ☎ 441/296–1940). Come here to find the famous monogram in ladies' handbags, men's and women's briefcases, carry-on luggage, wallets, credit-card cases, and other items. Prices here are the same as in the United States, except there is no tax. Small ladies' handbags start at about $750. Small soft leather monogram carry-ons cost up to $1,000, and natural cowhide briefcases start from $3,000.

The Yankee Store (✉ 15 Reid St., Hamilton, ☎ 441/295–2570). One of Bermuda's rare low-cost shops has a good range of very reasonably priced women's shoes downstairs, including extra-wide sizes. Quality varies, and some styles may be last season's, but it's one of the best places for a bargain. Upstairs (road level) sells everything from cedarwood ornaments and fashion jewelry to leather wallets and souvenirs.

WOMEN'S CLOTHING

Calypso (✉ 45 Front St., Hamilton, ☎ 441/295–2112; other branches at Princess Hotel, Hamilton; Coral Beach & Tennis Club; Sonesta

Beach Resort; Southampton Princess, Southampton; Clocktower Centre, Dockyard). This expensive women's clothing shop carries an array of sophisticated leisure wear. It has the island's largest selection of swimwear and is Bermuda's only purveyor of Jantzen merchandise. Accessories, including Italian leather shoes and straw hats, are plentiful. Eclectic novelty items from Europe make great gifts. Calypso's shop in Butterfield Place, Voila!, carries Longchamps leather goods, Oscar Leopold leather jackets, and Johnston & Murphy men's shoes.

Cecile (⊠ 15 Front St., Hamilton, ☎ 441/295–1311; ⊠ Southampton Princess Hotel, South Shore Rd., Southampton, ☎ 441/238–1434). Specializing in upscale off-the-rack ladies' fashions, Cecile carries such designer labels as Mondi, Basler, and Louis Feraud of Paris. There's a good selection of swimwear, including swimsuits by Gottex, and of European lingerie, especially La Perla. An expanded accessories department carries shoes as well as scarves, jewelry, handbags, and belts.

Cow Polly (⊠ Somers Wharf, St. George's, ☎ 441/297–1514). Phoebe Wharton's store brings together expensive hand-painted clothing and attractive accessories from the far corners of the globe. Beautifully crafted straw bags and hats are worth the trip from Hamilton. And you won't find the store's unusual pottery, jewelry, or men's ties sold anywhere else on the island.

Crown Colony Shop (⊠ 1 Front St., Hamilton, ☎ 441/295–3935). This branch of the English Sports Shop features quality formal and business wear for women. The shop's signature item is a line of Parisian-designed Mayeelok silk dresses and two-piece skirt and pant sets in polyester and silk, which sell for $235 and $295.

Frangipani (⊠ Water St., St. George's, ☎ 441/297–1357). This little store is filled with colorful women's fashions that have an island resort look. Cotton, silk, and rayon leisure wear are the backbone of the stock, but vibrant Caribbean art is also sold. Frangipani also stocks a collection of unusual accessories to offset various styles.

Stefanel (⊠ 12 Walker Arcade, Reid St., Hamilton, ☎ 441/295–5698). This small, trendy boutique is good for simple, stylish, modern women's clothes at reasonable prices. They have lots of cotton and natural fabrics, neutral colors, and delicate small-print fabrics. There is also a good children's section at the back of the shop.

Triangle's (⊠ Queen St., access next to Bermuda Bookstore, Hamilton, ☎ 441/295–5247). This boutique stocks a good range of designer labels and up-market outfits, some at almost half of what they would cost in the United States.

Crafts

Bermuda Clayworks (⊠ Dockyard, Ireland Island, ☎ 441/234–5116). Master potter Jon Faulkner and fellow artisans create on the potter's wheel colorful vases and planters, as well as lead-free cookware that withstands oven, microwave, and dishwasher.

Bermuda Glassblowing Studio & Show Room (⊠ 16 Blue Hole Hill, Hamilton Parish, ☎ 441/293–2234). A restored village hall in the Bailey's Bay area houses this glassblowing studio, where eight artists have created more than 200 examples of hand-blown glass in vibrant, swirling colors. You can watch glassblowers at work daily in the studio and purchase their work here. Prices range from $10 to $1,600.

Celia and Jack Arnell (☎ 441/236–4646). The miniature cedar furniture crafted by this husband-and-wife team is displayed in a dollhouse at the Craft Market (☞ *below*). The fine details on the breakfronts and chests of drawers include tiny metal drawer knobs, and the wonderful four-poster bed comes complete with a canopy. A four-poster bed sells for $125, chairs for about $35, depending on the model.

Craft Market (✉ The Cooperage, Dockyard, Ireland Island, ☎ 441/234–3208). Occupying part of what was once the cooperage, this large stone building dates from 1831. This is one of the few places that has island-made handicrafts. Anna and Glenn Correia's wooden creations are beautifully executed and reasonably priced. Outstanding is Judith Faram's exquisite—but expensive—handmade jewelry.

Kathleen Kemsley Bell (✉ 7 Seabright La., ☎ 441/236–3366). Ms. Bell creates exquisite dolls of persons from different periods of Bermuda's history. Each doll is unique, and each is researched for historical accuracy. The bodies are sculpted of papier-mâché, then hand-painted with marvelously expressive faces. Costumes are all hand-stitched. The base of each doll is signed and carries a description of the historical period on which the doll's fashions are based. Call to make an appointment at the studio, or visit the Bermuda Arts Centre at Dockyard, where her work is on display. Ms. Bell works on commission and will visit your hotel with samples of her work. Prices start at $325.

Ronnie Chameau. Ms. Chameau creates Christmas angels and dolls from dried palm, banana, and grapefruit leaves gathered from her yard and byways around the island. Dolls, ornaments, Christmas decorations, and doorstops are among Ms. Chameau's specialties. Trimingham's (☎ 441/295–1103) is the exclusive purveyor of her works.

Crystal, China, and Porcelain

Bluck's (✉ 4 W. Front St., Hamilton, ☎ 441/295–5367; ✉ Reid and Queen Sts., Hamilton, ☎ 441/292–3894; ✉ Water St., St. George's, ☎ 441/297–0476; ✉ Southampton Princess Hotel, South Shore, Southampton, ☎ 441/238–0992). A dignified establishment that has been in business for more than 150 years, this is the only store on the island devoted exclusively to the sale of crystal and china. Royal Doulton, Royal Copenhagen, Villeroy & Boch, Herend, Lalique, Minton, Waterford, Baccarat, and others are displayed in its two Front Street stores. There is a substantial stock of the popular Kosta Boda Swedish crystal, and a large gift section includes an abundant selection of Limoges boxes. The courteous staff will provide you price lists upon request.

Vera P. Card (✉ 11 Front St., Hamilton, ☎ 441/295–1729; ✉ 9 Water St., St. George's, ☎ 441/297–1718; ✉ Sonesta Beach Resort, South Shore Rd., Southampton, ☎ 441/238–8122). Lladró and Swarovski silver crystal figurines are widely available all over the island at almost identical prices, but this store has the most extensive selection, including open-edition and limited-edition gallery pieces. The Lladró Bermuda Moongate and several other works are carried here exclusively. The shop's collection of more than 250 Hummel figurines is one of the world's largest. The impressive selection of beautifully crafted Swiss and German watches and clocks includes the Bermuda Time collection; and the stock of fine and costume jewelry includes 14-karat gold earrings, charms, and pendants.

Gifts & Souvenirs

Flying Colours at Riihuolma's (✉ 5 Queen St., Hamilton, ☎ 441/295–0890). This family-owned and -operated shop, established in 1937, has the island's largest selection of T-shirts with creatively designed island logos in hundreds of styles. The selection of quality souvenirs and gifts is plentiful, and educational toys are a specialty. The shop also carries everything for the beach—hats, beach towels, toys, and more.

Hall of Names (✉ Butterfield Pl., Hamilton, ☎ 441/234–3410). This is a fun place to learn the origins of your family name, or of any nickname. Friendly owner John Doherty punches the pertinent information into a computer and for about $20 per surname gives you a nicely presented document with facts compiled from an extensive bibliography, with your family coat of arms at the top. The store is a franchise of a Canadian-based company, whose team of researchers and historians compiles the information into a database.

Hodge Podge (⊠ 3 Point Pleasant Rd., Hamilton, ☎ 441/295–0647). Just around the corner from the Ferry Terminal and Visitors Center Service Bureau in Hamilton, this cluttered little shop offers pretty much what its name implies: postcards, sunblock, sunglasses, film, and T-shirts.

Pulp & Circumstance (⊠ Corner of Queen and Reid Sts., Hamilton, ☎ 441/292–9586). If you are looking for a really unusual, quality gift, look no further than this cornucopia of delights. Exquisite, modern picture frames in all shapes and sizes and from all over the world are a specialty, as are baby gifts, candles, fresh herbs, bath products, and greetings cards.

Rising Sun Shop (⊠ Middle Rd., Southampton, ☎ 441/238–2154). This country store, the only one on the island, is easy to spot. A flag, a horse's head, and other eye-catching inventory usually hang outside the entrance. Owner Anne Powell's warmth and humor, not to mention her complimentary glass of sherry, infuse her novelty gift items, which may include toilet plungers, a ship's decanter, Portuguese wine coolers, or picnic hampers—though inventory changes frequently. There are usually scads of wicker baskets in stock, as well as more expensive items, such as antique hobby horses starting at $2,000. A large selection of quality tack (stable gear) is always on hand.

Sail On (⊠ Old Cellar La. off Front St., Hamilton, ☎ 441/295–0808, FAX 441/295–2712). Owned and operated by Hubert Watlington, a former Olympic windsurfer and top local sailor, this must-visit shop is tucked up a quaint alleyway, opposite No. 1 Shed and a cruise ship dock. It's the best place on the island for casual clothing and swimwear for adults and children, as well as gifts that appeal to those with a wacky sense of humor. Road Toad and Famous Onions clothing are sold here exclusively. T-shirts, designed by Bermudians, earn ongoing kudos for their originality in the Best of Bermuda merchant awards. Shades of Bermuda, a part of the shop, carries the island's largest selection of sunglasses. Mail order is available.

Treats (⊠ Washington Mall, Reid St., Hamilton, ☎ 441/296–1123). This candy store is filled with bulk candy in just about every flavor. Buy sweets by the piece or the pound. The Candygramme gift box is filled with candy of your choice and decorated with a balloon. Prices start at $15. You will find whimsical gifts here, too.

Grocery Stores

Many of the accommodations on Bermuda, usually guest houses and housekeeping apartments, allow you to do your own cooking. Self-catering vacations are cheaper than those where you pay full board or dine out at every meal. Considering how expensive Bermuda is, this option has widespread appeal for both families and budget travelers. Still, foodstuffs in Bermuda are expensive. For example, a dozen imported large eggs cost about $2.50 (locally raised eggs are even more expensive: about $4 a dozen), a loaf of Bermuda-made bread is $3 (U.S.-made bread is $5), a six-pack of Coke is about $5, and a 13-ounce can of coffee is $8. Listed below are some of the major supermarkets in Bermuda. Unless stated otherwise, grocery stores carry liquor.

A-One Paget (⊠ Middle Rd., Paget, ☎ 441/236–0351). This grocery is near Barnsdale Guest Apartments and the Sky Top Cottages. Be warned, however, that the route between Sky Top and the store takes in a significant hill, which could make for a difficult hike if you buy a large amount of groceries.

A-One Smith's (⊠ Middle Rd., Smith's Parish, ☎ 441/236–6673). Although part of the Marketplace chain, this mart doesn't have as large a supply of goods because it is smaller. It's near Angel's Grotto and Brightside Apartments, but not quite within walking distance.

Harrington Hundreds Grocery & Liquor Store (✉ South Rd., Smith's Parish, ☎ 441/293–1635). This is a must for those on special diets or seeking out unusual ingredients. It has the best selection of gluten-free foods on the island, including gluten-free pastas, breads and cookies. Near Spittal Pond and not far from Angel's Grotto apartments, it is still a long walk with bags.

Heron Bay Marketplace (✉ Middle Rd., Southampton, ☎ 441/238–1993). One of the island-wide Marketplace chain of stores, this one has a large selection of fresh vegetables. It's convenient to Longtail Cliffs and Marley Beach, but again, not on foot.

Lindo's Family Foods, Ltd. (✉ Middle Rd., Warwick, ☎ 441/236–1344). A medium-size store with a good selection of quality and gourmet foods, Lindo's is within walking distance of the several Warwick accommodations. But when you're heavily laden with groceries, you'll have to rely on a taxi.

The Marketplace (✉ Reid St. near Parliament St., Hamilton, ☎ 441/292–3163). The headquarters for a moderately priced chain with stores around the island, this is the island's largest grocery store. You can take out hot soups, stir-fried meats and vegetables, dinners, salads, and desserts for about $5 a pound. This branch is also open Sunday from 1 to 5.

Maximart (✉ Hog Bay Level, Sandys, ☎ 441/234–1940). Near Whale Bay Inn, this is a good place to stock up on snacks. There's a good selection of meats here, and they deliver.

Miles Market (✉ Pitts Bay Rd. near the Hamilton Princess, Hamilton, ☎ 441/295–1234). Here you'll find a large selection of Häagen-Dazs ice cream, an excellent choice of high-quality imported and local meats and fish, and specialty foods found nowhere else on the island. Many items are on the expensive side, but the quality here is unsurpassed in Bermuda. The market delivers goods anywhere on the island.

Modern Mart (✉ South Shore Rd., Paget, ☎ 441/236–6161). Part of the Marketplace chain, it is smaller than its flagship Hamilton store but has all the essentials. It is easily accessible from Sky Top Cottages, Loughlands, and other south shore accommodations.

Shelly Bay Marketplace (✉ North Shore Rd., Hamilton Parish, ☎ 441/293–0966). This Marketplace chain store, the only large grocer on North Shore Road, has a good selection.

Somerset Marketplace (✉ Somerset Rd., Sandys, ☎ 441/234–0626). The largest grocery store on the island's western end, it is convenient to Whale Bay Inn, but take a moped or taxi.

Somers Supermarket (✉ York St., St. George's, ☎ 441/297–1177). There's a large selection here despite its small size. Hot items, salads, and sandwiches are available and are made fresh daily. It's within walking distance of the St. George's Club and Aunt Nea's Inn at Hillcrest Guest House.

The Supermart (✉ Front St. near King St., Hamilton, ☎ 441/292–2064). In addition to the normal goods, there's a well-stocked salad bar, prepackaged sandwiches, and hot coffee. This store and Miles Market are a long hike—particularly with heavy bags—from the Ferry Terminal in Hamilton, but once aboard the boat it's an easy ride across the harbor to Greenbank Cottages and Salt Kettle House. Island-wide deliveries are available.

Jewelry

Astwood Dickinson (✉ 83–85 Front St., Hamilton, ☎ 441/292–5805; ✉ H. A. & E. Smith's, Front St., Hamilton, ☎ 441/296–6664). Established in 1904, this store is the exclusive agent for Colombian

Emeralds International. It has an exquisite collection of European jewelry, unmounted stones, and a wide range of Swiss watches. Elegant timepieces by Patek Philippe, Jaeger-LeCoultre, Omega, Breitling, Cartier, Baume & Mercier, Tiffany & Co., and Tag Heuer are sold for up to 35% less than in the United States. Jewelry from Tiffany & Co. is also available. The shop's exclusively designed gold mementos in the Bermuda Collection sell for $50–$1,000. Created in the store's workshop upstairs, they include a range of 18-karat and bejeweled replicas of the island's flora, fauna, landmarks, and traditions available as pins, pendants, and charms.

Vera P. Card (☞ Crystal, China, and Porcelain, *above*).

Walker Christopher (⊠ 9 Front St., Hamilton, ☎ 441/295–1466). For the past 10 years *Bermudian* magazine has named this goldsmith the island's best for fine jewelry. Classic pieces include diamond bands, strands of South Sea pearls, and the more contemporary hand-hammered chokers. The store also carries an excellent collection of rare coins, some salvaged from sunken galleons. Customers can work with the jeweler to design their own exclusive piece. The Walker Christopher workshop also produces its own line of Bermuda-inspired gold jewelry and sterling silver Christmas ornaments. There is also a small selection of antique and art nouveau jewels.

Crisson's (⊠ 55 and 71 Front St., 16 Queen St., and 20 Reid St., Hamilton, ☎ 441/295–2351; ⊠ Elbow Beach Hotel, South Shore Rd., Paget, ☎ 441/236–9928; ⊠ Sonesta Beach Resort, South Shore Rd., Southampton, ☎ 441/238–0072; ⊠ York and Kent Sts., St. George's, ☎ 441/297–0672; ⊠ Water St., St. George's, ☎ 441/297–0107). The exclusive Bermuda agent for Rolex, Ebel, Gucci, Seiko, Movado, and other famous names, this upscale establishment offers discounts of 20%–25% on expensive merchandise. Earrings are a specialty, and there's a large selection. The gift department carries English flatware, Saint Louis crystal, and imported baubles, bangles, and beads.

Jeweler's Warehouse (⊠ Walker Arcade, Hamilton, ☎ 441/292–4247). Astwood Dickinson's bargain jewelry shop offers unbeatable value for the budget-minded shopper. This informal store can give you savings of up to 50% off manufacturer's recommended retail prices. There's a good selection of diamond, sapphire, emerald, ruby, tanzanite, and other gemstone jewelry, as well as watches. With every purchase you can spin the Wheel of Fortune to win a prize.

Solomon's (⊠ 17 Front St., Hamilton, ☎ 441/292–4742 or 441/295–1003). Manager Allan Porter and his skilled staff custom design one-of-a-kind pieces of genuine stones and minerals. Ranging in price from $70 to upwards of $100,000, the designs are sometimes whimsical and charming.

Linens

Irish Linen Shop (⊠ 31 Front St., Hamilton, ☎ 441/295–4089). In a cottage that looks as though it belongs in Dublin, this shop is the place for Irish linen tablecloths. Prices range from $10 to more than $3,000. Antique tablecloths can cost nearly $2,000. The best buys are the exclusively designed Irish linen tea towels for around $10. From Madeira come exquisite hand-embroidered handkerchiefs for around the same price, linen sheets and pillowcases, and cotton organdy christening robes with slip and bonnet, hand-embroidered with garlands and tiers of Valenciennes lace (from $220 to more than $800). Pure linen hand-rolled handkerchiefs with imported Belgian lace are priced less than $20, while Le Jacquard Français cotton kitchen towels cost about $15. The shop's Bermuda Cottage Collection includes quilted tea cozies (around $30) with matching place mats and pot holders (less than $15). The store has an exclusive arrangement with Souleiado, maker of the vivid prints from Provence that are available in tablecloths, place mats, and bags, as well as by the yard—the last at a huge savings over U.S. prices.

Liquors and Liqueurs

The following liquor stores sell a good selection of wines and spirits. Each has branches sprinkled around the island from St. George's to Somerset; and each will allow you to put together your own package of Bermuda liquors at in-bond (duty-free) prices. Be aware that most spirits are sold at identical prices on Bermuda, so comparison shopping is not very fruitful.

Burrows Lightbourn (⊠ Front St., Hamilton, ☎ 441/295–0176; ⊠ Clocktower Centre, Dockyard, ☎ 441/234–5078; ⊠ Harbour Rd., Paget, ☎ 441/236–0355; ⊠ Water St., St. George's, ☎ 441/297–0552; ⊠ Main Rd., Somerset, ☎ 441/234–0963); **Frith's Liquors Ltd.** (⊠ Front St., Hamilton, ☎ 441/295–3544; Mangrove Bay, Somerset, ☎ 441/234–1740; Sonesta Beach Resort, Southampton, ☎ 441/238–8122); and **Gosling's** (⊠ Front St., Hamilton, ☎ 441/295–1123; ⊠ York and Queen Sts., St. George's, ☎ 441/298–7339; ⊠ Main and Cambridge Rds., ☎ 441/234–1544).

The Wine Rack (⊠ Emporium Building, 69 Front St., Hamilton, ☎ 441/295–1711). This is one of the best places in Bermuda to buy a quality bottle of wine, particularly the top-end California reds and whites, and French Bordeaux, the shop's specialty. There is also a great Italian selection. Free home delivery is offered, but not duty-free service.

Perfume

Bermuda Perfumery (⊠ 212 North Shore Rd., Bailey's Bay, ☎ 441/293–0627 or 800/527–8213). This highly promoted perfumery is on all taxi-tour itineraries. Regularly scheduled guided tours of the facilities include a walk through the ornamental gardens and an exhibit on the distillation of flowers into perfume. At the Calabash gift shop you can purchase the factory's Lili line of fragrances as well as imported soaps and an assortment of fragrances.

Peniston-Brown's Perfume Shop (⊠ 23 W. Front St., Hamilton, ☎ 441/295–0570; ⊠ 6 Water St., St. George's, ☎ 441/297–1525; ⊠ 21 Reid St., Hamilton, ☎ 441/295–5535). In addition to being the exclusive agent for Guerlain products, Peniston-Brown's stocks more than 127 lines of French and Italian fragrances, as well as soaps, bath salts, and bubble bath. Makeovers are available at the elegant Front Street shop where there's an in-store beauty consultant.

Perfume & Gift Boutique (⊠ 55 Front St., Hamilton, ☎ 441/295–1183). Trimingham's fragrance salon carries Chanel No. 5, Laura Ashley No. 1, Elizabeth Taylor's Passion and White Diamonds, and Calvin Klein's Obsession, along with most other leading scents.

9 PORTRAITS OF BERMUDA

Bermuda's Hidden Landscapes

America's Rebel Colonies and Bermuda:
Getting a Bang for Their Buckwheat

Off Bermuda's Beaten Track

BERMUDA'S HIDDEN LANDSCAPES

IN THE PUB on the square in St. George's, there is a sign on the second-floor veranda that everyone ignores. "Do not feed the birds," it says, but the clientele keeps handing out crumbs to the sparrows that dart through the open railings.

I sat on that veranda one sultry October afternoon, finishing a pint of Watney's and looking out over King's Square. I had just enjoyed my first cup of Bermuda fish chowder, which the Pub, like most local restaurants, lets you fine-tune with cruets of dark rum and a fiery concoction called sherry peppers.

At the next table an English toddler was singing a song about a little duck. The 18th-century square below was quiet, partly because it had just rained and partly because at the moment there was no cruise ship anchored at St. George's. I crumbled a few morsels from the bun of my fish sandwich, tossed them to the sparrows, and made up my mind on another Watney's. After all, I wasn't playing golf that afternoon.

Not playing golf? The Bermuda Islands, conventional wisdom has it, are a place where you live on the links. But I was after a different place—a traveler's Bermuda, if I could find it.

On an archipelago roughly 22 mi long and seldom more than a mile wide, traveling can be a difficult order—unless you severely limit your pace. Fortunately, automobiles are out of the question. Visitors can't rent them (even residents weren't allowed to own cars until 1946), and the only way to explore Bermuda on four wheels is to engage a taxi driven by an accredited guide. But why risk seeing the whole place in a day? If you move at any speed faster than a walk, you miss details like the sign I saw on a small, shuttered yellow building: "Dot & Andy's Restaurant. Operated by Barbara and Donna."

Until recently, walking in Bermuda has meant edging gingerly along the nearly nonexistent shoulders of narrow lanes, ready to press yourself into the hibiscus hedges when a car comes by. A few years ago, though, some enterprising Bermudi-ans got the idea of turning the right-of-way of the abandoned Bermuda Railway into an island-length hiking trail. (The entire railway, down to the spikes, was sold to British Guiana, now Guyana, in 1948.)

My first choice, as a rail enthusiast, would have been to have the narrow-gauge locomotive and cars still rattling along the tracks. But being able to walk the route, or part of it, is clearly the next best thing. My problem was that I chose a section that skirted a residential district along Bailey's Bay, near the northeastern end of the main island. Here the old roadbed was frequently severed by sharp inlets of the sea, and the trestles that had once bridged them had long since gone to South America. I'd walk a hundred yards or so and have to go back to the road, often finding no signs to tell me when I could pick up the trail again. (Farther west on the islands, the old route is less frequently broken.) On one side was the ocean, on the other a series of relentlessly suburban backyards—no raffish little island shacks here. Finally, after I had inadvertently wandered into my fourth backyard, it began to rain. It was the kind of rain that makes you so wet in the first few minutes that there's no sense in hurrying out of it. I walked to a bus shelter and admitted defeat . . . and some success, having gotten into a situation in which I could hardly be mistaken for a tourist, even in Bermuda.

It was in the bus shelter that I met a young American who was waiting out the storm with his two toddlers. He was a civilian worker at the U.S. naval air station, which has since closed. His most telling remark had to do with his younger child, who had been born in Hamilton: "She's a real Bermuda Onion."

He knew, of course, that genuine Bermudian citizenship requires at least one native parent, or jumping through more bureaucratic hoops than most people would care to contend with, but the fact that he liked thinking of his little girl as a Bermudian meant that he wasn't just serving a remunerative sentence in a faraway place. To a wet traveler like me, the message was that there was a community here, and that foreigners could join it.

The rain that ended my walk on the railway trail was part of the tail end of Hurricane Nana, which had threatened to strike the island in full force before being pushed off track by a continental cold front. "We don't have hurricanes in Bermuda," a hotel bartender had told me with a wink, obviously remembering 1987's Emily, with her 116-mph winds, 50 injuries, and $35 million damage.

"No," I replied. "I live in Vermont, and we don't have snow."

Nana was a hurricane that missed, but she faded and veered away with great dramatic effect. By 9 that evening the rain returned, sheeting sideways against the windows of the hotel restaurant while tall palms thrashed in wild abandon. From the hotel bar, the storm was a terrific backdrop—the room was all *Key Largo* atmosphere heightened by the adrenal tingle that comes with a sudden pressure drop. It didn't last long; within an hour, all that remained of Nana in Bermuda was a random gusting among the palm tops, and it was fine outside for a walk down to the bay.

The next day I reverted to the vehicle of choice for covering ground in Bermuda. Motorized or "auxiliary" cycles, and the more modern motor scooters—none for rent with engines larger than 50cc, but powerful enough for an island with a 20-mph speed limit—have become a virtual postcard cliché in Bermuda, and to strap on your de rigueur white helmet is to feel as though you've become part of the landscape.

A lot of visitors are afraid that the scooters will too easily help them accomplish just that (accidents are not infrequent), but the bikes aren't all that dangerous once you learn the controls and remember to stay on the left, British-style. There is, however, a common motorbike injury that the locals call "road rash," a nasty abrasion of whatever appendage happens to meet with the road, or with one of Bermuda's limestone walls, during a badly executed turn.

What I most wanted the bike for was exploring the Bermuda hinterlands. I had already visited St. George's, the islands' oldest settlement and former capital, with its narrow meandering streets, lovely State House (built in 1620), and cedar-beam, 18th-century Church of St. Peter. I had been particularly intrigued with a local attraction called the Confederate Museum, headquarters of blockade-running operations during the U.S. Civil War. What particularly caught my interest there was the attitude of the black docent—"proud," as she put it, of a building that housed the branch office of a desperate effort to keep her ancestors in chains. In Bermudian race relations, bygones are bygones to a remarkable degree.

Towns are best explored on foot (even if it did become great fun to breeze into the capital for dinner after dark and have a maître d' take my helmet), but the bike let me discover the countryside, with its quiet lanes, tended meadows, and fragments of old estates. One of those estates—Verdmont, in Smith's Parish, now a Bermuda National Trust property—lay at the end of a delightfully convoluted route I had devised, one designed to take me buzzing along as many back roads as possible.

It was on St. Mark's Road, rounding Collector's Hill, that the essence of this miniature landscape suddenly came clear: I was looking, I realized, at a near-perfect combination of Martha's Vineyard and the Cotswolds. On the Vineyard account was the gently rolling countryside with the sea not far away, as on a New England seacoast farm; the Cotswolds element was provided by a little jewel of a limestone Gothic church, by narrow byways with names like Pigeon Berry Lane, and by the faultless juxtaposition of every stand of trees, half acre of greensward, and carefully clipped hedgerow.

As it turned out, I wasn't the first to get this feeling about the place—I saw later that two of the local streets were named Nantucket Lane (close enough) and Cotswold Lane. And why not? The Cotswold Hills, Bermuda, and the Massachusetts islands are all essentially English places, the latter two offering their settlers a vaguely English landscape even before any art was applied to them. And that art, in all three locales, was the particular English genius for conjuring tremendous diversity within the most compact of areas. Consummately ordered yet always romantically picturesque, the English landscape aesthetic depends on constant variety and small surprises, never upon great vistas.

The result is a sense of much in little, of no space wasted. The effect in Bermuda is to shrink the visitor into the islands' scale, rather than to leave him feeling like a scooter-mounted giant in a hibiscus garden.

There was another aspect of Bermuda to consider, one that counters the islands' persona as a serene, ocean-borne fragment of English countryside. This is its past history as fortress Bermuda, a 22-square-mi dreadnought permanently anchored in the Atlantic. Fort St. Catherine, at the colony's extreme northeastern tip, is now decommissioned and restored to reveal its vast warren of tunnels, built to feed shells to guns commanding the island's northern and eastern approaches. St. David's Island, too, has its battery, a rusting line of World War II–era shore artillery where feral house cats pad about the empty magazines.

From the 17th to the 20th centuries, dozens of promontories and harbor entrances throughout Bermuda bristled with guns, reflecting Britain's confrontations with forces that ranged from imperial Spain to the newly independent United States to the U-boats of the Third Reich. And no single installation loomed so mightily as the Royal Navy Dockyard, at the barb of Bermuda's fishhook-shape western end.

From 1810 to 1950 the dockyard was the "Gibraltar of the West," providing a heavily fortified anchorage for British warships and a citadel of massive limestone support structures. Approaching by ferry from Hamilton, I immediately was struck by the orderliness and permanence of it all, by the twin towers of the main building with clock faces showing the time and the hour of the next high tide, and by the ubiquitous initials VR—"Victoria Regina," shorthand for one of history's most remarkable imperial achievements. The dockyard looks as though it was built to last a thousand years—and it may, though now it houses a cluster of museums, crafts galleries, restaurants, and boutiques. Like the rest of Bermuda's defenses, the dockyard was never tested by a serious attack; its bristles were too formidable a challenge.

Time and again in Bermuda, one encounters the opposing tidal pull of British and American influences. This, after all, is a place where they still call the panorama of harbor islands from the top of Gibbs Hill the "Queen's View," because Elizabeth II admired it in 1953. But this British colony conducts its financial affairs in dollars, not pounds sterling, and nearly 90% of its visitors are American.

Many residents do link one continuing Bermudian tradition with the long British military presence, and that is a certain formality of dress. I was reminded of this one day in downtown Hamilton, when I saw a white-haired gentleman wearing a blue blazer, a white shirt, and a rep silk tie along with pink Bermuda shorts, white kneesocks, and pink tassels on his garters. The shorts themselves are a throwback to the military, and got their start as a local trademark when Bermuda tailors began refining officers' baggy khaki shorts for civilian wear. They are now ubiquitous as Bermudian business attire, but the most striking thing about them is not the fact that they expose gentlemen's knees but that they are integrated into a very correct, very formal men's civilian uniform. I never once saw a businessman's collar and tie loosened on a hot day in Bermuda—a sure sign that the stiff upper lip can outlast even the presence of the Royal Navy.

In thinking about where I might find the quintessence of Bermudian formality and local tradition, I concluded that the place to look was probably afternoon tea at the venerable Hamilton Princess Hotel. I was staying elsewhere, and thought it might be appropriate to call the Princess first to see if outsiders were welcome.

"Are you serving tea at four?" I asked the English-accented woman who answered the telephone.

"Yes."

"Is it all right to come if you're not registered at the hotel?"

"Are you registered at the hotel?"

"No. That's why I'm asking."

"I'll switch you to dining services."

"Hello?" (Another Englishwoman's voice.)

"Hello, I'm wondering if I can come to tea if I'm not registered at the hotel."

"What is your name, sir?" I gave her the name and spelling. At this point, I was tempted to add "Viscount."

"I don't have you listed as a guest."

"I know that. I'm calling to ask if it's all right to come to tea if I'm not a guest."

"No, sir."

Now we were deep in Monty Python territory, and I had the John Cleese part. Clearly, there was nothing to do but get dressed, scoot into Hamilton, and crash tea at the Princess. But when I sauntered into the hotel with my best ersatz-viscount air, all I found was a small antechamber to an empty function room, where a dozen people in tennis clothes stood around a samovar and a tray of marble pound cake slices. I poured a cup, drank it, and was gone in five minutes. Crashing tea at the Princess had been about as difficult, and as exciting, as crash-ing lunch at my late grandfather's diner in New Jersey.

Hamilton is a tidy, cheerful little city, but as the days drew down I returned more and more to the countryside, particularly to the back roads where small farms survive. Bermuda was once a mid-ocean market garden, in the days before the United States restricted imports and property values skyrocketed beyond the reach of farmers; an occasional neat patch of red earth still produces root crops, broccoli, cabbage, and squash. I even saw a truck loaded with onions go by—a reminder of a Bermuda before golf.

–William G. Scheller

William G. Scheller is a contributing editor to *National Geographic Traveler.* His articles have also appeared in the *Washington Post Magazine, Islands,* and numerous other periodicals.

AMERICA'S REBEL COLONIES AND BERMUDA: GETTING A BANG FOR THEIR BUCKWHEAT

W**HEN THE AMERICAN** War of Independence began, Bermudians at first felt little personal concern. There was some sympathy for the colonists; quarrels between arbitrary executive power and people, which in America had now led to real trouble, had also been part of Bermuda's history, and besides this there were ties of blood and friendship to make for a common understanding. But for all that, Bermudians, while expressing discreet sympathy, were chiefly concerned for their ships and carrying trade, and, realizing their helpless position, they believed their wisest course lay in continued loyalty to the Crown. The wisdom of this policy was suddenly brought into question when the Continental Congress placed an embargo on all trade with Britain and the loyal colonies, for as nearly all essential food supplies came from the Continent, the island faced starvation unless the decree was relaxed. Thus there was a swift realization that Bermuda's fate was deeply involved in the war.

The drama now began to unfold and soon developed into a struggle between the governor, George Bruere, and the dominant Bermuda clique led by the Tuckers of the West End. Bruere's chief characteristic was unswerving, unquestioning loyalty, and the fact that two of his sons were fighting with the royalist forces in America—one of them was killed at Bunker Hill—made the ambiguous behavior of Bermudians intolerable to him, both as a father and as an Englishman.

Of the Tuckers, the most prominent member of the family at this time was Colonel Henry, of the Grove, Southampton. His eldest son, Henry, colonial treasurer and councillor, had married the governor's daughter, Frances Bruere, and lived at St. George's. There were also two sons in America, Thomas Tudor, a doctor settled in Charleston, and St. George, the youngest, a lawyer in Virginia. The two boys in America, caught up in the events around them and far removed from the delicacies of the Bermuda situation, openly took the side of the Colonists.

Up to the time of the outbreak of the war there had been warm friendship between the Tuckers and the Brueres, a relationship made closer by the marriage of Henry Tucker to Frances Bruere. But when it became known in Bermuda that the Tuckers abroad were backing the Americans, Bruere publicly denounced them as rebels and broke off relations with every member of the family except his son-in-law. But Colonel Henry was more concerned with the situation in Bermuda than he was with the rights and wrongs of the conflict itself, and he believed that unless someone acted, the island faced serious disaster. So, privately, through his sons in America, he began to sound out some of the delegates to the Continental Congress as to whether the embargo would be relaxed in exchange for salt. This move, never in any way official, had the backing of a powerful group, and before long it was decided to send the colonel with two or three others to Philadelphia to see what could be arranged. Meanwhile, another less powerful faction took form and likewise held meetings, the object of which was to oppose in every way these potential rebellions.

Colonel Henry and his colleagues reached Philadelphia in July 1775, and on the 11th delivered their appeal to Congress. Though larded with unctuous flattery, the address met a stony reception, but a hint was thrown out that although salt was not wanted, any vessel bringing arms or powder would find herself free from the embargo. The fact that there was a useful store of powder at St. George's was by now common knowledge in America, for the Tucker boys had told their friends about it and the information had reached General Washington. Thus, before long, the question of seizing this powder for the Americans was in the forefront of the discussions.

Colonel Henry was in a tight corner. Never for an instant feeling that his own loyalty was in question, he had believed himself fully justified in coming to Philadelphia to offer salt in exchange for food. But these new suggestions that were now being put to him went far beyond anything he had contemplated, and he was dismayed at the ugly situation that confronted him. It is evident that the forces at work were too strong for him. The desperate situation in Bermuda, verging on starvation, could only be relieved by supplies from America, and an adamant Congress held the whip hand. After some agonizing heart-searching, Colonel Henry gave in and agreed with Benjamin Franklin to trade the powder at St. George's for an exemption of Bermuda ships from the embargo.

Henry returned home at once, arriving on July 25. His son St. George, coming from Virginia, arrived about the same time, while two other ships from America, sent especially to fetch the powder, were already on their way.

O N AUGUST 14, 1775, there was secret but feverish activity among the conspirators as whaleboats from various parts of the island assembled at Somerset. As soon as it was dark, the party, under the command, it is believed, of son-in-law Henry and a Captain Morgan, set off for St. George's. St. George, lately from Virginia and sure to be suspect, spent the night at St. George's, possibly at the home of his brother Henry, and at midnight was seen ostentatiously walking up and down the Parade with Chief Justice Burch, thus establishing a watertight alibi. Meanwhile, the landing party, leaving the boats at Tobacco Bay on the north side of St. George's, reached the unguarded magazine. The door was quickly forced, and before long, kegs of powder were rolling over the grass of the Governor's Park toward the bay, where they were speedily stowed in the boats. The work went on steadily until the first streaks of dawn drove the party from the scene. By that time 100 barrels of powder were on the way to guns that would discharge the powder against the king's men.

When Bruere heard the news he was frantic. A vessel that he rightly believed had the stolen powder on board was still in sight from Retreat Hill, and he determined to give chase. Rushing into town, the distraught man issued a hysterical proclamation:

POWDER STEAL
Advt
Save your Country from Ruin, which may hereafter happen. The Powder stole out of the Magazine late last night cannot be carried far as the wind is so light.

A GREAT REWARD
will be given to any person that can make a proper discovery before the Magistrates.

News of the outrage and copies of the proclamation were hurried through the colony as fast as riders could travel. The legislature was summoned to meet the following day. Many members of the Assembly doubtless knew a good deal, but officially all was dark and the legislature did its duty by voting a reward and sending a wordy message expressing its abhorrence of the crime.

But no practical help was forthcoming, and after several days of helpless frustration Bruere determined to send a vessel to Boston to inform Admiral Howe what had happened. At first no vessels were to be had anywhere in the island; then, when one was found, the owner was threatened with sabotage, so he withdrew his offer. Another vessel was found, but there was no crew, and for three whole weeks, in an island teeming with mariners, no one could be found to go to sea. At last, on September 3, the governor's ship put to sea, but not without a final incident, for she was boarded offshore by a group of men who searched the captain and crew for letters. These had been prudently hidden away in the ballast with the governor's slave, who remained undiscovered. The captain hotly denied having any confidential papers, so the disappointed boarders beat him up and left.

In due course the ship reached Boston, and Admiral Howe at once sent the *Scorpion* to Bermuda to help Bruere keep order. Thereafter, for several years, His Majesty's ships kept a watchful eye on the activities of Bermudians, and in 1778 these were replaced by a garrison. It has always seemed extraordinary that no rumor of this bargain with the Americans reached Bruere before the actual robbery took place. It is even more amazing that within a stone's throw of Government House such a desperate undertaking could have continued steadily throughout the night without discovery.

The loss of the powder coincided with the disappearance of a French officer, a prisoner on parole. At the time it was thought that he had been in league with the Americans and had made his escape with them; but 100 years later, when the foundation for the Unfinished Church was being excavated, the skeleton of a man dressed in French uniform was disclosed. It is now believed that he must have come on the scene while the robbery was in progress and, in the dark, been mistaken for a British officer. Before he could utter a sound, he must have been killed outright by these desperate men and quickly buried on the governor's doorstep.

–William Zuill

A native Bermudian and former member of the Bermuda House of Assembly, William Zuill wrote several historical works about the island. This excerpt about the role of Bermuda in the American War of Independence is taken from his book *Bermuda Journey.* William Zuill died in 1989.

OFF BERMUDA'S BEATEN TRACK

ERMUDA IS LOVELY, but a walk along its narrow roads can involve close encounters with countless madcap moped drivers and a stream of cars. A more serene way to sample Bermuda's lush terrain, stunning seascapes, and colorful colonies of island homes is to follow the route of the railroad that once crossed this isolated archipelago. The Bermuda Railway Trail goes along the old train right-of-way for 18 mi, winding through three of the several interconnected islands that make up Bermuda.

Opened in 1931, the railway provided smooth-running transportation between the quiet village of Somerset, at the west end, and the former colonial capital of St. George's, to the east. But by 1948 it had fallen victim to excessive military use during World War II, soaring maintenance costs, and the automobile. The railroad was closed, and all of its rolling stock was sold to Guyana (then called British Guiana). In 1984, Bermuda's 375th anniversary, the government dedicated the lands of the old railway for public use and began to clear, pave, and add signs to sections of its route.

The trail's most enchanting aspect is its revelation of a parade of island views that were hidden from the public for nearly 30 years, scenes similar to what the first colonists must have found here in the early 1600s. The trail joins the main roads in a few places, but mostly it follows a tranquil, car-free route from parish to parish, past quiet bays, limestone cliffs, small farms, and groves of cedar, allspice, mangrove, and fiddlewood trees. Short jaunts on side trails and intersecting tribe roads (paths that were built during the early 1600s as boundaries between the parishes, or "tribes") take you to historic forts and a lofty lighthouse, coral-tint beaches, parks, and preserves.

I explored the Railway Trail on foot, moped, and horseback, using the 18-page guide available free at the Visitors Service Bureau in Hamilton. (You can also pick up the guide at some of the big hotels.) The booklet contains historical photos, a brief history of the railroad, maps, and descriptions of seven sections of trail, which range from 1¾ to 3¾ mi long.

Sporting a pair of proper Bermuda shorts, I revved up my rented moped and headed out to the Somerset Bus Terminal, one of eight former railroad stations and the westernmost end of the trail. From there I followed the paved path to Springfield, an 18th century plantation house used by the Springfield Library. A leisurely stroll in the adjoining 5-acre Springfield & Gilbert Nature Reserve took me through thick forests of fiddlewood. I also saw stands of Bermuda cedars that once blanketed the island but were nearly wiped out by blight in the 1940s.

Back on the trail I spotted oleander, hibiscus, bougainvillea, and poinsettia bursting through the greenery at every turn. In backyards I could see bananas, grapefruit, oranges, lemons, and limes growing in profusion, thanks to Bermuda's consistent year-round subtropical climate.

I parked the moped at the trailhead to Fort Scaur—a 19th-century fortress built by the Duke of Wellington, conqueror of Napoléon at Waterloo—and strolled up to its mighty walls and deep moat. Through a dark passage I reached the grassy grounds with their massive gun mounts and bunkers. A telescope atop the fort's walls provided close-up views of the Great Sound and Ely's Harbour, once a smugglers' haven. A caretaker showed me around the fort, one of the three largest in Bermuda.

On my moped again, I motored past Skroggins Bay to the Lantana Colony Club, a group of beachside cottages. I stopped to sip a Dark and Stormy—a classic Bermudian rum drink—and to enjoy the view of the sail-filled Great Sound. My post-swizzle destination: Somerset Bridge. Only 32 inches wide, this tiny bridge was built in 1620 and looks more like a plank in the road than the world's smallest drawbridge; its opening is just wide enough for a sailboat's mast to pass through.

I ended my first Railway Trail ride at the ferry terminal near the bridge, where I boarded the next ferry back to Hamilton. Had I continued, the trail would have taken me through what was once Bermuda's agricultural heartland. The colony's 22 square mi of gently rolling landscape, graced by rich volcanic soil and a mild climate, once yielded crops of sweet, succulent Bermuda onions, potatoes, and other produce. But tourism and international business have become bigger money-spinners here, and today only about 500 acres are devoted to vegetable crops.

JUST WEST OF Sandy's Parish the trail runs for some 3¾ mi through Warwick Parish. The path, now dirt, overlooks Little Sound and Southampton, where fishing boats are moored. Here the Railway Trail begins to intersect many of Bermuda's tribe roads, which make interesting diversions. Tribe Road 2 takes you to the Gibbs Hill Lighthouse, built around 1846; this 133-ft structure is one of the few lighthouses in the world made of cast iron. You pay $2.50 for the dubious privilege of climbing 185 steps to the lens house, where you can step outside and be rewarded with far-reaching views of the island and Great Sound. The 1,000-watt electric lamp can be seen as far as 40 mi away.

Spicelands, a riding center in Warwick, schedules early morning rides along sections of the Railway Trail and south-shore beaches. I joined a ride to follow part of the trail where it cuts deep into the rolling limestone terrain—so deep that at one point we passed through the 450-ft Paget Tunnel, whose walls are lined with roots of rubber trees.

We rode through woodlands and fields, past stands of Surinam cherry trees and houses equipped with dome water tanks and stepped, pyramid-shape roofs designed to catch rainwater. As we trotted through the cool darkness beneath a dense canopy of trees, it was hard to imagine a time when noisy rolling stock rattled along the same route, carrying some of the 14 million passengers who rode the railway while it ran. Finally, a tribe road led us through tropical vegetation to the clean, coral-pink beaches of Bermuda's beautiful south shore.

East of Hamilton, the Railway Trail follows the north shore, beginning in Palmetto Park in the lush, hilly parish of Devonshire. It hugs the coastline past Palmetto House (a cross-shape, 18th-century mansion belonging to the Bermuda National Trust) and thick stands of Bermuda cedar to Penhurst Park, which has walking trails, agricultural plots, and good beaches for swimming.

Farther east, the trail hits a wilder stretch of coast. The Shelley Bay Park and Nature Reserve has native mangroves and one of the few beaches on the north shore. After a short walk on North Shore Road, the trail picks up again at Bailey's Bay and follows the coast to Coney Island. The park here has an old lime kiln and a former horse-ferry landing.

The remaining sections of the trail are in St. George's; start at the old Terminal Building (now called Tiger Bay Gardens) and stroll through this historic town. The trail passes by Mullet Bay and Rocky Hill Parks, then heads to Lover's Lake Nature Reserve, where you can see longtails nesting among the mangroves. The end of the trail is at Ferry Point Park, directly across from Coney Island. In the park there's a historic fort and a cemetery.

Evening is perhaps the most enchanting time to walk along the Railway Trail. As the light grows dim, the moist air fills with songs from tiny tree frogs hidden in hedges of oleander and hibiscus. The sound sets a tranquil, tropical mood that has been undisturbed for nearly half a century by the piercing whistle and clickety-clack of Bermuda's bygone railroad.

–Ben Davidson

INDEX

NOTES

NOTES